Film Cultures

Film Cultures

Janet Harbord

SAGE Publications
London • Thousand Oaks • New Delhi

First published 2002

SAGE Publications Ltd
6 Bonhill Street
London EC2A 4PU

SAGE Publications Inc
2455 Teller Road
Thousand Oaks, California 91320

SAGE Publications India Pvt Ltd
32, M-Block Market
Greater Kailash – I
New Delhi 110 048

British Library Cataloguing in Publication Data

A catalogue record for this book is available from the British Library

ISBN 0 7619 6520 3
ISBN 0 7619 6521 1 (pbk)

Library of Congress Control Number available

Typeset by Keystroke, Jacaranda Lodge, Wolverhampton
Printed in Great Britain by TJ International, Padstow, Cornwall

for June Emily Harbord

Contents

Acknowledgements   ix

Introduction   1

Chapter 1   Breaking with the aura? Film as object or
             experience   14

Chapter 2   Spatial effects: film cultures and sites of exhibition   39

Chapter 3   Film festivals: media events and spaces of flow   59

Chapter 4   Marketing films and audiences   76

Chapter 5   Postmodern praxes: production on the national
             and global stage   93

Chapter 6   Aesthetic encounters   117

Chapter 7   Digitalization and its discontents   138

References   164
Index   177

Acknowledgements

As with most works, this book is the product of advice, criticism and encouragement from many people at different moments and in different places.

First, I would like to acknowledge with gratitude the invaluable support of a friend and colleague, Jan Campbell, for many conversations, discussions and debates that have helped shape this work, and for insightful comments on the whole manuscript.

I'd like to thank the following people for contributions of various kinds: Helen Cunningham, Alan Durant, Juliet Gardner, Jane Giles, Gary Hall, Stuart Hansen, Geof Hemstedt, Lucy Kimbell, Roshi Naidoo, Lawrence Normand, Jonathan Rutherford, Nelly Voorhuis. For conversations that went on late into the night, Lynda Dyson, Rachel Malik and Sylvia Shaw. Also my 'new' colleagues at Goldsmiths, and in particular Richard Smith who provided invaluable research support in the final stages of the writing of the book.

Finally, I want to thank Sarah Turner for challenging my taste in film and commenting on drafts of chapters. Also for countless conversations about the writing process and encouraging the use of the three-act structure in an academic text. I'm not sure that I ever got there, but the debates were none the less inspirational.

Introduction

In many accounts of social and cultural change, from modernity to post-modernity, Fordist to post-Fordist production, standardization to flexible specialization, national to multinational, the film text has stood as a metonym of such transformations. From the Benjamin–Adorno debates of the 1930s, to Jameson's postulation of the retro film as a sign of historical amnesia, through to David Harvey's use of *Blade Runner* to represent space–time compression, film has served as an emblem of the 'new', of mechanical reproduction at the beginning of the twentieth century to a culture of immediacy and spectacle at the beginning of the twenty-first. Film is part of, culpable even, in the former era of commodifying social relations, and latterly in the process of scrambling spatial and temporal co-ordinates, of bringing elsewhere into proximity, and lifting the local into a global circuit. As such, film has been central to an understanding of the alienation of modernism and the fragmentation said to characterize post-modernism. Yet these perspectives on the 'present' are a grand orchestration of a narrowly Western view of modernism and globalization. The diverse experiences of both global change and of film cultures mitigate against a universal fluidity, materially embedded in historical paradigms of identity and culture altogether less mobile. Doreen Massey articulates this materialism notably in her description of everyday practices: against the image of the sky-bus gliding across the horizon in *Blade Runner*, 'most people actually still live in places like Harlesdon or West Brom. Much of life for many people, even in the heart of the First World, still consists of waiting in a bus-shelter with your shopping for a bus that never comes' (Massey, 1993: 61).

One of the notable strains of critical discourse of recent decades has been the claim that postmodernism has collapsed boundaries, tastes and hierarchies, fragmenting social cohesion and social inequality at one and the same time. This debate has then entertained the argument of whether such splintering has produced a new equality of subcultural, multi-ethnic affiliations, or obfuscated political activity of various kinds. This book starts from a different premise, stepping back from this precipice of the postmodern to consider how film, beyond the representation of postmodern cities, enters our lives. Given that most of our experiences of film begin with waiting at a bus stop on the way to the multiplex, or slumped in the luxury or squalor of our front rooms in front of the television, film texts may offer us the view of the sky line, but we inhabit film as *culture* somewhere altogether more pedestrian.

The title of this book is a reworking of what and how we might think about and analyse film, not as the scrutiny of texts or studies of audience behaviour, but as a practice embedded in spatial and psychological contexts of social hierarchy and distinction.[1] Choices about film, our putative tastes, are derived from our position within what Bourdieu images spatially as a field, a matrix of relations structured by class, ethnic and national differences. We bring to film, and what brings us to film, is our own individual histories, which are none the less social histories produced through institutions of the family, education and work. Our tastes for film, located within our broader positioning of dispositions more generally, lead us to the social comfort and ease of certain texts and locations and the rejection of others. They propel us towards certain imaginary constructions of film as 'serious', 'entertainment', 'high brow', 'cult' or 'trash'. Yet filmic taste is not simply an arbitrary projection of individual preferences onto a range of film texts. Films themselves, as they are circulated through different paths and networks, different institutional and discursive domains, are produced and presented as a range of aesthetic objects and practices competing for status.

How then can we 'think' the spaces between production and consumption, the text and the bus stop, which open out onto a spectacular array of circuits, networks and pathways? The aim of this book is to trace the circulation of film in distribution, exhibition, official competition and marketing: sites where the value of film is produced and are yet elusive to trace. One example of this production is the meaning that accrues to a film, independent of what the film is in itself, when it travels a festival circuit. Festivals are events of competition and judgement, are inhabited by industry professionals and have limited access for the public. In Europe festivals are located in significant cities, flagships of creativity in the post-industrial era of culture as the new economy, competing against one another for attention in the global arena. Festivals carry the symbolic capital of select spaces of cultural competition, and as such, films that première at these spaces accrue this restricted distinction. Unlike Oscar ceremonial awards, festivals provide classificatory awards prior to a film's general release, based on expert opinion, a marker that appears in advertising and marketing materials. Film, in turn, reciprocates the status of the city as a centre of cultural prestige.

This is an argument that the 'value' of a film is produced relationally. The festival circuit provides a particular, restricted circuit of initial distribution, which takes on meaning in relation to the mass release of other films into the public domain as a media event, characterized by informational saturation. The relational discourse of value operates across a set of opposing terms extending beyond open access and restriction; it operates most poignantly in our conceptualization of the film itself. If we open a cereal box and a protagonist from a feature film clatters into the cereal bowl, if we open the pages of a magazine and the character of a film is promoting Diet Coke, the film slips into various practices and texts of everyday life. Whether we conceive of film as a discrete object with integral boundaries or as one component within a range of ancillary products is a distinction drawing on a historical opposition of purity and proliferation. The versioning of certain film narratives as games, toys, soundtracks and clothing repositions certain films as hyper-texts, creating links to other products and applications. The relational discourse of value operates across discursive domains where film as culture is produced – in marketing and journalism, the texts of advertising, promotion, reviews and features. The apparently 'neutral' decision of choosing which film to see is conditional upon where we recognize ourselves in the profiles of magazines, newspapers and television, where we share the language of reviews, identify with the 'you' and 'us' of advertising, and are reviled by the 'you' and 'them' of other texts. 'A comedy-romance', an 'action-adventure', 'Tunis new wave'; 'riveting, pure cinema', 'guaranteed to thrill', 'packed with testosterone' – such taxonomies speak 'our' language.

However, more than simply confirming existing tastes for individual films, this infrastructure of circulation affects and conditions our relationship to spatial practices. The paths of filmic circulation, whilst not strictly determined or fixed, deliver different film cultures to locations with diverse symbolic status. The multiplex at the outskirts of town is an environment that threatens to elide film exhibition with shopping, locating film within the context of commodity culture. It is a site, as Friedberg notes, predicated on social separation, a fabricated space cut off from the elements, a time capsule set adrift from the encounter of difference in urban life. Whilst the arthouse, a declining exhibitionary space under threat of closure in many parts of Britain, locates the cinematic experience within the heart of a historically dense fabric. More distinct still, the art gallery relocates film within a history of art practice and tradition, providing the intertextual referents for film within the surroundings of other artworks. Our taste for film is suggestive of our relationship to these spatial sites and whilst we may not inhabit each of these sites exclusively, foregoing all others, patterns of consumption fall into familiar routines rooted in the social comfort of environments, the ease and familiarity of the habitus as a spatial framework.

The methodology of tracing intermediary networks emerges as part of a conversation about how we might analyse and understand the part that film plays in forging connections between space and texts, between images of nationhood and social subgroups. Certainly, there are markers in the field where the study of filmic taste cultures occurs, in the analysis of popular film (Dyer and Vincendeau, Hollows and Jancovich, 1995), and in the exploration of film as social practice (Friedberg, 1993; Stacey, 1993; Staiger, 1992; Turner, 1992; Wasko, 1994; Willeman, 1994). Yet the methodology of these accounts has remained fairly peripheral in the canonized approaches to the study of film, evident in text books, readers, curriculum and conference schedules. These texts narrate a story of analysis that moves through film history, aesthetics and textual semiotic analysis, ideology and the apparatus, towards a more recent emphasis on audience research. Film studies is a broad church, of course, with greater nuances than this account can cover. Yet there is a particular shift in film studies from the text to the audience that for my own purposes of situating the debate that follows I will briefly reference.

The film text has been central to a range of methodologically and conceptually different approaches which I will gloss here. From the earliest writings on the nature of film, which strove to locate the 'essence of cinema' (G. Dulac, 1925), the notion of film as a 'new' art form and experience propelled a taxonomy of the technical and aesthetic features of the medium. Analyses of the effects of projection, editing and sound, the performance of the camera, contributed a broad and discursive sense of film language and practice. It is an approach that is not singular, nor singularly academic; from Eisenstein onwards, many contributors to the debate have been practitioners as well as writing about film. More singular in its approach, structuralism brought semiotics to bear on the text, drawing an alignment between wider ideologically motivated discourses of subjectivity and the particular ways in which the filmic experience had become sedimented. The psychoanalytic turn of 1970s *Screen* theory sealed an understanding of the filmic text as operating a compatible ideology through mainstream production processes, exhibitionary apparatuses and textual form. Continuing into the present, the desire to comprehend, codify, reread film language and effect centres the text as the subject of analysis.

In many ways, the empirical turn of audience studies has been a reflexive response to the difficulties that arise from the methodology of textual analysis. These are problems of determinacy, structure and agency. To render the argument crudely, the structuralist and poststructuralist readings of particular films or genres instates an ideological determinism to the practice of film spectatorship under the influence of Althusser. Emerging out of a movement where the critical imperative was to demonstrate how significant and forceful the effects of culture (rather than simply economics) were in reproducing dominant ideology, the danger of a structuralist account was that the spectator appeared as a two-dimensional walk-on part. In response to this, a more Gramscian notion of nuanced cultural engagement replaced the abstract spectator with the empirically grounded audience.

Influenced by a range of writings of the 1980s, most poignantly Michel de Certeau's *The Practice of Everyday Life*, audience studies repositioned the focus of film studies, or opened out a new dimension, with the study of the practices and tactics of viewers located in the cracks between ideological slabs. The notion of the active audience has redoubled textual readings, made them more complex, dissonant, at times backfiring against the perceived intentional effects of apparatus and formal textual positionings. With this renewed concept of ideological engagement as complex and indeterminate, has come the charge of ascribing utopian forms of resistance to audiences; audience studies are accused of placing the fulcrum at the farther end of the spectrum between structure and agency.

The starting point for this book is the space between these two approaches of text and audience – the spaces, networks, structures and flows through which film travels between these poles. Part of the argument is that film never finally arrives or is fixed at any one point but, like Appadurai's phases of the commodity, enters certain windows and arenas, before moving on to the next. And not only a deferral of the arrival of the one text but its afterlife, in a range of ancillary texts as the film undergoes metamorphoses of various kinds: animated as a computer game, reformatted as video, spliced into soundtracks, miniaturized as toys. The practices that shape the flow of film include (but are not exhausted by) production strategies, marketing, film festivals, reviewing, distribution channels and sites of exhibition. These are more than mediating processes suturing the path between supply and demand. The structures, patterns and formations produced by these practices in part inform production and shape consumption in a circle that never quite connects. What these practices engender, I argue, are particular film cultures, embedding film within practices of everyday life that are to a certain extent mapped out historically, filling the contours of the existing socio-cultural formations. Why might a seemingly innocuous manifestation of preference, that is 'taste', be a significant tool in understanding our relationship to film?

nausea

Paris, the late 1970s. Two French men are busy, labouring over the production of two different texts in different parts of the city's suburbs.[2] It is summer, afternoon, the air is thick with the smells of cooking mingling with a less distinct toxicity of car fumes. Voices, the sound of children playing, waver on the air. Bourdieu is writing up the findings of a large survey on taste conducted ten years before; the book has been a long time coming, a huge gestation. But the findings are conclusive; this is a game, he writes, the playing of culture and taste to win advantage but on a field that is far from level. Derrida, meanwhile, is putting the

6

final touches to a work on aesthetics, *The Truth in Painting*. It is a culmination of a different sort, expanding on the playful business of an earlier essay, 'Economimesis'. Smell, asserts Derrida, is simply taste distanced, held off. There is a sense of nausea for both writers.

'In matters of taste, more than anywhere else,' writes Bourdieu, 'all determination is negation and tastes are perhaps first and foremost distastes, disgust provoked by horror or visceral intolerance ("sick making") of the tastes of others' (1979: 56). In this account, the articulation of taste is not merely expressive, the indication of a preference, but a refusal, functioning through the necessary construction of others' tastes. To be able to express a taste, and if taste is always the taking up of a position, albeit unconsciously, this is then dependent on a knowledge of the social cartography of taste formations.

Otherness enters both accounts as that which is refused, dispelled. Both, like the majority of works on aesthetics in the past century, are in dialogue with Kant's thesis on aesthetics. For Derrida otherness represents the binary oppositions that Kant's work is predicated on: pure art against the copy, distanced pleasure against proximate enjoyment, creativity against mechanical production, infinite value against exchange value. Stumbling across the taste of others, Derrida writes, attempting to incorporate this difference, the subject of this masterful discourse chokes, vomits out what cannot be assimilated; the act of vomiting, like Bourdieu's sickmaking, is the expression of disgust. From these accounts, taste is returned to its corporal paradigm; not natural 'taste' but a refusal of the split between mind and body that Kant's writing enforces. Here, the body returns, explodes orally onto the scene as a loss of corporal control.[3]

Despite this common assault on Kant's thesis, Derrida and Bourdieu pursue different disciplinary approaches to taste, which lead in opposite directions. For Derrida, taste as the aesthetic is a category to be emptied out (as Armstrong, 2000 notes), deconstructed, pulled apart to show the fallacy of binarized thought; taste is the expulsion of difference. In Bourdieu's work in *Distinction*, on the other hand, taste is the site of difference, a mechanism no less, crucial to the operation of social ranking; binarized thought persists in naturalizing our differential relations to culture, suturing cultural preference with social position. Bourdieu's account pursues a neo-Marxist approach to the study of culture as social reproduction, but placing culture (rather than economics) more centrally and insidiously as the key mechanism through which social difference is unwittingly perpetuated.

How then does taste operate, and how do we acquire tastes? In the thick volume of *Distinction* Bourdieu presents empirical evidence of the patterns of cultural preference that correlate to the structures of class in French society. Through an

interpretation of the survey material, Bourdieu cross-references cultural preferences for a range of objects and practices with demographic information on
education, familial status, vocation and age. The findings dovetail into a range of
social predilections for particular cultural forms clustering into groups that
represent the divisions between classes. Why should this be so? For Bourdieu, the
sedimented histories of identity, indelibly shaped by education and the family in
particular, form an unconscious framework, at once a map upon which we orient
ourselves, and a set of approaches as automatic as speech, that enable us to respond
to the moment: taste as a knee-jerk reaction (again, the body). This Bourdieu
names the habitus.

In positing such an argument, there is an immediate risk of overemphasizing
social reproduction and the power of the infrastructure in determining behaviour.
This is a criticism levelled at Bourdieu, accused of overemphasizing the systematic
effects of social infrastructure whilst ignoring both the internal contradictions
inherent to social formations (Garnham, 1993), and underplaying individual
agency (de Certeau, 1984). Bourdieu has been cautious to situate his project
(beyond *Distinction*) across the dualisms of structure and agency, structuralism
and poststructuralism (Bourdieu, 1990).[4] Whilst his work draws attention to the
part that culture plays in reproducing the social formation, he is eager to point
out the contingency of social positioning, the ability of agents to shift position
and thereby move the dynamics of any given field whilst remaining within its
confines. His work is both riveted and riven by the forces of stasis and change
which, when not the subject of critique, are taken up in oppositional ways.
Susceptible to appropriation by both neo-Marxists and postmodernists alike,
Bourdieu is at times wheeled on to underscore the immutable nature of social
structures and, paradoxically, called upon to 'redeem' popular cultural tastes.

This book attempts to move away from the dilemma of reproduction and change,
structure and agency, the stark terms that trouble the emphasis of any critical
account of culture by holding these forces in tension. The way that this tension
is presented conjoins another dilemma of the present, the reading of modernism
and postmodernism. The debate whether modernity has succeeded, whether its
project was ever desirable, or whether we have moved beyond modernism into a
differently textured moment, has had extensive play (and canonization) in the
work of Habermas, Lyotard and Jameson. This exhaustive debate, and its many
critiques, circles questions of periodization and change without coming to
rest. The level of generalization that besets any such description as modernism
and postmodernism opens out onto other questions of individual perspective and
investment, of which dates are significant and for whom, of which cultural and
geographical terrain these terms claim to speak. Rather than falling into step with
these accounts, I have used the terms modernism and postmodernism as *processes*

8

which exist simultaneously, rather than as discrete epochs. Their co-existence has been remarked upon elsewhere; as Stuart Hall argues, 'postmodernism remains extremely unevenly developed as a phenomenon in which the old centre peripheries of high modernity consistently reappear' (Hall, 1996: 466). Yet the terms continue to strike a resonance; situated in tension, they speak of the dual forces at work in the present, of modernist forms of hierarchy and postmodern forms of fragmentation. Whilst not commensurate with the strain between structure and agency, modernism and postmodernism as processes offer a way of articulating the forces of change and stasis, of flow and fixity, that characterize the movement of culture, and film in particular.

The positing of modernism and postmodernism as process here owes much to the incisive critiques and critical reworkings of these terms from writers working in the area of postcolonial studies. Beyond the argument that modernism and postmodernism are historically redolent and geographically remiss, writers such as Ahmed, Appiah and Gilroy have reconceptualized the somewhat linear model of historical succession as a series of movements and effects that are scrambled in the ways that they take root globally. Appiah notes the co-existence of modernity and tradition in Ghana during his childhood as thoroughly imbricated facets of a culture. In a different context, Gilroy has written and recovered a history of black slaves as among the first postmodern peoples, displaced, transnational, acting within a double consciousness of cultures, identifications, allegiances.[5] Dispelling notions of mobility and displacement as symptoms of the present, Gilroy writes in a postmodern vein of ships as 'modern machines that were themselves micro-systems of linguistic and political hybridity' (Gilroy, 1993: 12). The critical endeavour of this work illustrates how the concepts of modernism and postmodernism appear as processes – of displacement, of hybridity, of transnationalism – that resist the orthodox account of temporal classification. The use of modernism and postmodernism in this text as processes suggest a dynamic at work between forms of mobility and stasis, networks of flow and centres of production, a horizontal surface and a vertical hierarchy. Here, the structures of nationhood manifest in institutions of policy formation and funding, in governmental reviews of national culture and in forums of European cultural legislation, are positioned as the modernist points of fixity in a system of cultural exchange and flow. In contrast, the mechanisms of circulation, the channels of dissemination that traverse national boundaries, and that proliferate film narratives across various media formats, are situated as the more liquid processes of postmodernity.[6]

The tension between these oppositional processes is often more a case of collision than of polite encounter, and film occupies a peculiarly important place in national cultures. Film is not simply a component part of the heavily ideologically invested 'cultural industries', but holds particular sway in several ways. First, as a product laden with the promise to generate employment as a 'creative industry', film reproduces the image of nations as productive, a crucial sign in an age of post-industrialism. Second, the film industry is also a service industry for international production companies, a facilities house with highly skilled labour. Third, film as a product is also constructed as an index of national attributes, representing the nation as an export intended for circulation elsewhere. In this multifaceted role, film inhabits a interstitial position between nations and transnational companies, between policy makers and film makers, and between various critics and audiences in debates on cultural worth. These fractious discourses are conducted in multiple forums – perhaps most obviously in the forums of international trade discussions such as GATT, where the modernist structures of the nation state attempt to place constraints on the processes of cultural flow. Yet they also occur in the pages of newspapers and on radio phone-ins, for example, in relation to the spending of lottery money on film in Britain. Perceived to be a tax on the poor, the allocation of lottery funds to films that proved to be commercially weak performers produced a debate in which filmic taste came to represent divisions of class, ethnicity and other differences of iden-tity and interest. The debate has a divisive edge in that class antagonisms emerge in resistance to what is perceived to be an erudite, avant-garde culture, suggesting in its place the possibility of a more popular, national film culture. Yet, this produces a sense of a preconstituted homogenous, national culture, whereas the major struggle facing European nations, and Britain in particular (whether evidenced on the streets of Bradford, school curricula or policing the Channel Tunnel), is the recognition of the ethnic and cultural diversity within its bounds.

An important part of discourses of value is that taste exceeds any simple adherence to class affiliations; taste for film cultures involves our imaginary identifications, our familiarity with certain institutions and cultural spaces. And whilst subtitled films are distributed by arthouse cinemas alone, and commercial success and competitiveness in overseas markets remains a priority for national film policy, the spectre of multiple, culturally diverse film cultures co–existing becomes more obscure. This book takes as a starting point the most polarized images of contemporary film cultures, the arthouse and the multiplex, in order to attempt to locate the origins of such a division, a path that leads back to early film and its institutionalization, and earlier still to the separation of the terms 'commerce' and 'culture'.

the chapters

The first chapter of this book returns to the beginning of the twentieth century and the emergence of cinema, to locate the divisions in film cultures in an historical context. Film is, of course, born into the moment of what has become known as European modernism, where technology takes on the dual charge of negative alienation through industrialization, and technology as progress, potentially breaking with tradition and simultaneously promoting enlightenment ideals of evolutionary progress. Cinema insinuates itself in the social fabric in various ways (Gunning), as multiple forms of entertainment drawing on popular forms of vaudeville, the spectacle of the fairground, the surveillance of anthropological travelogues and an imperial gaze, as the mimesis of local scenes of everyday life. The historical descriptions of early film emphasize the heterogeneous nature of cinema; its consolidation as a culture in particular exhibitionary practices and sites is predominantly read as a reduction of possibility, a paring down of the variety of cinema. The reasons for such a narrowing of scope are attributed variously to an economic imperative to standardize practice in the name of efficiency and economic return (Musser, 1990), to promote a respectability to cinema-going by eliminating its carnivalesque features, and institutionalization of production practices such as parallel editing, in line with recognizable features from other forms of fiction such as the novel. Whilst each of these points is persuasive, I would argue that the institutionalization of film, resulting in the production of a dominant mainstream and a peripheral avant-garde (or independent) sector, is also attributable to an earlier split between commerce and culture.

If Kant provides an origin of debates about the aesthetic, the context of Kant's work is also a moment in which the relationship of art to institutions of patronage is redefined. With the rise of the free market and the mercantile class in the eighteenth century came also fractures to the relationship between state, the production of culture and patronage. In brief, cultural production oscillates between the official art of state patronage, a bohemian rejection of such official practice, and culture as commerce. These divisions, I argue, are reproduced around film at the beginning of the twentieth century, and become located in different sites which acquire the values of their historic origins (the nickelodeon, the art gallery, the specialized film club). Each site cultivates a culture of film that distinguishes it from other sites (Neale, 1981).

These divisions of filmic cultures are complex configurations manifest in institutions, production practices, texts and exhibitionary contexts, and in ways that are not completely consistent with any neat polarization. My argument here is not that distinct aesthetic practices emerge with no traffic between them, but rather that film becomes recognizable through certain institutional and discursive domains: the film society, the political and oppositional discourse of manifestos, the shopping mall, film criticism. The sites and cultures that are given prominence in this account represent the outer edges of the field, the more extreme positions where such oppositions retain a particular symbolic charge. Chapter 2 pursues this extremity of film cultures in a polarization of arthouse and multiplex institutions, the former concentrated on the object of the text (and the gallery pushing this to a further extreme), the latter relocating cinema to the out-of-town leisure and shopping centre. As James Hay (1997) notes of recent geographic and architectural developments, contemporary cinema is less recognizable as a distinct site for some subjects, blurring into the experience of leisure pursuits and ancillary texts, whilst arthouse remains an object-focused practice within a clearly bounded space.

If Chapter 2 suggests that film plays a part in our relationship to and inhabiting of space, Chapter 3 pushes this enquiry further in a reading of European film festivals. Festivals provide a material text for the otherwise abstract circulation of film across national spaces. Festivals publicize the trajectories of film in the promotion of the event. Simultaneously film publicizes place, particular places, as symbolic capital accrues to the sites of events, restricted in access and mediated by journalists. Yet the festival provides an exemplary instance of the confusion that arises in the mixing of categories of commerce and culture. The relationship of art to commerce is troublesome, with sponsorship and marketing disturbing the 'seriousness' of this cultural arena. Similarly, festivals bring into tension the interests of regional, national and international bodies, foregrounding policies to promote cultural diversity with the desire to brand film nationally and circulate it beyond the borders of the nation state.

The fourth chapter addresses the issue of the imagined and constructed audience through marketing. Whilst it is claimed that marketing has shifted its focus from demographics to psychographics in a manoeuvre that represents a reconceptualization of audiences as fragmented rather than socially structured, the practice of market research suggests otherwise. With reference to research conducted on behalf of the cinema advertising association (CAVIAR), information on audiences is classified in demographic terms, utilizing categories of social class, age and gender. What emerges from the profiling of audiences is a desire to complexify the knowledge of the range of associated media and leisure practices of audiences rather than the audience itself. Marketing for film places emphasis on the inter-relation of media platforms, in a survey of cinema attendance, video rental and purchase, cable and satellite, computer games. In a reading of genre and marketing together, the desire to maximize the life of a film across different media operates in tandem with information on the social categories of audiences and their practices of consumption.

The debates about fragmentation and flexible specialization continue in the fifth chapter in relation to film production. The influential account by Christopherson and Storper (1986) of film production as a vertically disintegrated practice is reconsidered in relation to transformations of film texts, and in relation to global and national policy. In terms of film production, the developments of the high budget and high concept feature suggest that mainstream film has developed formally as spectacle and effects, whilst capitalizing on narrative segmentation (Wyatt, 1994). The vertical disintegration at the level of production is replaced by an emphasis on horizontal reintegration (Wasko, 1994) in the versioning of film across different media forms. Such syncretic integration of multinational interests provides both the impetus for and the resistance to global trade negotiations in GATT, and more recently through the World Trade Organization. The particular focus of the debate here is how spatial and cultural affiliations are redrawn. Whilst global negotiations have effectively consolidated a European suprastate of audiovisual partnerships, in policy if not practice, the union is troubled by national and ethnic differences, and by its relationship to a multinational presence within its borders. Cultural diversity is presented as a solution, but it is also a troubling factor in attempts at unification (Schlesinger, 1997).

The final two chapters of the book pursue questions of filmic effect and cultural transformation, questioning to what extent film cultures are fixed. Chapter 6 addresses the subject of aesthetics in terms of the relationship between viewing subjects and film texts. In surveying cultural theorizations of the aesthetic, it is argued that the effect of film can not be guaranteed or assured, and that whilst an analysis of film circulation emphasizes the constraints of our relations to film, this does not extend to individual texts; the aesthetic encounter, its actual effect, remains a potentially enabling relation across film cultures. The final chapter of the book considers the impact of digitalization on the circulation of film, on the practices of production, distribution and consumption. Whilst digitalization opens up possibilities of extending our experience of film through new distribution systems, digitalization, like other technologies, remains embedded in the historical context of its emergence. Digitalization potentially redirects our viewing experiences to the home, where the ambient space of consumption may be enhanced by surround-sound, wide-screen and other developments. The practices of home viewing are not purely postmodern in nature, but practices such as collecting film (reformatted digitally or supplied with additional information) are cut through with the modernist impulse of ordering, collecting and controlling. Digitalization, perhaps more than any other framing of film culture, emphasizes our relationship to films as culture as both enabled and constrained.

Notes

1 The title of this book, I have come to discover in the writing, resonates with an earlier usage of the singular 'film culture' as the title of an American magazine devoted to avant-garde film making. In 1955 Jonas Mekas, a poet and an immigrant from Lithuania, discovered cinema in New York and founded the magazine, devoted to European-influenced experimental cinema in America. The title of the magazine underscores the ways in which taste for film extends beyond the text to embrace a whole culture, a matrix of shared values; in so doing, 'film culture' provides an exemplary instance of the ways in which the value of film exists in a wider body of texts that might, in Foucauldian terms, be thought of as discursive formations. For further reading see P. Adams Sitney (ed.) (1971) *Film Culture: An Anthology*.

2 The imaginary setting for both writers is of course of my own creation. Although the texts were published within a year of each other, I have no knowledge of where they were produced.

3 Apart from their common national origins, the two writers are distinguished from each other in many ways, not least in writing in different disciplinary traditions. Where Derrida is the flighty philosopher, musing on the abstraction of thought, Bourdieu digs around in the empirical matter of 'real' lives; the split of mind and body, and its attendant social values (where philosophy wins out), play on in disciplinary distinctions.

4 In the book *In Other Words*, Bourdieu redresses these criticisms and positionings of his work: 'If I had to characterize my work in a couple of words, that is, as is often done these days, to apply a label to it, I would talk of *constructivist structuralism* or of *structuralist constructivism* . . . By structuralism or structuralist, I mean that there exist, in the social world itself, and not merely in symbolic systems, language, myth, etc., objective structures which are independent of the consciousness and desires of agents and are capable of guiding or constraining their practices or their representations. By constructivism, I mean that there is a social genesis on the one hand of the patterns of perception, thought and action which are constitutive of what I call the habitus, and on the other hand of social structures, and in particular of what I call fields and groups, especially of what are usually called social classes' (1990: 123).

5 Moreover, the canonized uses of the terms modernism and postmodernism have mitigated against such an understanding, keeping in place the defining binary of modern, developed world versus traditional, under-developed world, a division that has facilitated the recent and devastating imaging of Islam as a pre-modern religion.

6 Zygmunt Bauman uses the property of liquid to describe modernity; in his account, the process of liquification has won out over the the features of resistance, of what I would want to call the continuing modernist structures. See Bauman (2000).

CHAPTER ONE

Breaking with the aura? Film as object or experience

If the starting point of this book is the notion that film is embedded in taste cultures, and therefore part of a system of social reproduction, this assertion immediately raises questions about how taste cultures are manifested and their mode of operation explicitly as film cultures. Further, where have taste cultures emerged from, and what historical and discursive formations provide for the current situation of film embedded in systems of opposition? These questions are complicated by the different historical lineages that they are connected to and, to an extent, are situated within. In addressing the first part of this formulation I turn to the work of the sociologist Pierre Bourdieu, and in particular his thesis in *Distinction* (a culmination of many of his writings prior to this publication) of how tastes are mobilized relationally, that is in tension with other positions within the social field. Yet Bourdieu's work, based on ethnographic research conducted in France in the 1960s, opens a vista onto another historical plane of the late eighteenth century. From the opening pages *Distinction* makes it clear that it is written in explicit dialogue with the philosophy of aesthetics set out by Immanuel Kant (1790), a philosophy worked out in an historical milieu of social transformation of relations of state and subject, art and patronage. For Bourdieu, the mechanism of reproduction travels onwards into the present, untroubled by the effects of modernism and, more recently, the postmodern; in *The Rules of Art* (1992), Bourdieu affirms the narrative albeit with adjustments to the particular artistic movements.[1]

Against Bourdieu's fairly linear account of the history of taste and social reproduction, I want to suggest that the narratives of modernism and postmodernism have and continue to exist simultaneously, providing a tension between the forces of change and stasis operating in taste cultures. This is a view that sits uneasily not only with Bourdieu's account, but also the argument in film scholarship that film is indelibly marked by modernism and, in turn, reveals something of modernism's essence. 'If we cannot understand the birth of cinema without the culture of modernity,' writes Leo Charney, 'we also cannot conceive modernity's culture of moments, fragments, and absent presents without the intervention of cinema, which became a crucible and a memorial for modernity's diverse aspects' (1998: 7). Unlike Charney, I do not envisage cinema as a memorial to modernity, nor modernism as a temporally defined epoch. The characteristics of modernism carry forward the discourses of the Enlightenment (centredness, imperialism, the hierarchy of races, knowledges, classes), as much as rupture. Into this context of order and disruption, a nascent cinema evolves, caught within paradigms of social tradition and a discourse of radical futurism. In returning to this moment, there is a specific juncture at which old paradigms of taste are inflected by a new concern: the imbrication of culture and technology. The tension between individually crafted artworks and the industrially produced cultural commodity is fundamental to the discourses of value and discrimination in which cinema developed. In early cinema we find the struggle for film as either art or commodity, its affinity with older forms of culture (vaudeville performance, songs, novels) and a concern to locate the particular new 'essence', the innovative nature of cinematic culture in the moving image. This chapter traces the tension between, on the one hand, historical continuities of aesthetic discourse within the institutionalization of cinema, and on the other, the disruptions to paradigms of value that film evokes. The first point of this analysis turns to the historical roots of discourses of taste, before moving on to the specificity of film as a 'new' cultural form at the end of the nineteenth and beginning of the twentieth centuries.

distinctions

Bourdieu opens *Distinction* with the analogy between sociology and psychoanalysis; confronted with a subject such as taste, the task of the sociologist is to dig beneath the surface of received cultural wisdom that taste is natural, a given, to upend such ideas through the illumination of less visible structures of interest and claim. Indeed, Bourdieu's notion of accumulated cultural preferences, the habitus, situates taste across the spheres of conscious and unconscious psychic life. The habitus is the sedimented effect of our individual histories, created through the systems of family and education, legitimated and consolidated by systems of reward (the titles of nobility), and the assumption of social position within a hierarchy (aristocracy). The analogy with psychoanalysis is a telling one, for it sets the tone for an argument that is a denaturalization of commonly held assumptions (not a particularly radical treatise for an academic work), but, moreover, points to the difficulty to *prove* the manifestation of taste empirically. Bourdieu's recourse to science in the introduction (and subsequent claims to objectivity) trouble the text as it shifts between the statistical 'evidence' of research, the suturing in of almost anecdotal extracts from interviews, and polemical analysis.

Part of Bourdieu's recourse to a late eighteenth-century text is perhaps motivated by a desire to locate the abstract effects of aesthetic distinction in a material textual form, an origin of sorts. Against Kant's thesis of judgement as disinterested, free-floating as it is applied to cultural works, Bourdieu asserts that such forms of valuation derive from and in turn reproduce the structure of the social classes; taste is interested, motivated. The move that Bourdieu makes in the initial moments of the book is reminiscent of Raymond Williams's reworking of the term 'culture', conventionally referring to artworks, to culture as the practices of everyday life.[2] For Bourdieu, culture extends beyond the discrete boundaries of texts into the myriad practices of daily life; the survey traces the discourses of taste through preferences for food, interior design and politics, as well as particular cultural forms and genres. The horizontal reach of taste (as lifestyle) is not Bourdieu's trump card. Rather, the ranking of such preferences within a system of hierarchy, or the imposition of the value of those tastes is what concerns Bourdieu – the ability of the dominant class to impose its judgement across the social terrain, and therefore to reinforce its position within the structure. Here culture, rather than bare-faced economic capital, is the site of social discrimination and the enforcement of class difference; discrimination manifest in the micro details and semi-conscious acts of choice in everyday life.

How then does a system of classification operate as a dominant set of ideas? Here Bourdieu springboards from Kant's thesis more directly, mapping out particular class relationships to culture. This set of relationships operates through a grid of binary oppositions concerning distance and proximity, luxury and necessity, pleasure and gratification. In a Kantian aesthetic, the ideal relationship to the work of art is distant, retaining a critical space between the artwork and subject, a space of abstraction and reflection. This approach Bourdieu characterizes as the aristocratic gaze. In contrast, argues Bourdieu, a popular relationship to culture is proximate, involving a recognition of self within the space of representation. This spatial relation to the text is underpinned by an economic imperative; the popular appreciation of culture turns on a concept of necessity, whilst the aristocratic gaze is removed from the context of need and practical purpose. This in turn helps define the cultural preferences each class makes as well as the relationship to the work. Working-class subjects, through necessity, value use, which in the sphere of culture becomes self-recognition, a validation of art as life, culture that is recognizable and that can be incorporated within a system of daily life. Bourdieu describes it thus:

> Everything takes place as if the 'popular aesthetic' were based on the affirmation of continuity between art and life, which implies the subordination of form to function, or, one might say, on a refusal of the refusal which is the starting point of the high aesthetic, i.e., the clear-cut separation of ordinary dispositions from the specifically aesthetic disposition. (1979: 32)

The relational element of taste is clear here: the aristocratic cultural taste is predicated on a refusal of culture as life, as ordinary, whilst the working-class preference is forged in opposition, the refusal of the aristocratic denial of culture as ordinary. But a further binary division opens up here in the description of the relationship to culture, which is a way of thinking culture as either form or content. For Bourdieu, the popular appreciation of culture blurs the distinction between life and art and in so doing prioritizes the content of work, its expressive function. Conversely, the aristocratic relationship, through its insistence on a division between art and life, the ordinary and the sublime, places a premium on form. The apprehension of cultural objects then is tied into our socially stratified systems of classification, where the working-class subject has few cultural resources to contextualize artworks, therefore reverting to everyday life as a yard-stick, whilst the aristocratic subject, wielding significant amounts of cultural capital, situates the work within an intertextual paradigm of previous art movements and practices.

The relationship forged by Bourdieu between individual competencies, relation-ships to cultural forms and preferences for particular types of culture roll the argument into the general and macro universe of class antagonisms. These are problems that cause us to pause and point to the limits of this account. One difficulty is the formulation of the working classes through this set of elisions. In *Distinction* Bourdieu's 'objectivity' (assuming that we accept this as a possibility) gives way to a more active skewing of cultural value, reversing the dominant legitimization of disinterest with the proximate engagement of the working classes. Indeed, a positive notion of participation is counter-posed to cold con-templation when Bourdieu claims 'popular entertainment secures the spectator's participation in the show and collective participation in the festivity which it occasions'. In a manner that echoes a Bakhtinian celebration of the popular, he continues in the same paragraph to argue that moments of collective 'festivity' 'satisfy the taste for and sense of revelry, the plain speaking and hearty laughter which liberate by setting the social world head over heels, overturning conventions and properties'. The popular relationship to culture is then warm-hearted, engaged, bodily, which in turn is potentially revolutionary, threatening to 'overturn' convention. Apart from the radical proposal of this statement, Bourdieu's description of the working classes, valorizing the underdog, spills over into a sentimentalization and, I would argue, infantilization of this social category. They are the group rendered simple in need by their dependence on necessity. Further, their proximate relation to culture, unable to discriminate between life and art, suggests an over-investment, a collapse into the space of identification. If the aristocracy are imaged as narcissists, the working classes are stuck in the ill-defined and powerless space of the preoedipal.

There are further critiques of Bourdieu's work from various quarters. John Frow, in a text committed to the exploration of cultural value, diagnoses a double essentialism at work in *Distinction* that unifies cultural tastes and class affiliations. The first essentialism involves the projection of a single class experience onto a range of disparate groups that form the dominant class (we may add that the same is true of the forging of a unified working-class experience). The second refers to the unified aesthetic logic which adheres to each class. As a result, Frow argues 'the effects of this is a binary construction of the concepts of a "high" and a "popular" aesthetic understood as something like class languages, fixed and ahistorical class dispositions with a necessary categorical structure' (1995: 31). Whilst this is a valid criticism up to a point, there are two responses that might be made to this. The first is that Bourdieu's project is ambitious in its claims for the central importance of taste in structuring the class system, and in such an account the most extreme symbolic charge of the high and the low, of good and bad taste, appears to make the case most forcefully, if somewhat parodically. Yet, these are only the outer parameters or poles of the field, the middle distances of which Bourdieu goes on to elaborate. This leads to the second point, that Bourdieu does offer a more nuanced account of class fractions in his subdivision of the social structure into the dominant (the aristocracy), the dominated fraction of the dominant class (artists and intellectuals), the middle classes as petite bourgeoisie (or the nouveau riche) and the conservative middle classes, as well as the working classes.

Where Frow refutes Bourdieu's claims as too generalized, his turning to de Certeau's account of the uses of culture is a substitution of a different kind. In de Certeau we are offered a picture of the tactics and strategies of consumers as agents operating against and between the structures of social classification. This is altogether a different project, pursuing different goals. In *Distinction* the questions concern the role that taste plays in obfuscating social interest and in reproducing social relations, whilst in *The Practices of Everyday Life* the pursuit is precisely to locate the practices of subterfuge that obscure social control (de Certeau, 1984). Yet Bourdieu cannot be positioned simply as a structuralist; indeed, in his work we find a constant movement between structure and agency, objectivism and subjectivism in a dialectic that is a refusal of these categories of approach. In his concept of practice (a regulated range of perceptions and responses within which improvisation occurs) we find the possibility of trans-formation or change. But this is always a process conducted within specific social structures, and in a culture in which politics has become culturalized (the socially given narrative of the conformist anti-conformist; 'political' positions fulfil given socio-cultural roles). If Bourdieu emphasizes the structure of social relations in *Distinction* at a cost to agency, his particular rendering of how power operates through culture offers, in compensation, the nuances of the lived, bodily effects and the nuances of structural relations. In comparison, de Certeau removes culture to the private sphere, takes it out of the circuit of value and the terms of exchange that determine its worth, and pits agency against a monolithic power that simply dominates, or which we escape.

Frow's most pertinent criticism is in his dispute of Bourdieu's splitting of form and content. This division occurs in *Distinction* as a consequence of the aristocratic and popular relations to culture, outlined above. For if the popular aesthetic values content, and conversely the aristocratic aesthetic values form, there is the implication that culture can be divided into two separate parts. Of course, it would be possible to defend this split in terms of how culture is perceived by particular groups rather than a division that can be made; in other words, the binary is the result of class interest, determined to establish different systems of value that support their own disposition and classificatory system. It is a split that retains a common usage, for example in debates on pornography and art – the representation of erotic or explicit sexual acts is framed by supporters as art valued for its formal qualities and relationship to a history of other representational practices, defended in the discourse of liberalism and freedom of expression, whilst it is condemned for its explicit 'content' by its critics. The split however does effect a certain reductiveness to debates on cultural value and cultural effect (MacCabe, 1992). A more central division that operates in the institutionalization of culture, as I shall go on to argue in relation to film, is the desire to establish a singular pure cultural object against the demand for culture to proliferate into practices and experiences.

taxonomies: art and life

Distinction contains a ghostly presence of Kant throughout its pages, hovering over the contemporary divisions and struggles, and yet there are reasons to question whether this demonized figure is representative of all there is to say of Kant's work? Isobel Armstrong argues otherwise, suggesting that Bourdieu's emptying out of the aesthetic is fighting a rearguard action (Armstrong, 2000). For Armstrong, the moment of Kantian influence has passed, killed off critically and thoroughly through the discourses of structuralism and poststructuralism, stamped on as the ruling ideology by Eagleton and Bourdieu among others, leaving little in its place; aesthetics rendered a cartoon of a flattened body. In her account, the pressing issue has become how to think the aesthetic progressively, without which aesthetics remains a discourse abandoned to the forces of conservatism (see Chapter 6 for a fuller discussion of aesthetics). What Armstrong

20

draws our attention to is the context of Kant's thesis as a key moment in the disengagement of aesthetic and economic value. This is a digression worth pursuing here as it informs the ongoing debate of the relationship between art and life, which returns at the moment of film's emergence in the latter part of the nineteenth century.

Viewed in the broader context of eighteenth- and nineteenth-century history, Kant's work ironically returns us to issues of economy and social structure. If the late eighteenth century witnessed the increased separation of art and economy, it was a movement that claimed some autonomy for art from its affiliation with Church and State, a shift away from explicit ideological control through patronage. As part of the enlightenment project, art, and cultural ideas more generally, were resituated in civic society within and as facilitators of a discursive space (albeit a bourgeois forum), free from state control (Garnham, 2000). Kant's thesis on judgement figured thus purports to a different set of principles based on rational discrimination and guaranteed by freedom from economic interest. The fact that such a disinterested position then becomes a new aesthetic ideology less apparent in its social affiliations and support (Eagleton, 1990) does not detract from this moment of social restructuring as progressively imagined.

The implications of this freeing up of art from the sphere of economics are several-fold. First, the liberation of art from economics was simultaneously a process of increased social regulation, as spheres of economic and cultural mixity came under scrutiny and administration. Stallybrass and White offer a pertinent example of such a process in the late eighteenth-century reorganization of the fair as either commercial trade event or a site of pleasure:

> As the bourgeoisie laboured to produce the economic as a separate domain, partitioned off from its intimate and manifold interconnectedness with the festive calendar, so they laboured *conceptually* to re-form the fair as *either* a rational, commercial trading event *or* as a popular pleasure-ground. (1986: 30)

The separation of a range of cultural practices from economic interest inculcated both a freeing up of the realm of artistic production, a movement reflected by Kant's text, and the increased presence of state administration in all spheres of life. In a Foucauldian reading this movement of the social classification of space and practice is, of course, a less overt manifestation of power; the discrete entity of the fair as a site of pleasure removed it from the 'real' world, withdrawing any threat from social festivities, whilst the trade fair emerged as an instrument of modernization, clarified in intent and more productive in its service of trans-actions. A similar argument concerning the separation of art and economics is developed by John Giullory in a re-reading of Adam Smith's writings on eighteenth-century laissez-faire economics (Giullory, 1993). In Giullory's account the whole process of unhinging aesthetics and economic value pertains to a more general aestheticization of the social structure, whereby the component parts of the economy and social life exist in harmony, unlegislated. Thus the autonomous existence of art comes to represent the values of the free market in general. This separation of art from economics, and art from life, returns in a more extreme way in the nineteenth century and the movements of art for art's sake, by which time the enclosed circuit of bourgeois cultural exchange effectively made the gap unbridgeable (Burger, 1984).

In *The Rules of Art*, Bourdieu returns to this history himself to argue that, following Napoleon III's seizure of power in France in the 1850s, the artistic world undergoes a division into that of a market of restricted production (bourg-eois art) and large-scale production (mass culture). The separation of artistic production from particular forms of patronage, coupled with the ideology of the free market, provokes a further split according to Bourdieu: the division between official art of the bourgeoisie belonging to the salons, and Bohemia, a current of artistic production that opposes both the market economy of mass production and the ideological values of the bourgeoisie. For Bourdieu, the critical focus here is the situation of individual interest within a social paradigm, connecting the individual to a broader canvas. What is lacking from this analysis is a recognition that this structure is fundamentally tied to the micro-effects of bureaucratic state power, and is part of a larger movement to administrate and classify social life – processes of organization that Foucault argues is the permeation of state power in social and subjective spheres. For Foucault it is a power effective through administration rather than control, complicit with the processes of taxonomy and ordering common to European imperialist states (1977, 1980). Yet, rather than reading these works adversarily, placing the readings of Bourdieu and Foucault side-by-side offers both an overview of eighteenth- and nineteenth-century social formations (Foucault) and the more specific ways in which this process of classification was realized in the cultural sphere (Bourdieu).[3] The desire to separate art from the economy effectively rendered the economy as the real, and art as the supplement, simultaneously repositioning cultural practice outside economic relations and into Kant's space of free-play and critical disinterest.

If the organization of art and economy as separate spheres frames this further division of art and life, this becomes more specifically rooted in the binary of form and content. These terms are relational positions rather than commensurate dualisms; as art becomes removed from life, from concepts of the everyday, the critical focus falls on form (the formal properties of a work) rather than content (culture as a mimesis of life). These divisions become more pronounced in the moment in which film emerges, and the cultural value attached to each, I argue, undergoes a reversal, a contortion in which popular forms of film as performance, trickery and magic oscillate on the periphery of film culture and return as avant-garde properties. Thus, the splits that Bourdieu posits as a continuous historical process undergo a particular transformation as a result of the bringing together of technology and culture. In the processes of institution- alization narrative realist film, the mimetic, conversely moves towards the centre. This reversal of fortune of the formal and the mimetic in film culture makes for its unstable, volatile status within the broader field of cultural value.

'new' technology: film

The emergence of film as a *technological* culture at the end of the nineteenth century had a profound impact on these dualisms, an impact felt differently by the diverse groups of cultural producers, institutions and audiences of the time. Photography had of course pre-empted part of the response to film, yet the differences between the media effected different expectations and threats (Sobchack, 1994). Photography lent itself to the taxonomic social imperative as well as the artistic practices of portraiture (Tagg, 1988). Film, however, with its fascination of projected mobile images, lent itself more specifically to spectacle rather than surveillance. The two strands of spectacle and surveillance were manifest less explicitly in the difference between the films of Lumière and Méliès. Lumière's films of natural vistas extended film into the realm of travel, connected to practices of mobility and taxonomy found in the discourse of colonialism (Friedberg, 1993), whilst the films of Méliès invoked the spectacle and perfor- mance of the music hall, of entertainment. Yet the sites of exhibition of both types of work located film within the domain of entertainment and leisure rather than institutions of government surveillance or within the paradigm of collection in the museum, the sites across which photography had been dispersed.

What then did a technological culture of entertainment mean for diverse groups, or perhaps a better way of asking the question, what interests were at work in the institutionalization of film? The coupling of the terms 'technology' and 'culture' brings together two relatively distinct discourses, discourses that have ideo- logically been held apart. On one side of this coupling, technology belongs to the realm of the workplace and industrialization, embedded in the narrative of progress and civilization, but it also belongs to another story, of alienation and the fragmentation of the social fabric in the industrial cities of the nineteenth century. Culture, on the other hand, bears the emphasis of the Kantian discourse, of the cerebral, the abstract, the noble. In the forged relationship of these two discourses, the binary of art and life, art and economics threatens a collapse as the identity of each is potentially put under erasure by the hybrid form of film. For the avant-garde,[4] this suggested a potential political radicalism in the bringing together of these two terms, tumbling the bourgeois separation of art and life. In the dialectic of the avant-garde–bourgeoisie, the bourgeois reproach would be either full-scale rejection of the new form from the realms of culture, or its appropriation into the sphere of art by tracing lines of continuity between traditional artworks and film (the gallery).

In the annals of film history, the two traditions of the avant-garde and bourgeois, of non-narrative and narrative film have become the canonized way of reading the work of Méliès and Lumière respectively. Yet Tom Gunning warns against this mapping as overly simplistic and in denial of the crossings and braidings that make up the non-linear historical fabric (1990a).[5] For Gunning the hetero-geneity of early cinema thoroughly mixes these terms until the institutional-ization of film after 1906, or thereabouts. Life and film culture were elided, for example, in films that presented local scenes, thereby offering the audience the possibility of viewing themselves, or at least recognizable locations. The programming of films further mixed these categories: fiction and documentary were shown consecutively, along with novelty films based on visual jokes and tricks, together with formats borrowed from vaudeville and popular theatre. In addition, the exhibition experience blurred the boundary of the film and the 'real' space of viewing through spoken commentary, music and off-screen sound effects. Life and art, then, were thoroughly imbricated.

In Gunning's account the appeal of early cinema was not necessarily narrative, fictional forms (although these existed within many of the early film formats), but rather the unique spectacle and event of film presented most poignantly in the direct address of the audience, the returned look. This appeared in a variety of ways – magicians bowing to the audience, actors directly addressing camera, the comedian's sly asides. In short, the thrill of cinema was the excitement of solicitation, rupturing the enclosed world of the screen. The particular mani-festation of narrative in early film is, for Gunning, secondary to this experience: 'Theatrical display,' he writes, 'dominates over narrative absorption, emphasizing the direct stimulation of shock or surprise at the expense of unfolding a story or creating a diegetic universe' (1990a: 59). Early film draws heavily on popular attractions as well as narrative-based arts, on the fairground and its physical, sensational form of pleasure, the corporal shock of sensory confusion. As Gunning notes, the notion of attractions is a term utilized by Eisenstein in his search for a theatrical tradition invoking an impact, and underpins his theory of montage in film. The motivation to 'shock' continues in avant-garde film making where, Gunning notes, the innovative nature of film as a new, mass culture suggested 'a new sort of stimulus for an audience not acculturated to the traditional arts' (1990a: 59). 'Shock' also returns as a key term in Benjamin's understanding of and investment in popular narrative film.

If early cinema thoroughly mixed the distinction of art and life and promoted a cinema that realized corporal shock and participation, what were the forces that shaped its demise in favour of a narratively driven, sealed diegetic cultural form? In Gunning's argument, the new features presented by film were overtaken by earlier cultural forms, in particular the 'legitimate' theatre. The known dramatic stories of theatre may have been an obvious choice for fictional representation that lacked the explicatory powers of sound. But if familiarity with a dramatic story becomes a prerequisite to the film, the intertextual nature of cinema becomes a more tightly focused set of relations linked to cultural taste: the social class of audiences becomes a key factor in its development. Again Gunning, in a different essay, argues that the consolidation of film as a form and industry after 1907 is characterized by a drive to attract and become desirable to middle-class audiences (1990c). The twin processes of this development he cites as a censorship of content, and a standardization of exhibition sites as respectable venues. In the United States, this consolidation took the form of a patents company, the Motion Picture Patents Company (MPPC), a body representing the industry's interests. In 1909, in response to the lobbying of reformist groups campaigning against the moral degradation of nickelodeons, the MPPC, in association with the People's Institute, set up the National Board of Film Censorship. This manoeuvre effectively allowed film companies to steer censorship away from state regulation, and to present film content as 'improved'. The experience of film viewing significantly changed during this period (until 1913) with the elimination of 'sidewalk barkers' standing at the periphery of theatres, the introduction of refreshments and improved lighting. In addition, the entertainment function of film was redressed through the discourse of education; trade journals, notes Gunning, increasingly advertised films as educational and instructive. Gunning notes the impact on 'content' and structure: 'Along with the drive to eliminate gruesome melodrama or vulgar comedy, we find during this period a lobbying for the happy ending as a requisite for all films' (1990c: 339).

In opposition to Gunning's emphasis on respectability and the social status of audiences, Charles Musser argues that the institutionalization of a particular narrative form occurred as the result of the consolidation of film as mass culture. For Musser, the consolidation of film as linear, narrative form was produced through a shift in the organization and responsibility for film from the exhibitor to the producer. Prior to 1907, the heterogeneous mixed format programme, it is argued, presented a problem of comprehension; evidence of audiences struggling to follow sequences, connecting segments of film located in different places and possibly moving back in time suggests a level of confusion only partially allayed by the practices of lectures, the use of intertitles and the array of intertextual knowledges that audiences might bring. The notion of a mass audience of course forestalled the appeal to specific knowledges of cultural forms and stories. In order to overcome the limited circulation of film, narrative was by necessity clarified at the point of production. Musser cites the formalization of temporal sequences, moving forward in a linear manner, as a major transformation. In support of this, the practice of parallel editing, of cutting between two scenes of action occurring simultaneously, as the particular formal practice that standardized the linear narrative structure developed. As a result, the significance of the exhibitor as interpreter and administrator of the cinematic programme was severely curtailed. Sound was, of course, to further the redundancy of the exhibitor. The standardization of narrative form resituated responsibility and power with the producer. Thus, the form of narrative cinema, associated strongly with the work of D.W. Griffith, 'won out for many reasons, standardization, narrative efficiency and maximization of profits were among the most crucial determinants' (Musser, 1990: 272).

excess

From these accounts, the shift from early cinema's heterogeneous programme mixing art and life, entertainment and commerce to the institutionalization of film as narrative cinema suggests a redrawing of those lines of demarcation; film becomes fiction, drama, a culture of viewing rather than participation. But this is too crude an opposition to map squarely onto a large corpus of films and a broad history of development; certainly, narrative film as a mainstream form incorporated some forms of the cinema of attractions, whilst more marginal avant-garde practice enlisted narrative to its services. In place of a formal division, there is a paring down of the multiple formats of early film and viewing experiences in general to a standardized range of texts and practices. Rather than conceiving of this transformation as complete, I want to suggest that these polarities of film culture exist in a dialectic, constantly shifting and realigning in relation to one another; narrative and experimental film, mimesis and abstraction, standardization and non-conformity are forged within a paradigm where each identity is produced in relation to its opposing term. Thus, although these cultural formations appear entirely opposed, the dialectical identity does not preclude crossings and appropriations across boundary lines, which in turn serve to realign the field.

What occurs to the 'excess', the theatre of attractions? For Gunning 'the cinema of attractions does not disappear with the dominance of narrative, but rather goes underground, both into certain avant-garde practices and as a component of narrative films, more evident in some genres (e.g. the musical) than in others'

(1990a: 57). In terms of this project, the displacement of the cinema of attractions from the centre to the periphery of film culture represents a crucial reversal. If the performative cinema of attractions is rooted in everyday life, in forms of popular culture and participation, this culture moves into the sphere of the avant-garde, and into the narrative of art that in Kantian terms is reserved for formal play over and above mimesis. This provides the scene of a new encounter that changes both the avant-garde and what has been conceived of as the cinema of attractions. The avant garde is in possession of a potentially mass cultural form in film, whilst the cinema of attractions takes root in a tradition of artistic practice.

This encounter is staged in all its complexity in the British film journal of the late 1920s, *Close Up*. The emergence of written texts about film are a further form of institutionalization and cartography; whilst trade magazines had existed since the inception of film as a source of technological information, reviews and journals contributed to this discursive formation of film culture by characterizing the lineage and purpose of film. *Close Up* emerged out of a modernist literary tradition and a political affiliation with Soviet film makers, a tradition shared with other European countries. In 1914 *Le Film* had been founded in France, in addition to the movement *Association des artists et écrivains révolutionnaires*, commissioning fiction writers such as Colette to write on film, and in Germany *Kulturkritik*. Anne Friedberg comments on *Close Up* that 'it typified a vanguard modernism less directly allied with political action than with experimentation in aesthetic form' (1998: 9). Here, 'experimental' film culture became appropriated by a literary modernism, as the writer 'advocated a cinema that mirrored the aesthetics and production of their own written discourse' (1998: 3). Significantly, art and commerce become separated once more, not only in the articles published but also in the economic foundations of the journal. Independently financed, it functioned free from the constraints of advertising and the pressures of circulation, and was run by a collective of independently wealthy writers and artists known as 'POOL'.

The appropriation of film culture by an artistic-literary tradition was clearly in dialectic with institutionalized (or what had become 'mainstream') film (Street, 1997). The cover of the journal articulated its identity in opposition to other discursive texts: 'Theory and analysis – no gossip' (Friedberg, 1998: 3). The October 1928 edition of the journal foregrounds the tradition of aesthetics through its cover: 'The only magazine devoted to films as an art.' The cultural paradigm of the POOL collective was not simply literary: the editorials present an aggressively hostile attitude to the pervasive influence of literary realism and theatrical tradition in mainstream film. Their cultural references were of a particularly modernist kind – the abstraction and formal play of Woolf, H.D., Gertrude Stein and, of course, the wider context of artistic movements such as surrealism and Dada, and Russian expressionist work. Motivated by the constricting institutionalization of Hollywood films, the collective aspired to a multiply conceived cinematic culture, on the one hand broad enough to incorporate various forms of experimentation, and on the other, circumscribed by the modernist perspective of what experimentation entailed.

In many ways the call to arms that characterizes *Close Up* is a demand for the exploration of the form of film at a moment when the possibilities for this 'new' medium are foreclosed through the processes of standardization outlined by Gunning, Musser and others. The excitement and enthusiasm for film permeates the writing, coupled with a political narrative that conceives of the radical potential of culture for social transformation.[6] The journal presents the confused ways in which the class-based aspirations for film are played out. An implicit faith in the internationalism of film as a language cutting across national and cultural specificity, opening up dialogue on art and politics, represents the aspirations for a mass culture of broad appeal. Indeed, sound was perceived to threaten this universal appeal of film, creating language barriers. Yet the articulation of this vision through a polemic opposing entertainment – indeed, denigrating the tastes of the mass audience – effectively redrew lines of class boundaries. This division is all too apparent in the culture of exhibition supported by the journal. The founding of film societies with a membership fee, whilst a necessary protocol for the screening of films outside socially sanctioned cinematic spaces, circumscribed the culture within specific sites removed from the everyday practices of cinema. The POOL collective may well have been ready to lead the vanguard of avant-garde film, but whether the working classes would follow was an issue less readily addressed.[7]

The questions of access to film feature as a central concern of the collective in initiatives to address distribution and exhibition. Yet the political possibilities of expanding access, of creating a popular alternative film culture, are mired by the issue of form. An example of this displacement from access to form appears in a report on the Independent Cinema Congress, an international forum which met at 'the chateau of Madame de Mandrot at la Sarraz'. What the group were opposed to was far easier to articulate than what independent film should be, or indeed whether there should be a prescribed set of criteria. 'The nature of the independent film (formerly *avant garde* film) was not understood in the same way by different members of the Congress', writes Jean Lenauer (Donald *et al.*, 1998: 274). Debate ensued about the inclusion of the film maker Pabst, who made films with 'mainstream' qualities of plot, action and professional actors. 'At last a basis was found', we are told as though to arrest 'our' anxiety, although what that agreement may have been is omitted from the account. Instead, the article moves on to announce that the result of the discussion was the creation of an

International League of Independent Cinema, and of 'co-operative production'. 'The League will have for its principal aim distribution among the already existing clubs (such as the Film Society or Film Liga) and the creation of *films of note*' (emphasis added). Films will be distributed whose 'cinegraphic value justifies the idea', yet the idea itself is obscured. In the pages of the journal, the aspiration for an expanded cinema is curtailed by the sense of aesthetic judgement and taste – films of note – an unspecified distinction naturalized by and specific to the community of members.[8] What is also noteworthy in the report is the replacement of the term 'avant-garde' with 'independent' film. The reasons for this change are not clear, but certainly the effect was to cleave a distance between the 'old' art-based movement and the 'new' radical technology of film, whilst also positioning this particular type of film culture as heir to the avant-garde tradition. At another level, this assertion of identity was also a production, a generic lumping together of all film cultures outside of this particular definition. Thus, the perjorative term 'mainstream' develops as a term defined by the boundary that circumscribes 'independent' film.

In opposing the institutionalization of film as a commercial mass culture of standardized product, the avant-garde, here represented by *Close Up*, returned the debate to form, to the distracted base of aesthetics. Here, I would argue, the distinction between art and life potentially ruptured by a technological culture, re-emerges as the distinction that holds apart mainstream and alternative film cultures. As Huyssen notes, the potential use of technology as art to destabilize the distinction between art and life, and work and culture, is profound: 'by incorporating technology into art, the avant garde liberated technology from its instrumental aspects and thus undermined both bourgeois notions of technology as progress and art as "natural", "autonomous", and "organic"' (1986: 11). The reintegration of life and art in film, however, was to occur in the mainstream if it did at all, a film culture of psychological realism and narrative drama soliciting audience identification. The formally 'radical' aspects of the cinema of excess, the Méliès tradition of magic and trickery, was to take root in the avant-garde tradition of art and aesthetic experimentation, splitting once again a culture of mimesis from a culture of formal play. It is a split that, I would argue, lives on in what becomes a reconfigured relation of avant-garde and mass culture in specific film cultures. Huyssen describes the psychology of the ongoing dialectic thus:

> Or, to put it differently, as modernism hides its envy for the broad appeal of mass culture behind a screen of condescension and contempt, mass culture, saddled as it is with pangs of guilt, yearns for the dignity of serious culture which forever eludes it. (1986: 17)[9]

shock, perception, subjectivity

The eternal unfixity of positions within the socio-cultural field is, however, demonstrated neatly by the discourses on film in the following decade, a context in which the rise of fascism in Europe, predicated in part on an aesthetics of political power, created a new urgency for thinking the role of culture in social reproduction.[10] The splits between film and everyday life, avant-garde and mainstream, undergo a critical reworking in the 1930s in the work of Walter Benjamin and Siegfried Kracauer. Benjamin's artwork essay is a thesis on the ways in which film may unsettle the complicit relations of art, privilege and social distinction, and advance a revolutionary culture. It wields a dialectic between the older-tradition cultures of painting and theatre, and the new form of film. Technology, as the title suggests, plays a key part in shifting the definition of art from that of the original, unique object of individual contemplation, to that of the endlessly reproducible text, closer to the commodity. Film, in its elision of presence and absence, the referent in the real world and the screen as referent, reconfigures the conventional definition of art as an object whose authority resides in the nature of its originality, its singular presence. The notion of aura that Benjamin attributes to this paradigm in which the artwork exists is then jeopardized by the multiple form of film, whose reproducibility lends itself to widened access, and is spread out across the terrain of the social in sites of exhibition. Yet the threat that reproduction appears to present to the singular work of art takes a reverse turn. In a footnote to the essay Benjamin notes, 'To be sure, at the time of its origin a mediaeval picture of the Madonna could not yet be said to be "authentic". It became "authentic" only during the succeeding centuries and perhaps most strikingly so during the last one' (1936/1999: 243). The disruption that reproduction presents is not to the singular art work, whose authenticity is doubled in relation to the new forms of reproducible art in the sense in which fakes, forgeries and copies consolidate the status of the 'original'. The threat is rather to the concept of and our relationship to culture itself.

The effect of technological reproduction in the form of film in the first half of the twentieth century forces a disruption and subsequent realignment in the categories of cultural value. The 'original' work of art weathers the storm to emerge as more authentic than in earlier times, whilst the status of film oscillates between the varied statuses of avant-garde experimental works, the emergence of classic narrative form in sound film, and the mass spectacle of newsreels and explicitly politically motivated film (Hansen, 1987). In this context, as Hansen points out, Benjamin's essay is both an intervention and an act of critical redemption, attempting to draw film and photography back into the folds of a political project in which culture was to play a key part in social transformation.

The detailed thesis that Benjamin sets out relies on a shift in the collective organization of perception. Influenced by Brecht's work on distanciation (particularly in the section on acting), Benjamin proposes that film, through the process of editing, fragments and disrupts the field of vision in a dialectic of continuity and discontinuity. Drawing an affinity with industrial modes of production, which fragment social reality by disembedding workers from social contexts of creativity and use by placing them in an isolated context of mechanical labour, and by removing the commodity from contexts of production through means of transportation, the spatio-temporal reconfiguration of the modes of production are replayed to the viewer through the spatial and temporal disjunction of film. Denied the contemplative moment in the presence of the artwork (identification, absorption), the audience instead is faced with the shock of modernity returned in the experience of film.

The decline of the aura in Benjamin's account suggests a shift in audience perception facilitated by the new technology of film production, positing a polarity between the auratic work (aesthetics) and the masses. This is explicated more fully in the wielding of the binary distance/proximity. For while the effect of shock in the Brechtian sense implies a distance from the object, in Benjamin's account the terms are reversed. It is the original artwork that imposes the critical, contemplative distance, whilst the reproducible representation of film initiates a desire in the masses to 'bring things "closer" spatially and humanly, which is just as ardent as their bent toward overcoming the uniqueness of every reality by accepting its reproduction' (1936/1999: 217). For Benjamin, the insatiable desire for reproduced images is a desire to unhinge the object from its context, to destroy its uniqueness and perceive an equality between things, a perception fed more broadly by the plethora of reproduced commodities. Here, the particular qualities of film are crucial to the thesis. The description of 'closeness' is dependent on the film's mixing of scale in the range of shots (he cites the close-up in particular), a kind of denaturalization of perception. This is compounded by the process of editing that mixes the sequence of images ('their constant, sudden change'), and the shifting focus of perception on 'hidden details of familiar objects' and 'commonplace milieus'. Finally, space and time are rendered plastic, malleable: 'With the close-up, space expands; with slow motion, movement is extended' (1936/1999: 229), supporting the barely metaphorical claim that 'we calmly and adventurously go traveling'.

Importantly for Benjamin, film's invocation of a distracted spectatorial gaze is not a negative hypothesis regarding loss of critical faculty. In a somewhat surprising move, Benjamin reads the distracted gaze as facilitating a particular form of perception, a look turned awry, coming from left field. The experience of cinematic perception is one of unexpected association rather than prescribed response, linking the past through memory, the everyday through detail, the unconscious involuntary mechanism that feeds our relationship to vision.[11] This description of distraction and its effects is worked through in greater detail in Benjamin's other work, most explicitly in the arcades project, where the phenomenological relationship between objects and the subject concerns Benjamin in a redemption of commodity culture. The distracted gaze shares affinities with the *flâneur*'s lack of engagement and absorption on the one hand, and subjective responses to the environment on the other. Vision here is not an optical mechanism akin to the camera, but a bodily response, an 'intimate fusion of visual and emotional enjoyment' (1936/1999: 227).[12]

The notion of distraction and sensory perception appears also in the work of Kracauer. Like Benjamin, Kracauer turns distraction into a positive. 'They [the spectators] are not prompted by a desire to look at a specific film or to be pleasantly entertained,' he writes. 'What they really crave is for once to be released from the grip of consciousness, lose their identity in the dark, and let sink in, with their senses ready to absorb them, the images as they happen to follow each other on the screen' (1960: 159–60). As Miriam Hansen argues, both writers are working at a time of historical urgency and bleak political events, the 'all out gamble of the historical process' manifested in the rise of fascism. The application of technology to the machinations of war presented a dystopian narrative of social possibility, hinged to a rationalism that tipped over into its opposite.[13] In the face of this, Benjamin and Kracauer sought a different ending to political events of the time and the applications of technology in the mass media:[14]

> Like Benjamin, Kracauer invested the mass media's double-edged implication in the crisis of modernity with therapeutic or cathartic intentions: the hope that a public, and sensory, recognition of "innervation" (Benjamin's term) of contemporary reality could deflect the fatal course of history, so that the final catastrophe in this crisis could yet be averted. (Hansen, 1997: xii)[15]

What we find in their work is a return of 'art' (or here mass culture) to life, a mixing of these Kantian divisions within practices of cinematic, mass culture: memory and screen image, street-life and cinematic narrative overlap, and converge at the point of the spectator. Where Benjamin locates the dialectical moment in the shock of the edit, Kracauer invokes 'chance', the necessarily disordered and confused spectacle of events in the slapstick film. Here, objects and subjects are misrecognized, doubled, reversed in their meaning; importantly, for Kracauer, the outcome is not knowable, for slapstick represents a discontinuous narrative where seriality replaces closure.[16] The potential for film to endlessly replay events, to present images and scenes from different moments and contexts in juxtaposition, butting up against one another, offered both writers an allegorical way of reversing the inevitability of history.

What is also suggested in their writing is a notion of subjectivity decentred by its encounter with this 'new technology'. In the artwork essay Benjamin explicitly references Freud and *The Psychopathology of Everyday Life*, as a text that changed everything. This is a poignant historical configuration of the unconscious, the seat of irrational forces, the experience of modernity and film. The influence of Freud is traceable in Benjamin's account: film re-presents ourselves on the screen but as an alienated form, absent, lacking corporal substance; the haunting of the modernist subject by his/her otherness. Leo Charney writes of this convergence of cinema and modern sensibility as a process of drift, casting us free of the notion of identity as positivist presence. 'In the techniques of cinema,' he writes, 'the ephemeral moment became the engine of motion, the peak moment the spur for stimulation, the empty moment the site of spectatorship' (1998: 7). Film represents the moment at once past (a recorded otherness) and contemporane-ously fleeting in the passing of images across the screen, the 'engine of motion'. The cinema presents us with our own loss of presence to ourselves whereby our ability to apprehend the given moment always takes place after the event, therefore temporally we are split off from the present and our own presence. Anne Friedberg casts this relationship in a different light through the notion of the virtual mobile gaze, but leads to similar conclusions. The notion of mobility of vision presented by cinema (Benjamin's travelling) offered an alternative to the panoptic surveillant gaze, a mobility of vision that decentred the subject's concrete existence 'emphasizing mobility and fluid subjectivity rather than restraint and interpellated reform' (Friedberg, 1993: 16). In both accounts, the technological apparatus of the cinema ushers in a new form of perception and subjectivity, characterized by the alienation and fragmentation of experience that serve as the tropes of modernism.

climates of change

From Benjamin through to Charney and Friedberg, the cinematic form is itself endowed with the ability to transform audience perception to various political ends. In Benjamin's work, the suggestion is that cinema will reverse the tendency of fascism to aestheticize politics by 'politicizing art'. For Charney and Friedberg the consequences of a shifted subjectivity are less overtly rendered. Yet, the diffi-culty of these theses which propose a shifted structure of perception attributable to cinema is a latent technological determinism. The political potential lies in its form, and its effect on an undifferentiated mass; for Benjamin this is manifest in the shock of the viewing experience. Yet, as Gunning and Huyssen argue, the shock effects of early cinema live on in both the avant-garde and mainstream cinema with no guaranteed return (special effects, for example, can claim no inherent radicalism). For my purposes, this attribution of the political to the cinematic apparatus relocates politics within a generalized effect of technology.

To return to the original concerns of this chapter, the discrete relationships of film culture that become manifest in particular sites of exhibition and circuits of distribution are lost to a generalized effect of technology. The claim to radicalness in this context is as limited in its scope as the avant-garde preoccupation with the formal characteristics of the text. For what remains in play throughout the twentieth century is the cultural value and legitimation of various cultural practices in relation to one another. As I will argue in the following chapter, film viewing is located within socially specific sites, and our access to these formations is dependent upon our position (enunciative modalities) within the discourses of information that circulate with film. To return to Bourdieu's thesis, the divisions of Kantian aesthetics continue to trouble the value of diverse film cultures. And whilst the binaries of art and life may not appear as resolute as they once did, their imbrication within a discourse of commodity culture is no longer perceived to be the radical mixing that is proposed in Benjamin's thesis, or that of the avant-garde. The elision of art and life has become reworked in a context in which film spills out across the bounds of the text into various commodity forms. The apprehension of film as either separate object or commodified experience produces a new twist to the Kantian distinction – a twist concurrent with the seismic shift from national to global cultural production.

The thesis that film presents potentially a rewriting of the bourgeois conceptions of culture as disinterested takes as its foundation a belief in the ability of culture to change the world. For Huyssen, and Rodowick, this belief is rooted in the European avant-garde and political modernism respectively (Huyssen, 1986: Rodowick, 1988). Huyssen argues that a revival of the avant-garde is not the solution:

> Any such attempt would be doomed, especially in a country such as the United States where the European avant garde failed to take root precisely because no belief existed in the power of art to change the world. (1986: 7)

In place of a call to arms, Huyssen suggests that motivations of the avant-garde are not best served by art, but by 'decentred movements which work toward the transformation of everyday life' (1986: 15). Similarly Rodowick, in a study of political modernism, critiques the focus on the textual form of culture inherent to what he calls the discursive formation of political modernism. In a castigating conclusion he writes 'political modernism's particular delimitation of the text as a site of "political" activity can now be understood as naive' (1988: 287). In a reading of theory and practice together, Rodowick argues that the valorization of formal properties of avant-garde texts as promoting new modalities of subjectivity fails to engage with the institutional relations that constrain and enable what film culture may be.

What then happens to modernism, its binary splits and political project? By way of ending, I want to bring attention to a metaphor of temperature that has come to characterize the movements of modernism and postmodernism, and which I think is suggestive of the process of dissolve that is seen erroneously to characterize the transition of one era to another. Time and again in reading the texts of or about modernism, the concept of coldness, or even freezing temperatures, occurs in the writing. Adorno writes of Benjamin 'he was drawn to the petrified, frozen or obsolete elements of civilization', and again, 'Small glass balls containing a landscape upon which snow fell when shook were among his favourite objects' (in Friedberg, 1993: 49).[17] Here Adorno captures Benjamin's fascination with the miniature, the detail that speaks of another time and space but which exists simultaneously to burst in upon the present: the frozen image, the object which splits open to reveal its relationship to other moments of time. For Benjamin, the frozen aspects of commodity culture presented both the problem of temporal separation and the potential re-reading of the object of the past. In a different context, a discussion of the demise of ideology, Kracauer images the decline of the old belief systems as becoming 'increasingly cooler . . . it is only the cooling process which is irreversible' (1960: 295). Modernity, then, is figured as an era of coldness, fixity in the frozen image. Borrowing a metaphor from thermodynamics, Kracauer invites us to think of ideology as a central system losing its energy, its heat which 'in the course of time can no longer flow back to it'. Writing in the postwar period, Kracauer describes a type of thawing of modernity, a loss of power figured here as heat.

This metaphor of thermodynamics appears again in the work of Charney. Writing on the loss incurred in modernity (the loss of presence), Charney turns to a text from 1852 by Sir William Thomson, which articulated the law of thermodynamics. In brief, the law that every exchange that creates heat must also waste heat; the law of an impossible return to a prior state before exchange (friction) takes place. Science then steps in as the explanatory parallel that illuminates the condition of modernism, the movement towards zero degrees. If modernism is thought through this metaphor of coldness, then postmodernism is conceived as the opposite, the thawing of modernism, a heating up that takes us into a final meltdown. It is present in Marshall Berman's title *All that is Solid Melts into Air*, the recycling of Marx's phrase, and occurs in more virulent form in Baudrillard's 'hot ecstasy' of communication. These metaphors of temperature suggest a natural shift from one era to another, experienced as a different climate of opposing characteristics. It suggests the shift from modernism to post-modernism is the melting of binaries, the dissolve of systems of power and the ability to classify (the melted form becomes liquid). Such tropes encourage us to think of the two terms as oppositional, separate, that a culture of modernist film is separate from a postmodernist framework. I want to suggest in the following chapter a different weather system, where the climates or extreme temperatures co-exist.

Notes

1 'The definition of cultural nobility is the stake in a struggle which has gone on unceasingly, from the seventeenth century to the present day, between groups differing in their ideas of culture and of the legitimate relation to culture and to works of art, and therefore differing in the conditions of acquisition of which these dispositions are the product' (Bourdieu, 'Introduction' to *Distinction*, p. 2). In *The Rules of Art*, Bourdieu reproduces this historical narrative as linear: speaking of the literary field in the 1880s, 'From now on, the unified literary field tends to organize itself according to two independent and hierarchised principles of difference: the principle of opposition, between pure production, destined for a market restricted to producers, and large-scale production, oriented towards the satisfaction of the demands of a wide audience, reproduces the founding rupture with the economic order, which is at the root of the field of restricted production' (p. 121).

2 Bridget Fowler illuminates the biographical similarities between Bourdieu and Williams: 'The son of a postman in a village in the South-West Pyrenees area of Bearn, in France, Bourdieu is very like his late contemporary, Raymond Williams, in being from the marchlands of a metropolitan country, that is to say, in a peasant area within a late capitalist society' (1997: 1).

3 Where Foucault concentrates on the discourses of medicine, law, hygiene and punishment as they impact on individuals through an eventual interpellation of the docile subject, the discourse of culture is an under-represented area in his work.

4 Huyssen cites the existence of the avant-garde as preceding the French Revolution: 'Historically the concept of the avant garde, which until the 1930s was not limited to art but always referred to political radicalism as well, assumed prominence in the decades following the French Revolution. Henri de Saint Simon's *Opinions litteraires, philosophiques et industrielle* (1825) ascribed a vanguard role to the artist in the construction of the ideal state and the new golden age of the future, and since then the concept of an avant garde has remained inextricably bound to the idea of progress in industrial and technological civilization . . . Throughout the 19th century the idea of the avant garde remained linked to political radicalism' (Huyssen, 1986: 4–5).

5 Gunning's point is that concern with narrative has overshadowed the similarities between them: 'The history of early cinema, like the history of cinema generally, has been written and theorized under the hegemony of narrative films' (1990a: 56).

6 The 'magic' of cinema, appearing to connect with the Méliès tradition of film making, appears in the journal. In an article entitled 'A New Cinema, Magic and the Avant Garde', Robert Herring writes: 'But we can't get on unless we keep a firm hold on magic. As that is our foundation, it comes to keeping our feet on the ground. It is surprising that many prefer a tight-rope.' Yet Herring's definition of 'magic' bears recourse to the aura of the artwork rather than the visual play of Méliès. The article ends: 'A bit less quackery, a bit more appreciation of magic which is not camera tricks in black and white.' In *Close Up*, Volume IV, no. 4, April 1929, reprinted in Donald *et al.*, 1998: 50–7.

7 The collective was not immune to the ways in which class was manifested in and through film culture. An article by R. Bond gives an account of the censorship of exhibition in class terms ('Acts under the Acts'). The article reports an incident in 1929 of the London Workers' Film Society applying to London County Council for a licence to screen uncensored films on Sunday afternoons. The LCC refuse on this occasion, and again in 1930 for an application to exhibit Eisenstein's *Battleship Potemkin*. The report comments that the decision was 'actuated by class' (Bond, 1930, 1998: 301). What emerges is differential treatment of the Film Society, whose members paid 25 shillings to join, and other societies (such as the obviously working class Workers' Film Society) which charged a shilling. The account poignantly captures the contradictions of the licensing criteria, '*any* member of the general public can join these latter societies. You see, if you pay twenty-five shillings to the Film Society, you are not a member of the general public' (1998: 302).

8 As a counter-tendency to this tradition, Kracauer provides a commentary that locates the specific nature of film within the medium itself, necessitating a break with former artistic traditions. In an essay entitled 'Basic Concepts', Kracauer writes, 'When calling the cinema an art medium, people usually think of films which resemble the traditional works of art in that they are free creations rather than explorations of nature. These films organize the raw material to which they resort into some self-sufficient composition instead of accepting it as an element in its own right.' He continues in a new paragraph, 'Yet such a usage of the term "art" in the traditional sense is misleading. It lends support to the belief that artistic qualities must be attributed precisely to films which neglect the medium's recording obligations in an attempt to rival achievements in the fields of fine arts, the theater, or literature. In consequence, this usage tends to obscure the aesthetic value of films which are really true to the medium' (Kracauer, 1960: 39).

9 A similar point is made by Bourdieu in his analysis of the restricted field of production (the avant-garde) and the general field of production: 'One should beware of seeing anything more than a limiting parameter construction in the opposition between the two modes of production of symbolic goods, which can only be defined in terms of their relations with each other. Within a single universe one always finds the entire range of intermediaries between works produced with reference to the restricted market on the one hand, and works determined by an intuitive representation of the expectations of the widest possible public on the other' (1993: 127).

10 At the time that Benjamin and Kracauer both struggled over the role of culture, Alfred Rosenberg, a leading spokesman on the subject in Germany, produced *Der Mythus des 20. Jahrhunderts* (1930). Where Benjamin and Kracauer were responding to the democratizing potential of the mixity of the city, the metropolis figured in Rosenberg's work as a condition of 'mongrel art', the forms of expressionism and impressionism that constituted modern art: 'The metropolis began its race-annihilating work. The coffee-houses of asphalt men became studios; theoretical bastardized dialectics became laws for ever-new "directions". A Race-chaos of Germans, Jews and anti-natural street races was abroad. The result was mongrel "art"' (1930/1992: 394).

11 The artwork essay ends with a section connecting futurism and the aestheticization of war with war and spectacle more generally. In the final lines Benjamin argues 'Its self-alienation has reached such a degree that it is capable of experiencing its own destruction as an aesthetic enjoyment of the highest order. So it is with the aestheticization of politics, which is being managed by fascism. Communism responds with the politicization of art.' The shift of gear in this passage is quite remarkable, and Susan Buck-Morss writes illuminatingly on it: 'This paragraph has haunted me for the twenty-odd years I have been reading the Artwork essay – a period when politics as spectacle (including the aestheticized spectacle of war) has become a commonplace in our televisual world. Benjamin is saying that sensory alienation lies at the source of the aestheticization of politics, which fascism does not create, but merely "manages" (*betreibt*). We are to assume that both alienation and aestheticized politics as the sensual conditions of modernity outlive fascism – and thus so does the enjoyment taken in viewing our own destruction' (Buck-Morss, 1993: pp. 123–44).

12 See Jan Campbell, *The Embodied Gaze* (forthcoming, Polity Press) for a further development of the bodily relationship to the cinematic image.

13 See Zygmunt Bauman for a reading of the Holocaust as the 'rational' conclusion to industrialization (Bauman, 1989).

14 The different fates of Kracauer and Benjamin are flagged up by Miriam Hansen in her introduction to *Theory of Film*. She relates the story of a meeting between the two writers in the midst of the political catastrophe for the two Jewish men: 'Soma Morgenstern, novelist and former Vienna correspondent of the *Frankfurter Zeitung*, describes how he and Benjamin, on their way to the prefecture, ran into Kracauer, seated in front of a cafe, scribbling eagerly. At the end of the familiar desperate conversation about expired transit visas and the perpetually delayed French exit visa, Morgenstern recalls asking Kracauer, "What will become of us, Krac?" To which the latter replied, without thinking twice, "Soma, we will all have to kill ourselves here", and quickly returned to his notes. As they reached the prefecture, Benjamin turned to Morgenstern and remarked, "What will happen to us cannot be easily predicted. But of one thing I'm sure: if anyone will *not* kill himself, it's our friend Kracauer. After all, he has to finish writing his encyclopedia of film. And for that you need a long life"' (Hansen, 1997: xiv). Ironically, it is Benjamin of course, who

commits suicide on the border, attempting to leave France through Spain. In a series of events that read with all of the disorder and chaos of slapstick, but without the redeeming possibility of reversal, the border is closed when Benjamin reaches it; he commits suicide during the night; by the morning the border is reopened.

15 Hansen comments on Kracauer's postwar work, *Theory of Film*, that 'the elided historical object of the book is not film as a phenomenon of late capitalism but, more specifically, the question of film after Auschwitz' (1997: xiv). This concern of the place of culture after such a momentous, dehumanizing event is echoed by A. Alvarez's questioning of the purpose of poetry after Auschwitz, yet the affinity of mechanization in both film and the concentration camps places film in a more complicit relation to inhumanity.

16 This is a feature that returns in the format of the computer game in the age of digital imaging: see Chapter 7.

17 Friedberg interprets this quote brilliantly through the narrative structure of the film *Citizen Kane*: 'The glass enclosed snow scene, a souvenir like the one Kane clutches on his deathbed at the beginning of *Citizen Kane*, serves as a symptomatic clue to Benjamin's unfinished project' (1993: 49).

CHAPTER TWO

Spatial effects: film cultures and sites of exhibition

A century on from its inception, the public, institutionally organized collective spaces to view film within Europe are the multiplex cinema, the independent arthouse cinema and the art gallery.[1] These diverse institutional locations offer different experiences of film, locating it within diverse histories and socio-cultural networks. If, in the early part of the twentieth century, film appeared to offer a multiplicity of possibilities (of political transformation, of bodily pleasure, of an imbrication of art and life), a century later the institutional locations on offer represent a radical paring down of those possibilities.

It might be argued in response to the framing of these three various sites of film cultures that the institutional identity presents a coherence that belies the crossing of films across such boundaries. Further, that to identify institutional sites of exhibition as representative of different film cultures is a further polarization of aesthetic traditions. In response I would argue that my concern is not to classify, and thus delimit, aesthetic filmic practices. Film as a media is multiple, infinite, always in excess of strict categorical definitions. Nor am I arguing that film cultures present a coherent body of work existing in discrete domains (the multiplex, the arthouse, the gallery). Mutual influence and cross-referencing, co-existence and appropriation subvert any definitive sense of boundary. What I am proposing is that the context of exhibition contributes to the social value of film cultures. In the exploration of these sites, certain formal aesthetic traditions adhere to film texts more strongly than others, but none are definitive features of 'arthouse' or 'multiplex'. In the first part of this chapter I address the problem of the homogeneous meanings that have come to accrue to film as mass culture and avant-garde production; returning briefly to the critical debates framing the history of different film practices, this section troubles the notion of a singular avant-garde and a monolithic tradition of film as mass culture. The following sections then turn to an understanding of film cultures as institutionally and spatially located.

instituting a dialectic

40 If the history of media studies is coloured by the play-off of oppositional readings on the value of culture (Adorno versus Benjamin, Lukacs versus Brecht), the focus of debate falls on the value of mass versus high culture, a political avant-garde practice against the fetishized commodity. What is implicit in these rivalrous claims is the clarity of these apparent divisions between cultural forms and practices. The key questions for an enquiry into the effects of culture then become either redemptive (mass culture is redeemed through its appropriation into popular cultural appropriations and uses), or transformative (how to undermine the hegemony of dominant market forces either through critical readings of texts or in the manufacture of 'political' culture). I want to pursue a different type of enquiry, which is concerned and dealt with somewhat briefly here, with the historical development of specific film cultures. This returns to the ongoing framing of film as mimetic or abstract in Chapter 1. Second, I want to argue that particular film cultures develop within specific institutional and social spaces, that the purported value of film, and our understanding of it as precisely a culture, derives in part from its place within spatial contexts, particular sites within cities and regions, related to other cultural practices, and connected to larger networks of circulation.

The multiplex and the arthouse cinemas present an extreme division of film cultures, a divide that speaks the triumph of capital; as the multiplex proliferates, the arthouse increasingly takes on the appearance of a rare species, endangered and in need of protection. Yet this gloss evades the central dynamic at work in the relationship between these cultures, one in which positions are both carved out in relation to the other and also in a dynamic structural play. To conceive of each homogeneously overlooks the complex formation of cultural fields as historical and spatial entities. How then do we read the lineages of the arthouse and the multiplex as complex formations? Friedberg argues against the divide between modernism and mass culture: 'one must, instead, examine the bifurcated lineage of art and its relation to mass culture' (1993: 165). To begin with, what we have come to understand as arthouse film culture elides the diverse practices and movements of modernism and the avant-garde. For Andreas Huyssen (1986) the elision of modernism and the avant-garde is a retrospective reading enacted by the discourses of art criticism. Whilst art criticism has enhanced this divide, the opposition of a modernist avant-garde to mass culture is traceable at least to Clement Greenberg's essay of 1939, 'Avant-Garde and Kitsch'.

As the title of the essay indicates, Greenberg's reading reproduces a division between a serious art practice and a frivolous, stylized mass culture. The argument that the avant-garde is the last bastion of valuable cultural production is a familiar one, although as Mary Kelly points out, Greenberg's 'core of modernist criticism' is 'far from coherent' (1981: 49).[2] What is interesting about this essay is its perspective on the creation of an internal art world, self-referential and coiled in on its own concerns:

> The avant-garde's specialization of itself, the fact that its best artists are artist's artists, its best poets, poet's poets, has estranged a great many of those who were capable formerly of enjoying and appreciating ambitious art and literature, but who are now unwilling or unable to acquire an initiation into their craft secrets. (Greenburg, 1939: 37)

Greenberg sounds an ambiguous note in the hinging of 'unwilling or unable', unsure of whether the avant-garde can be accused of exclusivity or the disinterest is an indictment of the modern audience. Whichever way, the spatial metaphor of a loss of ground dominates the piece. For Greenberg, the retreat of the avant-garde is a result of a split of this group of artists from its social base 'from which it assumed itself to be cut off', that is, the patronage of the bourgeoisie. Through its negation of bourgeois values, the avant-garde separates itself from public contexts and becomes established through an autonomy which proclaims the values of art alone. This, Greenberg postulates, leads to the formalist pre-occupations of art for art's sake. Thus, whilst avant-garde art withdraws from audiences in its critique of commodification and instrumentality, kitsch, main-stream culture appropriates the centre ground.

However, as Juan Suarez argues, echoing Huyssen's reading, the avant-garde and the mainstream are not simply homogeneous cultural entities of high and low culture respectively (Suarez, 1996). Where Greenberg's formulation characterizes the avant-garde as a singular movement in opposition to bourgeois values, and thus formalism against mimesis, Suarez argues that the avant-garde and modernism are two distinct features of cultural practice at this time. Drawing on Peter Burger's more Marxist interpretation, *The Theory of the Avant-Garde* (1974), Suarez quotes Burger's assertion that the separation of art from the social sphere is an 'ideological' moment, dating from the last decades of the eighteenth century, a moment where aestheticism prefigures modernism, as transcendent: 'The relative dissociation of the work of art from the praxis of life in bourgeois society becomes thus transformed into the (erroneous) idea that the work of art is totally independent of society' (Suarez, 1996: 12). The rise of aestheticism for Burger is consonant with the separation of politics and private life; in effect, the aesthetic transcendence of the Kantian aesthetic manoeuvres to become the official culture, whilst the avant-garde is rendered isolated, critical of the separation of art and life. For Burger, and Suarez, the avant-garde effects 'a break with bourgeois *and* artistic values' which predates the modernist moment.

What occurs in this account then is a splitting of artistic practice, a split predating modernism, in which there emerges two movements: an avant-garde opposed to both mass culture and bourgeois values, and a more official, legitimate artistic tradition of 'disinterested' practice. According to Wollen, in a reading of avant-garde film, under modernism the avant-garde splits again, but we might read this division as a more extreme reproduction of the separation in existence. In 'The Two Avant-Gardes', Wollen proposes a formalist cinema and a political avant-garde, one derived from a painterly tradition, the other from a literary one. Both traditions are profoundly affected, if not set in motion, by a break in representational history in the work of cubists. Thus, for Wollen, the dissembling of the mimetic relation of art, 'a disjunction between signifier and signified' (1976: 79), is common to both as an ideological critique. Yet the trajectory of each differs, as one takes the painterly tradition of concern with light, colour, form and the abstract language of the specifically cinematic (rendered as the visual rather than audial), the other borrows the literary concerns of montage, association and meaning. Wollen's project is to realign these two traditions within a semiological model, in which the project of modernism may be restored through an acknowledgement that meaning does not reside outside of the text (practices of reference) but within its own code or system of signification.

Wollen's text is both seminal and exemplary of the *Screen* tradition of film criticism, profoundly influenced by Althussarian Marxism (the ideological critique) and poststructuralism (the centred subject displaced through ellipses in language). The prioritization of the text, and representation as the locus of political concerns, fetishizes aesthetics to the exclusion of other social conditions. As Sylvia Harvey notes, the critical focus on the internal organization of the text neglects 'the insertion of that text within a particular apparatus, within a system of consumption, distribution or exchange specific to a particular society and a particular historical moment' (1978: 69). In response to this, I want to suggest that the avant-garde in these two modes of development becomes located in the institutional contexts of the gallery (formalist, abstract film) and the arthouse (the 'political' tradition). These sites represent more than situations of viewing of course; they are indicative of the modes of production, distribution and exchange of film within different institutional networks.

Within the gallery, film is firmly located within a history of art; the context provides the intertextual references of a filmic practice concerned with traditions of formal representation both in terms of the relationship to other artifacts within the immediate surroundings, and by the descriptive frameworks of catalogues and themed exhibitions. Here, film acquires the status of the collectible, limited in transmission (unlike film which moves to video and broadcast), and ascribed an exchange value (the gallery buys the work or offers it for sale at a fixed price).

The film culture of the gallery carries forward the tradition of the formalist bourgeois avant-garde, not predominantly through particular representational practices but through its economic dependency on the system of bourgeois patronage and latterly commerical sponsorship. In contrast, arthouse exhibition is a system of distribution characterized by its independence from mass cultural dissemination. The context of exhibition is derived from the location, the building (which I address in more detail below) and the programming of arthouse cinema. Whilst there are no explicit criteria for arthouse exhibitions, the label of 'independent' invokes both political affinities (anti capitalist monopoly) and aesthetic traditions. At its best, arthouse cinema attempts a heterogeneous pro-gramme of films made outside of the studio system, embracing at least three forms of filmic classification: the formally innovative film, the social realist text and foreign films (mainly including American films that fall outside the former two descriptions). In his exemplary article on art cinema, Steve Neale argues for distinct formal features of art film, providing an analysis of aesthetic features of art films in French, German and Italian culture. He adds the corollary that 'Even where the marks of enunciation themselves are heterogeneous, they tend to be unified and stabilised within the space of an institution which reads and locates them in a homogeneous way' (Neale, 1981: 15).

If arthouse cinema functions through a notion of independence, implicit to its identity is that which it is independent of. Thus, inscribed in its own programme is the dialectic of mainstream, monopolized filmic culture and a tradition separate from and acting against its definition of film. This dialectic suggests that the mainstream is homogeneous, coherent and consistent in its production of a film culture. Certainly this reading of Hollywood history as institutionally coherent has been proposed by film theorists as a reading of the studio system, dominating film production from the 1930s to at least the 1960s, and for Bordwell, Staiger and Thompson, beyond this point (Bordwell *et al.*, 1985). But before turning to this familiar narrative, I want to pick up on the label that Greenberg uses for mainstream film – kitsch. For Greenberg, kitsch is a formulation of the derivative nature of mass culture. In a paragraph striking for its pre-empting of Sontag's treatise on camp, he outlines its principal characteristics:

> Kitsch, using for raw material the debased and academicized simulacra of genuine culture, welcomes and cultivates this insensibility . . . Kitsch is mechanical and operates by formulas. Kitsch is vicarious experience and faked sensations. Kitsch changes according to style, but remains always the same. Kitsch is all that is spurious in the life of our times. (1939: 35)

For Greenberg, this is clearly a judgement of a moral order: mass culture as the ungenuine, the fake, the pretender. It draws its powers from its pretence of serious culture, which becomes 'debased', a 'simulacra' of the real. In this exercise,

44

Greenberg effects a polarization that simultaneously denigrates mass culture and centres the avant-garde as the genuine article. Mass culture is not original; in fact it borrows from the originality of high culture and distorts it as a formula.

Sontag's essay of course offers another reading of the fake. In 'Notes on Camp', the kitsch is rendered a sensibility, 'a mode of aestheticism' (1999 [1964]: 54). Connecting camp explicitly to the work and life of Oscar Wilde, Sontag renders camp as a style concerned with artifice, or rather not concerned with but appearing only in surface phenomena; it has no depth. Camp is not, importantly, an intrinscially subversive text or act ('Probably, intending to be camp is always harmful') (1999 [1964]: 58), but a general mode of being 'alive to a double sense in which some things can be taken' (1999 [1964]: 57). Hollywood film permeates the list of examples: *Trouble in Paradise* and *The Maltese Falcon* are cited as examples of great camp film for 'the effortless smooth way in which tone is maintained'. Part of the Hitchcock repertoire meets the criteria, and Sternberg's six American movies with Dietrich. Camp is an excess without the ambition to exceed: 'Camp is art that proposes itself seriously, but cannot be taken altogether seriously because it is "too much"' (1999: 59). Ultimately, camp is all that nature is not, it is in excess of the real, or what can pass as the real in terms of physical or emotional mimesis: 'Nothing in nature can be campy . . . most campy objects are urban' (1999: 55).

If Greenberg's statement on kitsch positions mass culture as a replica attempting the status of the original, Sontag rewrites it as a sensibility cut off from the original and yet illuminating the distance. It is at once innocent and performative, a 'way of seeing the world as an aesthetic phenomenon' (1999: 54). Mass culture as the seat of camp is then an acknowledgement of the derivative nature of all appearances and artifacts. Importantly, it renders nature as an impossible real, a relationship lost to a former age of innocence. Here, film retrieves or reproduces the excess of the cinema of attractions, its bodily sensations, its sensuousness. Mass cultural film exposes us to the theatrical nature of the real, the artwork without the aura, the representation detached from the referent of the physical world. Whilst this is in some senses a utopian reading of camp film, it pushes us towards the contexts in which film emerged and has continued to develop in the sites of the multiplex; a world of cultural commodification which extends across the bounds of different artifacts and texts.

In summary, different traditions of film culture (the avant-garde, modernism and mass culture) have been read historically through the debate of a relationship to the real, of form and content. I am suggesting that the relationship of form and content, of mimesis and abstraction, becomes reconfigured through the different contexts of exhibition. What emerges is a binary of a different order: on the one

hand a desire to maintain the purity of the singular object of the film text, and
on the other, the dissolution of the film into a range of ancillary products in a
context of consumption. Or, more simply, film as a discrete object or film as an
experience. The institutional context of viewing film becomes central to an
understanding of how different film cultures operate. My interest in institutions
is not their internal hierarchical structure of management, but their spatial
location, their position within networks of exchange and the types of social
practice that they facilitate.

flânerie, space and time

In *Window Shopping: Cinema and the Postmodern* (1993), Anne Friedberg traces
the relationship of film to commodity culture. The culture firmly in place in the
multiplex, situating film as one commodity among others, is traced back to
the modernist innovation of commodity display in arcades, boulevards, and later
the department store and shopping mall. In this reading, the context of film's
emergence in the moment of modernism consists of a type of confluence in the
acts of looking, at both shop displays and cinematic images. For Friedberg,
borrowing extensively from Benjamin's arcades project, the new commodity
culture of the first part of the century invokes a particular form of looking
and being in the urban environment. This she names the mobile virtual gaze, a
look that moves position like the camera, shifting across a range of objects, each
separate and unconnected. Like Benjamin, Friedberg reads this movement across
objects as incurring a dialectical splitting, whereby the montage of objects
produces a response: 'The shopper enacts the social relations between things.' Like
Baudelaire's impassioned observer, the *flâneur* shifts anonymously through the
crowded streets of the metropolis, both seer and seen.

Friedberg's reading traces a commodified type of cultural experience to the late
nineteenth century, where the twin forces of an emergent tourist economy and
a consumer culture, it is argued, realized a particular form of 'looking'. Whilst
tourism engendered a culture of interest in other places (underpinned by a
colonial infrastructure), consumer culture brought goods from elsewhere into
proximity. In addition to these encounters with otherness, read as a type of
cultural tourism, the newly formed urban centres brought a clustering of peoples
and commodities; moreover, these metropolitan centres were constructed around
the possibility of mobility and a mobile cultural gaze, directing the populace to
the wide central streets of boulevards in Paris, of shopping arcades and department
stores. Friedberg argues that these new spaces of consumption reorganized the
subject's relation to space and time. The manufactured structures of the shopping

mall and department store effectively insulated the consumer against the elements, providing the conditions of an 'endless summer' (1993: 3), a simulacral environment detached from any sense of 'nature'. Here, Friedberg's reading plays into Sontag's notion of mass culture as artifice, detached from nature or the real. And with the decontextualization of goods from various parts of the globe, rendered equivalent by their commodity status, spatial co-ordinates are jumbled. Such spatial disorientation for Friedberg is matched by a temporal disjunction: 'these architectural spaces were, in a sense, machines of timelessness, producing a derealized sense of the present and a detemporalized sense of the real' (1993: 4).

Within this analysis of a newly commodified gaze, cinema assumes a position of priority offering a convergence of the tourist and consumer gaze: 'Cinema spectatorship,' argues Friedberg, 'brought together the mobilized gaze of the shopper and tourist into a "virtual mobility"' (1993: 147). The presentation of images from elsewhere (often unidentifiable places or studio constructions of place), and from another time, coupled with the techniques of editing that facilitate the manipulation of sequence, produce what Friedberg identifies as the emergent virtual gaze of postmodernism. The past is rendered a commodity experience with a price attached, available to the consumer at any time, open to repetitive viewing. Drawing on Bergson's account of the temporal in *Matter and Memory*, whereby duration becomes the contemporaneity of the present and past, Friedberg cites the cinema as the privileged vehicle for an understanding of subjective time in opposition to standard time. Indeed, the argument is pushed further to claim that the mobile virtual gaze, residing at the nexus of tourism, consumption and cinema, becomes 'paradigmatic of a postmodern subjectivity' (1993: 132).

Friedberg provides a lucid and complex account of the various historic transformations that converge at the moment of cinema's emergence. There is, however, too great a sweep in the claims for a generalized shift in subjectivity, eliding the double meaning of the term 'mobility'. For Friedberg, mobility refers predominantly to a form of social meandering in the metropolis, a *flânerie*, characterized by a restless, distracted gaze across the displays of commodities. The second sense of mobility as a social fluidity, the ability to move within the hierarchical system of social categories, plays at the edges of the account. In a passage drawing out the implications of the argument, Friedberg states 'the fluidity of flanerie (once offered predominantly to men) was now offered as a pleasure to anyone – of any race, ethnicity, or gender – who had the capacity to consume' (1993: 147). The already generalized sensibility, the mobile virtual gaze, becomes a levelling social practice. Pushed into the present, the mobile virtual gaze reaches its apex in the context of the multiplex. Effectively relocating the cinema to the shopping mall, the multiplex is the realization of a spatial and temporal dissolve. Private time replaces public time in the proliferation of films and viewing times, as if the multiplex 'is a set of contiguous VCRs' (1993: 141). The mannequins of the mall come to life in the context of the cinema figured here as the '*not now* in the guise of the *now*'. The cinema, in this account, becomes the forum for a dialectic of past and present.

The main thrust of Friedberg's narrative is to posit a particular form of gaze, indicative of a decentred subjectivity, within the socio-historical context of modernism and postmodernism. The difficulty of this reading is the way in which cinema becomes a generalized practice, potentially offering to facilitate a social fluidity, an unhinging of the social differences reproduced through culture prior to an encounter with film. Whilst Friedberg maintains a sensitivity to the gendered nature of cinema culture, she neglects the dialectical relation of opposing film cultures, and their manifestation in social hierarchies, as cinema evolves. If the development of cinema as a social practice is closely related to the divisions in art practice of earlier centuries, such divisions were reconfigured differently at the beginning of the twentieth century by a new, technologically based media. Whilst I agree with Friedberg's account of the emergence of cinema within the paradigm of commodity culture, which culminates in the multiplex, I would argue that this is one part of a narrative which produces the avant-garde, and arthouse, as its subtext. The social divisions that accrue historically to the text of 'art', the value of abstract formalism above mimetic representation, become displaced onto the contexts of exhibition. Here, the marked distinction between the avant-garde film and the mainstream, studio-produced film resides in the conceptualization of film as a discrete object (within arthouse and to a greater extent the gallery) and the practice of film as an experience (the multiplex), a diffuse experience leaking out into various associated commodities.

film in the experience economy

James Hay, speaking of the American context of cinema development, remarks 'Cinema may be less recognizable for some social subjects as a distinct site' (1997: 224). Clearly, the cinema that Hay has in mind is the multiplex, characterized by its relocation of film viewing within a context of shops, sporting activities and outlets supplying food and drink. The *distinct* practice of film viewing is exchanged for a consumer practice where film viewing is but one option among many, or one possibility to combine with other activities. For Baudrillard, this relocation would signify an equivalence between practices, a levelling of all consumer practices under the logic of the commodity. Yet this universalizing reading of the multiplex glosses over the particular qualities of the experience, and the relationship which is forged between cinema and shopping. Whilst there have been many accounts of consumption that have challenged the negative and passive associations of consumerism (Abercrombie 1994; Featherstone, 1991; Lury, 1996; McRobbie, 1994), and provided a more nuanced analysis of particular practices, the specific alignment of consumption and cinema produces a particular frisson. Cinema, historically conceived of as a specific cultural practice, is reconfigured in the context of the multiplex as leisure, a more general and hybrid activity.

If the multiplex represents a convergence of leisure, entertainment and 'cultural' practices, a dissolution of the specific nature of each activity, this convergence is pushed further by changes to the film text itself. No longer a singular object, the mainstream film is produced as one component of a chain of associated products – indeed, as Wasko notes, the film may be imagined as the advertisement for ancillary products. In the spatial realignment of cinema, shopping and leisure, the film sustains an intertextual relationship to other practices within the location: the soundtrack of the film, the video and DVD, and the computer game provide a reformatted version of the film text available to purchase within the same location. Through its relationship to other outlets, the multiplex provides a context for the extension of the life of the film in other media, and a spatial extension as an experience that can be purchased and taken home. This signifies an important transformation of both the practice of film-going and the conceptualization of the film text. If both the activity and the text are less bounded or discrete, the blurring of definitions shifts film culture from object to an experience. This is a transition identified by Lee as a more general trend in the organization of production and consumption away from material forms towards the ephemeral, dematerialized experiential commodity (1993). The experiential economy is characterized by time-based goods, simultaneously used up in the moment and extended in the souvenir-like ancillary products. The experience economy is predicated on an intensity of experience, a sensual pleasure that burns brightly but does not endure in its original form. It is manifest not only in the shopping malls and multiplex centres, but in the theme parks and holiday centres where a particular experiential world is created.

In *A Cinema Without Walls*, Timothy Corrigan reads such changes in cinematic culture (from the 1960s and 1970s onwards) as a freeing up of subjectivity and identification. In an argument that is similar is some respects to Friedberg's, Corrigan states 'viewers emptied of subjectivity by the homogeneous address of a blockbuster industry can become mobile viewers across heterogeneous identities' (1991: 228). For Corrigan, the proliferation of film products, in tandem with the range of other images that we expose ourselves to, sets in play a mobility, 'viewing now means continually reinventing oneself and one's spatial and social location' (1991: 229). Yet, there is something of a short-circuit in the argument that exposure to more images produces a mobility. In one sense the convergence of different cultural and leisure practices affords a transgression of categories, which may be imaged as a type of mobility. Read from another direction, the collapse of categories of classification, invoking an imbrication of everyday life and culture, signifies an inability to orientate the self. Such fluidity does not necessarily suggest a social mobility, but can be turned around to figure as a regression, a social stasis within the confines of the imaginary. If, as Bourdieu forcefully argues, social distinction rests on the recognition of boundaries, the Kantian logic of disinterest and distance, a convergence of culture and everyday life signifies an indiscriminate social position. Whilst it may be argued that this is an imposition of a class judgement which is refused in the immersion of the self in the culture of the mall and multiplex, it does not negate the system of social stratification that resides as the dominant; it merely puts them in tension. Corrigan's argument begs the question, are we ever outside the imposition of value judgements, even or especially in those spaces presented as environments of social mobility? `

The argument I am making here does not reinvoke an account of social determinism against the postmodern re-evaluation of consumption. Rather, it is an argument for the coexistence of two narratives that mutually reproduce each other. The narrative of social reproduction I have traced back to the moment of modernism in terms of film culture, a moment in which film emerged within the shifting terrain of cultural value, but within which a modernist aesthetic centred back to become the institutional authoritative term, enforcing the markers of distinction that some artistic practices had set out to challenge. This modernist narrative refers also to the infrastructure of cultural funding, production and institutionalization supported by the state, therefore reinforcing the coherence of the nation in the face of an increasing internationalization of cultural commodities. This narrative is not displaced by the postmodern challenge, with its potential unfixity of social categories and identifications, its aestheticization of everyday life and its multinational system of production and distribution, but both movements (if we can call each a movement) co-exist more often in conflict than in co-acquiescence. These narratives are in tension precisely in the relationship between multiplex culture and arthouse culture.

This notion of relational value is modelled usefully by James Clifford, in what he terms the art–culture system (1988). Clifford's interest in the distinction between art and culture is specifically in the incorporation of 'other', 'primitive' cultures during the modernist period. The diagram that he produces to account for the way in which authenticity or value is ascribed to objects rests on and produces the distinction (art and culture). Whilst culture refers to all routine and symbolic activities in its widest application, it accrues a particular devalued meaning in

49

relation to art. Where art rests on notions of individual production, originality and transcendence, culture is rendered collective, material, reproduced. For Clifford, the 'system' consists of the institutional sites and paths of circulation through which objects travel. Transposing this model to film, the site of exhibition is an integral part of the system of circulation, albeit an end point. This is a particularly useful way of framing the system into which film emerges; the tendency for film to be situated within either sphere of art or culture is manifest in the exhibition-ary sites of the multiplex, arthouse and gallery. In the imbrication of culture and everyday life in the location of the mall, the value of that culture is at least in part configured by its relationship with its absent opposite.

How might this be so? The relationship of conflict between film as mass culture and film as a discrete practice is not predicated on the claims to symbolic status, but on a broader terrain of struggle between a multinational saturation of markets and the demise of arthouse, which in the present is largely national, film cultures (the postmodern and modern respectively). Paradoxically, the problem that arises in the discourse of opposition mounted by proponents of 'independent' cinema is that the dual history of modernism, the political and the formalist avant-garde, return within the narrative. The discourses through which oppositional identity is produced reinvoke the social status of art as distinct, in contrast to its political remit to invoke a more pluralist agenda for film making. The case of Dogme is a recent example of the playing out of these tensions. In 1995 a Danish group of film makers formed a collective and produced a manifesto, 'The Vow of Chastity' (www.dogme95.dk). The case of Dogme has provoked much media attention, and may legitimately be regarded as a successful intervention into marketing from a 'local' position (similarly *The Blair Witch Project* and self-branding). The Dogme manifesto, however, provides a richer example of how film cultures operate dialectically. For the manifesto is not a call explicitly proposing a broader definition of film culture, but rather it provides a series of rules to which film makers must adhere upon signing. Ostensibly, 'The Vow of Chastity' proposes a further delimiting of practice, a more circumscribed conceptualization of film making; only in dialectic with the mainstream, an oppositional culture that has monopolized markets, can the manifesto be understood as an intervention for a more heterogeneous culture.

The dual narratives of the avant-garde are invoked by Dogme in the following ways. In one sense, the manifesto declares an allegiance to the political avant-garde; indeed, the use of a manifesto references the earlier manifestos of the modernist period: the futurist cinema (1916), the realist manifesto (1920), the AKHRR 'Declaration' (1922), the Red Group Manifesto (1924), surrealist manifesto (1925), the ARBKD manifesto and statutes (1928). The avant-garde of the 1960s is cited as a worthy but failed attempt at filmic dissent, its failure analysed as a reliance on the concept of the *auteur* and an individualistic practice of 'bourgeois romanticism'. In recognizing this earlier failure, Dogme carries forward the tradition of counter-cinema as a political project of remaking film culture. Yet, the avant-garde, anti-bourgeois position is overlaid with a second opposition, to mass cultural cinema. Most explicitly this is formulated in clause eight, which states 'Genre movies are not acceptable'. Yet mass culture is present through a series of binaries; improvisation against superficial action, location shooting against a constructed set, truth against illusion. The two tropes that give a coherence to the manifesto are nature and purity. Where the film has been 'cosmeticized to death', the Dogme solution is an appeal to the spontaneous, the unconstructed, all that is not artificial. Thus, the technical qualities of film such as lighting, dubbed sound and special effects are eliminated in a return to a pure notion of film as the recording of dramatic interplay. This appears to shift attention to the 'content' of the film, the 'force of truth' in the terms of the manifesto. Yet the prescriptive measures of course determine a distinctive aesthetic: hand-held camera, long takes, long and middle shots as opposed to close-ups and cross-cutting, grainy texture, filmic features reminiscent of Super 8 and other 'experimental' formats which have remained at the margins of mainstream film making. The trope of purity, whilst ironic and self-parodic, refers not so much to the chastity of the collective, but to the manifesto itself as a chastisement of the mainstream. Here, the political and formalist tendencies of the avant-garde converge; in the presentation of an oppositional film culture, the focus of critique is not predominantly the infra-structure of production, distribution and exhibition, but a type of aesthetic which then becomes naturalized once again in the arthouse site.

spatial effects

If the argument so far has traced the historical divisions between filmic traditions, and has pointed to their manifestation in different sites of exhibition, can we know whether this distinction is played out in the use of such sites? Do these historical trajectories impact on the perceptions and practises of sites of exhibition? In place of my own ethnography, I draw on some of the research on audience behaviour conducted by groups reporting to the industry. This type of research is conditioned by its own interests in shaping and defining cinema practice; the narrative of the Cinema and Video Industry Research (CAVIAR) in producing annual reports, is unremittingly upbeat in its presentation of cinema attendance and trends.[3] For example, the report summary selects seven key points and presents them within the guise of the pub-quiz knowledge test, 'Did you know?' Statistics selected have the status of both trivia and economic forecast: '1999 saw a 5% increase in regular cinema-going', '70% of cinema-goers buy food, drink and merchandise at the cinema' (CAVIAR 17), and 'Average journey time to the cinema is 19 minutes' (CAVIAR 15). Yet the reports also offer a wealth of information on cinema and its related practices: the research surveys not only cinema attendance, choice of films and ancillary products, but also home-based 'lifestyle' activities such as video rental and purchase, access to digital and satellite channels, newspapers and magazines. What is more interesting is that whilst the range of subjects researched might lead us to speculate that lifestyle consumption has replaced demographics in industry analysis in pursuit of individual patterns of consumption, conversely, the material is subsequently cross-referenced by categories of class, age and gender. A postmodern consumer fluidity is overlaid by a grid of social classification showing the flows and blockages in the ebbing of cultures and identities.

The CAVIAR reports elucidate the differences in film viewing by class in three domains: the arthouse, the mainstream cinema including the multiplex, and the home. Indeed, the emergence of the multiplex reveals its origin as a response to a crisis of declining cinema attendance, exacerbated in the decades of the 1970s and 1980s by the inception of video, redirecting entertainment from public cinema sites towards the home. In order to reinvigorate the field, the multiplex was defined against both home entertainment and former cinema culture. In the drive to distinguish cinema practice from home entertainment, the multiplex was designed to maximize the corporal, sensory affect of cinema; thus investment in technology created surround-sound, wide-screen exhibition (Allen, 1998; Wasko, 1994). In distinction from arthouse cinema, with its ability to exhibit one film at a time, the multiplex offers greater choice of film from a menu of 8 to 10 screens (recent plans for 'megaplexes', for example at the site of the former Battersea Power Station in London, boast up to 32 screens; Birmingham's Star City, recently opened, has 30 screens) (Hanson, 2000).

As Sylvia Harvey notes in an essay collection dedicated to the centenary of film, significant sections of the population do not attend the cinema at all (1996). The picture constructed through the advertising industry studies supports this view. Crudely drawn, the statistics evidence a predominantly middle-class culture of the arthouse, a mixed band of middle- and lower-middle-class culture of the multiplex, and a working class culture of home view. The 1998 report summary cites 79 per cent attendance of 'art film' as comprising the social categories of A, B, C1 and 21 per cent C2, D, E. The information collated on promotional materials reveals another difference; specialist sources of information, which include specialist film magazines and listings produced by individual circuits, provided information for only a low percentage of those surveyed overall, and were used by the higher social categories. The main source of information about films screened at multiplexes is provided by the local press. Asked whether films are selected in advance of attendance, a quarter of visits to mainstream cinema were decided on the day of the visit, and similar percentage decide on arrival at the cinema. What emerges from these statistics is a division between a cinema culture produced through specialist sources of information and focused on the film itself, and a culture where the activity of cinema-going takes priority over the film viewed.

The social demographics utilized by the industry bodies neglect any mention of ethnicity as a social category, nor do the surveys include films from other ethnic traditions such as Hindi cinema. This omission is supplemented by a state-funded study conducted by the British Film Institute (BFI), 'Black and Asian Audiences' (2000),[4] which aims to determine how public sector bodies 'might help improve film-related products and services, in order better to meet the self-defined needs of people of African-Caribbean and South Asian descent living in the UK' (2000: 3). The study revealed that the location for viewing most films was the home, with a quarter nominating the five terrestrial channels, a fifth stating cable/satellite, and a fifth selecting video/DVD. Attendance at non-Asian multiplexes was 22 per cent overall; the proportion was slightly higher for South Asians (26 per cent) than for African-Caribbeans (20 per cent), possibly because a few multiplexes (for example, in Birmingham) show Bollywood films. The home-view figures again divided the respondents by ethnic group, with double the proportion of African-Caribbeans watching film at home rather than the cinema (almost a quarter). Cross-referenced by the material surveying problems with the cinema, the issue of representation arises. Concern about films (such as Tarzan movies and *Independence Day*) 'which were seen as demeaning or offensive to Black minorities' produces an alienation from mainstream cinema culture not evidenced in the industry research. The different system of data presentation makes for problematic comparisons with the CAVIAR reports. The BFI report does not explicitly list arthouse cinemas as a category, but lists non-Hindi multi-plex, non-Hindi 'smaller' cinema and Hindi/Bollywood. Using these categories, and assuming 'smaller' cinema to at least include arthouse, the findings of the study reveal that the majority of cinema-going for ethnic minorities surveyed is split between the multiplex and home view; both smaller cinemas and Hindi cinemas gain significantly smaller audiences. Cross-referenced by social grade, the information suggests a reversal of the former picture of lower-middle class attendance of multiplexes; 29 per cent of social grades A, B, C1 attend non-Hindi multiplexes against 16 per cent lower social grades, and a slight differential in terms of the Hindi cinema, with only 3 per cent of higher social grades citing this exhibitionary space against 8 per cent of lower categories (BFI, 2000: 24).

The picture that emerges from these various sets of statistics is an 'independent' film culture existing in the arthouse spaces for white and higher social grade audiences. The multiplex emerges as a more mixed social space in terms of ethnicity and class, but revealing itself to be a culture for the lower-middle-class respondents in particular. What are the implications of this for the use of social space, for networks of affiliation and for an understanding of the significance of film cultures for spatial practices?

exhibitionary cultures and spatial networks

The relationship between the cinema and the city has been subject to much critical analysis and debate over time. The coincident emergence of cinema and the modernist city (the first full realization of European metropolitan life) at the turn of the century inscribes more than an historical accident; each, it has been argued, inflected the development of the other, as camera work pondered the structures of cities from aerial shots, and cities developed attributes of what has become known since Debord as the society of the spectacle.[5] Travelling forward to the present, fewer cinemas in Britain remain at the centre of city life, and far more exist on its periphery, multiplexes built as 'out of town' developments, satellite spaces orbiting and, in turn, centring the city.

'Did you know: Average journey time to the cinema is 19 minutes?' (CAVIAR, 1997). The multiplex is a culture of car travel, rarely built near stations, the privatized transport of the car is often a necessity. A rather more interesting 'fact' resides in another report to the industry produced by Dodona Research, entitled 'Cinemagoing Europe' (1998). In a report that provides a forecast for the industry, Dodona states 'In 1992 nearly two-thirds of the new screens that had been built in Europe since 1975 were in the United Kingdom. By the end of 1997 the figure was still over 40%' (1998: 9). What emerges from this report is that the focus of multiplex development in Europe has been Britain; by 1997, Britain had 1089 multiplex screens, compared to the next highest statistic of Germany with 487 screens and France with 429 screens (Dodona, 2001: 47). The possible interpretations of this development are of course multiple and complex. The siting of multiplexes at the periphery of towns and cities has coincided with a project of urban renewal where the town centre has been the privileged focus, leaving the outskirts to weather various types of satellite formations. Urban renewal has also provided multinational companies with a train of potentially thriving city centres to link their services to; certainly, multiplex development is the province of the large multinationals. Exhibition ownership is characterized by the dominance of four leading multinational companies: Odeon Cinemas (having recently acquired ABC), UGC, United Cinemas International and Warner Village. Similarly, distribution is dominated by four related companies: UIP, Buena Vista, Columbia and Twentieth Century Fox, with Warner Bros trailing the main field. The location and ownership of cinema exhibition contributes then to a understanding of the narratives of the city, and their connectivity to larger networks of circulation, exchange and flow. This is not a claim that individual cultural practice adheres to specific narratives and pathways; the complexity of urban formations, a fabric characterized by difference and dissent, denies a coherent mapping of lived cultural practices. Rather, this account contributes to a sense of the conflicting narratives at work in the formation of cities, narratives that operate spatially (creating boundaries, territories for certain uses, paths that link certain practices with others) and temporally (invoking various historical notions of community, citizenship, nationhood and identity). The siting of the multiplex at the periphery of the city creates a cinema culture that is removed from the historical centre, which is possibly part of its appeal for groups marginalized by ethnicity, excluded from the narratives of a national past (a similar point to Miriam Hansen's reading of early cinema and immigrant populations in America[6]). Yet this is not simply an issue of spatial use. Issues of location and ownership of exhibition are related to the types of film circulating within the multiplex network. Despite the apparent crudity of arguments wielding a cultural homogeneity, the monopolization of distribution and exhibition in Britain has effectively excluded all but the most commercial of British, and nearly all films from other parts of Europe (Dodona, 2001). The notion of a pluralized culture of choice is severely challenged by the reports: 'Cinemagoing' suggests that 'as much as 60% [of the total film market], is constituted by the top twenty films at the box office' (2001: 36).

Multiplex culture is characterized by a form of spatial remove from the hub of the city, and an involvement with films that are predominantly from the Hollywood studios. What the multiplex culture offers is a type of connection between the individual and the global, bypassing local and national particularity. This engagement can be read positively, as Iain Chambers argues, in the spirit of democratization, as 'a distracted reception in which we all become "experts" and learn to move around inside the languages of the mass media' (1993: 191). Chambers's argument echoes Friedberg's sense of the new spaces of consumption as distracted and socially unaffiliated, a refusal even of the narratives of historical nationhood. Conversely, it can be read as the further institutionalization of a socially isolated and functional culture of 'spatial segmentation' (Morse, 1990). The multiplex culture may indeed operate contradictorily in the terms of both of these accounts. But what I want to argue is that it is a culture in dialogue or in tension with its other – the centred, modernist, historical narrative of the arthouse and gallery film culture. Where Chambers argues that 'modern mass culture involves the shattering of tradition in the secularization of the image', I would argue that tradition creates a different spatial and cultural intensity elsewhere. The 'contaminated' quality of metropolitan life that Chambers cites does not register a necessary collapse of prior narratives and networks, but rather a co-existence of forms.

The arthouse and gallery, in contrast, are ensconced in the centre of cities, and are often the subject of renovation and protective legislation (Jones, 2001[7]). The arthouse cinema in Britain is typically an old cinema that has retained independent ownership; its situation within towns and cities in a contemporary context of urban renewal is one of authenticity, a marker of the specificity of place. The cinema then becomes embedded in a social discourse of place, of the narratives of 'postmodern' architecture where the local historical markers of the urban fabric have become emblems of particularity. For David Harvey (1989), this process of urban renewal is part of a shift in policy and governance of the city, from a modernist technologically imaged and functionally designed concept, to a postmodernist image of eclecticism and vernacular traditions. In this reading, Harvey is keen to inflect a complexity to the concept of change, stressing the contradictory and unknowable outcomes of various practices of urban development. I would argue that cinema cultures contribute to this unevenness of epochal shift. The arthouse cinema, in the context of urban renewal, contributes to the postmodern vernacular of a mixed architectural heritage. Yet it also signifies an enduring narrative of modernism in a different context, that of film cultures. In a curious reconfiguration of the avant-garde movement, which historically emerged at the moment in which civil society developed independently from the state, the culture of arthouse realigns avant-garde and 'independent' film with the state through the funding of 'national' film and, in some cases, subsidy for exhibitionary sites.

In summary, film cultures are then social practices, materially rooted and connected to larger networks of exchange and flow. This terminology is of course borrowed from Castells in his analysis of the global, network society. For Castells, as for Soja, space is not an inert or static physical matter, but 'the expression of society' (1996: 440). Spatial forms and processes are created by the contradictory dynamics of the 'overall social structure', where different groups have opposing interests and values. Importantly, Castells represents the space of flows as more than 'complex' or dense, as some descriptions of 'postmodern' space report in an anodyne manner. In his account, the dynamics of local, national and global are the playing out of particular interests. Like Bourdieu, Castells has an account of social hierarchy; whereas for Bourdieu the élite is manifest in the aristocracy of the national structure, for Castells, the élite is the managerial actors of the new global economy:[8]

> Articulation of the elites, segmentation and disorganization of the masses seem to be the twin mechanisms of social domination in our societies . . . In short: elites are cosmopolitan, people are local. The space of power and wealth is projected

throughout the world, while people's life and experience is rooted in places, in their culture, in their history. Thus, the more a social organization is based upon ahistorical flows, superseding the logic of any specific place, the more the logic of global power escapes the socio-political control of historically specific local/ national societies. (1996: 446)

Thus, in addition to Bourdieu's account of culture as symbolically and socially invested, the tensions between film cultures open out another plane of antagonism, between the global élite and the nation state. The manifestation of film cultures as spatial practices bears testimony of our relationship to both those networks of flow, and to the narratives of modernism and postmodernism that manoeuvre around and against each other as we operate within them.

Notes

1 The viewing of film in the space of the domestic is addressed in Chapter 7. This categorization of exhibition focuses on the institutional sites of exhibition; films are also exhibited publicly, but in far fewer instances, in commercially sponsored open-air screenings, and for educational and training purposes.

2 Kelly notes: 'Greenberg's attempt to establish the objective purposiveness of the art object, to define its particular forms of adaptation to definite ends in terms of material substrate, is continually undermined by the exigencies of a subjective judgment of *taste*. And here an altogether different order of purpose emerges. The only necessary condition for *judging* good art is common sense; but for *producing* good art, genius is required. With reference to Kant's *Critique*, genius is the mental disposition (*ingenium*) through which nature gives the rule to art' (1981: 51).

3 The CAVIAR reports are a study carried out by BMRB International: 'Face to face interviews were conducted in the home amongst a representative sample of 3,000 individuals age 4+ across Great Britain. For 4–6 year olds, interviews were conducted with parents' (CAVIAR 17, 1999).

4 The research was undertaken in 1999/2000 by Surrey Social and Market Research. A quantitative interview study was undertaken with 400 respondents, and five discussion groups conducted with respondents from South Asian backgrounds and five discussion groups with respondents from African-Caribbean backgrounds. In addition, 37 interviews with film professionals were conducted by telephone.

5 Paul Virilio develops this moment of modernist emergence with a logic of perception linked to aviation and the military: 'At the turn of the century, cinema and aviation seemed to form a single moment. By 1914, aviation was ceasing to be strictly a means of flying and breaking records . . . it was becoming one way, or perhaps even the ultimate way, of *seeing*' (1989: 17). Virilio traces the convergence of a logic of perception through architecture, film and war communications in relation to the Eiffel

Tower, which was at once a monument to the modernist vision of command from the height of the tower, of interest to Thomas Edison, and used as a giant aerial when war broke out in 1914 (1989: 23).

6 See Miriam Hansen, *Babel and Babylon: Spectatorship in American Silent Film* (1990).

7 Janna Jones, in 'Finding a Place at the Downtown Picture Palace: The Tampa Theatre, Florida' (2001), provides an analysis of the project of restoration of a cinema in an American context.

8 Castells's description of the élites of the informational society bears the imprint of Bourdieu's account of the new bourgeoisie, manifest in the detail of diet, leisure activities, interior design and clothing: 'Furthermore, there is an increasingly homogeneous lifestyle among the information elite that transcends the cultural borders of all societies: the regular use of SPA installations (even when travelling), and the practice of jogging; the mandatory diet of grilled salmon and green salad, with *udon* and *sashimi* providing a Japanese functional equivalent; the "pale chamois" wall intended to create the cozy atmosphere of the inner space; the ubiquitous laptop computer, and Internet access; the combination of business suits and sportswear; the unisex dressing style, and so on' (Castells, 1996: 447).

CHAPTER THREE

Film festivals: media events and spaces of flow

If there is one story that represents the complexity of interests, pressures and contradictions of film festivals at the dawn of a new century, it emerges out of the relocation of the Berlin Film Festival in the year 2000, as reported in the British press. In that year, the 50th anniversary of the festival and the 10th anniversary of German re-unification, the Berlin Film Festival relocated from Zoo Palast to a new site, the Potsdamerplatz, 'surrounded by American hamburger venues and buildings that look like burst cushions' (O'Hagan, 2000: 25). The festival site, according to reports, is caught in the process of its own construction, covered in advertising boards, largely for L'Oreal products. The confusion of who or what is fronting the festival, and the doubled significance of a face cream cosmeticizing the building site, is thrown into a further state of chaos as the hoardings contain the image of the chair of the jury, Gong Li. Further still, the L'Oreal advertisments feature an actress from the festival's opening film, Milla Jovovich, who stars in *Million Dollar Hotel* (Wim Wenders). A huge image of the actress hangs over the entrance to the main festival site. Jovovich however, if we are to believe the reports, is less worried by the commercial branding of the festival than by the incongruous siting of her image: 'It's over a giant building site and I don't see that construction workers are going to be big buyers of the products' (Rose, 2000: 9). Clearly, within a situation that is far from clear, we can at least say that there are different concerns and interests being expressed. For Jovovich the confusion lies in the incongruity of her image (read 'glamour'), the product (face cream) and context (manual workers). For other participants, the problem lies more squarely with the relationship of commerce to culture, of the serious to the cosmetic. In an attempt to rebuff the slapstick appeal of the festival as cosmetic dressing, jury member Dr Peter Jansen asserts: 'We are a serious festival and we want to stay that way' (Rose, 2000: 9).

Some may be tempted to pursue a Baudrillarian exit into the simulacra of signification and the hype of a lost referent for the 'real'. But rather than disappear into the 'ecstasy' of communication, I want to stay with the material hybridity of the festival site. Film festivals are mixed spaces crossed by commercial interest, specialized film knowledge and tourist trajectories. So far I have talked of film cultures as discursive formations, produced in opposition to each other (as well as responding to other determinants), bearing testimony to the historical legacies that strike across concepts of 'art', 'culture' and 'technology'. I have tried to describe the formations of film cultures not as coherent, rounded hypotheses advanced by a propositional logic, but as discourses that come into being in transactions and exchanges, redefining limits and boundaries as they shift around one another. If exhibitionary circuits provide a complex interplay of these discourses, then the festival, a market place, a designated space of transaction, brings together the determinants of film culture under the duress of space–time compression or the media event. Within the boundaries of the festival, at least four discourses operate in the field. First, discourses of independent film makers and producers circulate in catalogues, press releases, interviews and other texts. These statements draw on concepts and unformulated assumptions from the avant-garde, opposing not one 'other', but variously the values of bourgeois culture, nationalism and commercialization. Second, discourses of media representation, particularly the press, provide a commentary on events, on controversies, spec-tacles and the 'new'. These are the texts of local, national and international press and magazine publications. Third, a business discourse of purchase, price and copyright, existing in the texts of legal transactions and contracts, in verbal discussion, reported partially in the trades press. The traces of commercial dis-course also appear in logos evidencing sponsorship. Fourth, the discourse of tourism and the service industry, the local press releases, brochures, advertisments and guide books that provide an intertext between the filmic event and the location. All of these constitute what we experience, whether in proximity or at a distance, as the media event of film festivals, and what I will call the discursive formation that constitutes the film festival.

'How does one "think" a marketplace?' ask Peter Stallybrass and Allon White of a different context – the eighteenth-century rural fair (1986: 27). They con-tinue: 'At once a bounded enclosure and a site of open commerce, it is both the imagined centre of an urban community and its structural interconnection with the network of goods, commodities, markets, sites of commerce and places of production which sustain it.' A timely reminder that place has been crossed, opened out and produced as a limit through its relationship with 'elsewhere' for centuries, this description of the fair of the past also highlights the intensity of those operations in the present. The 'network' of global commerce creates link-ages between sites, creating centres and peripheries, eclipsing other spaces altogether. More than the hybrid mixing of goods and cultures, the festival as marketplace provides an exemplary instance of how culture, and cultural flows, produce space as places of flow, in Castells's terms. One part of the argument of this chapter is then that the film festival is a particular manifestation of the way that space is produced as practice (as opposed to inert materiality). Festivals advertise cities, set them in competition, region against region, global city against global city. More than this, festivals are implicated in the structure, design and use of cities, are part of the fabric of city life and its annual calendar. Festivals set a beat to the rhythms of city living wherever they occur, in competition and connection with other festival events.

A second stage of the argument that I want to make is that festivals produce a regularity of organization to the different discursive formations that cut across its site. Certain propositions and assumptions appear in various discourses, echoed and repeated in ways that are sometimes conflicting and, at other times, congruent: that 'art' film is in conflict with commercial forces, that European film struggles against American dominance, that 'serious' film festivals are opposed to the cosmeticized industries of tourism and a service economy. The repetition of assumptions gives rise to a certain naturalization of oppositions; such oppositions are productive of types of authenticity, purity, marking off domains from areas or objects by definition impure, inauthentic and outside. These oppositional markers demarcate not only art and commerce, and in so doing, invoke narratives of the nation in its struggle to reinstate a territorial space within the deterritorializing effects of multinational capitalism. Film festivals have since their inception (Venice, 1932), entwined film culture within the organization and materialization of national and regional space. And whilst, as Stringer notes, there are more than five hundred film festivals world wide, my focus here will be the European context (Stringer, 2001).

rebuilding Europe

According to Bordwell, Staiger and Thompson (1985), film festivals emerged within a particular moment of urban regeneration of Europe in the aftermath of the Second World War (Bordwell and Thompson (1994). Certainly a cluster of 'major' festivals originated in this decade: Cannes, 1946; Edinburgh, 1947; Berlin, 1951. In this moment of postwar regeneration in Europe, the project for Berlin is particularly pertinent. The reconstruction of the city, unlike other European sites, involved the task of unifying a city out of a divided organic fabric, to make the part a whole. The festival facilitated or brought into being (west) 'Berlin' as a new cultural centre, yet this performative gesture depended on acts of expulsion as much as affirmation.[1] The communist East Berlin, sealed off by a physical barrier yet proximate, had to be distanced, an act effectively commandeered by the first selection committee. The committee invited films from a select number of countries, privileging Europe and America, and excluding Eastern bloc countries (Jacobsen, 2000: 12). Other means of maintaining the boundary between east and west were temporal and economic. The timing of the festival was a controversial decision for a number of reasons, but the rationale for the final decision to stage the festival in June was that it coincided with plans for Welt-Jugend-Festspiele (World Youth Festival) in East Berlin. The conflict of events was, according to Jacobsen, intentional – the International Film Festival Berlin (IFB) presenting a counter-event designed to attract East Berliners (particularly youth) to West Berlin. Economically, the festival drew support from America as part of an international effort to stabilize a former war zone: as Tiratsoo argues, the American perception of the European postwar economies was that 'unless the Europeans changed economically, they would not be able to withstand the challenge of Communism' (1999: 97). Indeed, the initiative for the festival came from an American, Oscar Martay, who from 1948 had acted as film advisor to the city council of Greater Berlin. The financing of the first film festival depended in part on government subsidy, and a substantial donation from the American military authorities.[2] The origins of the IFB were clearly located in national political networks as much as cultural relations concerning film.

Yet if the festival consolidated Berlin as a Western city of cultural influence, there was also competition between European countries for ascendancy, with a European hierarchy of symbolic power. The Federation Internationale des Associations des Producteurs de Film (FIAPF), which had a partial monopoly on international film festivals, convened in Venice in September 1950 and passed a resolution that severely curtailed the remit of the new festival. It ruled that national productions of that year were to participate in festivals at Cannes and Venice only. A further meeting negotiated a relaxation of this ruling, on the condition that films were exhibited but not entered into competition. In effect this was an attempt to curtail the ambition of the IFB, which was denied the 'A status' classification as a festival for some duration. Clearly, the condition effectively placed IFB in a lower category of film festivals by disallowing the authority of endowing significant awards on film makers. In return Berlin enacted its own claims for distinction in the naming of the festival. Reluctant to appear derivative of existing major festivals, the title 'Berlinale' was rejected for its similarity to the Venice Film Biennale; following deliberation, the festival was named the International Film Festival Berlin (IFB).

The establishment of a film festival in Berlin during the postwar period was clearly an attempt to locate the city on a map of European cultural centres. Venice, Locarno and Brussels are cited in the documentation as key references.

In addition, the Municipal Department of Tourism was drawn in by the planning committee to advise on the structure and appeal of the event (Jacobsen, 2000). The notion of 'planning' the festival spatially within this city recalls Kracauer's earlier remonstration against the new in 'Streets Without Memory', that in Berlin 'new enterprises are always absolutely new', leaving no traces of a past (cited in Wilson, 1997[3]). Yet, within this vision of a new Berlin, the historic emerges out of the films themselves: Ruttman's *Berlin, Symphonie einer Großstadt* (1927), Lang's *Metropolis* (1927) and the first filmic rendition of Doblin's *Berlin Alexanderplatz* (Piel Jutzi, 1931). This intertextuality emerges as something of an ongoing tradition, in Fassbinder's adaptation of *Berlin Alexanderplatz* (1979–80), Wenders's *Wings of Desire* (1984) and *Faraway, So Close* (2000). For Marin Jesinghausen, Wenders recreates the aura as a metaphysical presence out of the physical 'reality' of the city as it is filmicly represented (Jesinghausen, 2000). Filmic representations provide a metatextual commentary on the city, the city becomes poetically magisterial within the films themselves, and in turn, films retain some authenticity in the representation of 'real' locations (Nowell-Smith, 2001).

If European film festivals are organized in part through the historical discourses of reconstruction and urban regeneration, an investment in the establishment of a European film culture perhaps invigorated by the Paramount decision of 1947, which curtailed the oligopolistic control of distribution and exhibition of the major studios, they are also connected to the discourses of film as a developing cultural form (both political and artistic). The history of the Edinburgh Film Festival leads back to affiliations with a theatrical tradition and established societies. Officially launched in 1947, the Edinburgh Film Festival emerged out of the Edinburgh Film Guild, founded in 1930: the Edinburgh International Festival of Music and Drama was already in existence. The Guild was established in part as an extension of the London Film Society (1925), itself an emulation or equivalent of the Stage Society. The Edinburgh Film Guild was established for interested members of the public with the remit to exhibit 'interesting films':

> The Film Society has been founded in the belief that there are in this country a large number of people who regard the cinema with the liveliest interest and who would welcome an opportunity seldom afforded the general public of seeing interesting films of intrinsic merit, whether new or old. (Hardy, 1992: 2)

Whilst this statement foregrounds issues of distribution and access in Scotland, and gestures to the widest possible membership, the association with the London Film and Stage Societies situates the Guild within a particular, and more limited, social strata. Here, the legitimacy of film is in the process of being established through association with older cultural forms (theatre). The first 29 members enrolled reinforces the intellectual nature of the society and its social location; among the members were H. G. Wells, George Bernard Shaw, Roger Fry, J. M.

Keynes, the actor Ben Webster, Dame Ellen Terry and Lady Swathling. According to Hardy (1992), the Guild was ridiculed by the press of the time for attracting Bohemian audiences, and indeed the fact that the society contained members of the Bloomsbury group, a self-proclaimed cultural élite, supports this notion of the Guild. Like the collective of POOL who produced the journal *Close Up*, the Film Guild were committed to experimentation in film and to the exploration of the potential of film as an aesthetic form.[4]

The origins of European film festivals are marked by two different discourses. One is a broad historical project of rebuilding Europe, a rebuilding of the social infrastructure ravaged by the Second World War, and a consolidation of Europe as a significant player in a global economy. Importantly, by the post-war period, culture has become a means of representing the status of place and facilitating local economies through cultural events. The other discourse, from film societies and guilds, is concerned with the definition of film as a form, with the aim of broadening categories of definition in contrast to the studio format of Hollywood film. Here, the oppositions of national cultures, and of aesthetics practices, align in opposition to a mainstream American film product. The festival then represents an attempt to separate out national cultures, to distinguish certain practices, and in so doing, places a critical emphasis on the value of the text. This separation, however, becomes increasingly strained by the end of the twentieth century as the 'event' of the festival is caught in tension with the practices of aesthetic evaluation. Where the mainstream film text, as I have argued, is dispersed into ancillary products in the context of the multiplex, the culture of the festival threatens to disperse festival film into the spatial practices of tourism.

rebuilding for the twenty-first century

The phenomenon of the film festival as tourist attraction and an anxiety about scale begin at least as far back as the 1970s. Commenting on the Cannes festival in 1976, Houston, writing in *Sight and Sound*, opens her review with the spectacle of the festival as mass event. The notion of overexposure poses questions of scale, but also of definition. Houston writes:

> 'Cannes suffocated by success', said a *Figaro* headline, the article going on to claim, alarmingly enough, that the Festival now rates as 'the biggest international attraction after the Olympics'. 40,000 visitors; 1700 journalists; nearly 500 films: the statistics of overkill. (1976)

The Cannes festival, even in 1976, the year of its 30th celebration, teeters on the edge of a tourist attraction, a theatre of mass spectacle. In journalistic accounts, the business of film festival culture, the process of evaluation and marketing, is slipping into a liminal space of leisure that merits comparison with the Olympics, but perhaps more poignantly, with the themed parks of Disney. The nature of the festival as an event that spills out into the business of international travel and tourism, the culture of pleasure versus business, of entertainment versus art, where the local infrastructure of the festival site impinges on the definition of the event. The event cannot be separated, extracted from the context of its geographical location; indeed, the reciprocal relation between festivals and sites emerges in this discourse of anxiety surrounding scale. Festival cities, in the latter part of the twentieth century, are characterized by redevelopment, constructing new architectural feats as the twenty-first-century venues for such occasions. Rotterdam in 2001 unveiled its new development on the waterfront, in the year in which it held the title of Cultural Capital of Europe. Culture as an international tourist attraction has fertilized local economies, underpinning and shaping the contours of development in cities. Thus the paradox – festivals contribute significantly to the regeneration of economies in Europe, yet in so doing, the restricted notion of art as separate from commerce is increasingly unviable. The tensions of definition, of what festival culture becomes, what it includes and excludes, is played out in all discursive domains.

Again, the Berlin Film Festival provides a exemplary case of struggles of definition. Rebuilt as West Berlin in the postwar period within the rubric of a national centre consolidated by its cultural activities, the collapse of the Berlin Wall in 1989 represented the loss of a spatial, but more importantly, a symbolic boundary of identity. The project to reconfigure the identity of Berlin included the festival site as a prime cultural showcase and annual event. Whereas in the earlier redevelopment, Berlin was reconstructed largely through municipal planning strategies and foreign and national subsidy, in the latter redevelopment the function of the state is eclipsed by corporate bodies. The IFB festival director, Moritz de Hadeln, describes the development as 'a new town centre built by Mercedes and Sony', with Mercedes responsible for real estate and Sony for the cinema theatres (Jacobsen, 2000: 535). The decision of where to locate the festival was influenced by 'modern architecture, a theatre with a large capacity, the proximity of many cultural landmarks, several museums, the national library, the philharmonic hall, and above all the film museum, the film school, the film archives not to mention the many restaurants and entertainment facilities'. De Hadeln continues, 'By saying farewell to Budapester Strasse, we have also had to clean up our appearance, and somehow renew our corporate identity' (Jacobsen, 2000: 537), a process overseen by a major Berlin company, MetaDesign. In place of a national or regional festival, the IFB emerges with a corporate branding.

The summative point of the festival director's sentence, the throw away 'not to mention' of entertainment and restaurant facilities, underscores the value of certain activities of the global city over others. From the list of credited local features, the service industry appears last and in least detail, as an 'add on' to the culturally symbolic status of the other facilities and objects. As Saskia Sassen argues, the service industry is crucial to the operation of the global city yet rarely referenced as a key component. The less visible sector commands positions that are characterized by low pay and 'unsociable' working hours, positions often held by immigrants and women:

> Although these types of workers and jobs are never represented as part of the global economy, they are in fact as much a part of globalization as international finance is. We see at work here a dynamic of valorization that has sharply increased the distance between the devalorized and the valorized – indeed over valorized – sectors of the economy. These joint pressures have made cities a contested terrain. (Sassen, 1994: 72)[5]

What Sassen draws our attention to in the case of Berlin is the strategic development of the film festival as a global city, the economic significance of which is masked by the emphasis on cultural exchange. Sassen's work on cities in the global economy draws the perspective out from a local or national vision to the international situation. Redevelopment of major cities is not a matter simply of a struggle for ascendancy in competition with other strategic sites, but the organization of command points and 'production sites for the information economy'. Film festivals serve a global function in advertising cultural products, generating information about them and situating a point of information exchange.

If this argument tells us something of the value of film for the global economy, how do we begin to theorize the reverse, the impact of the globally connected festival on the cultures of film? I want to suggest that the various discourses of the festival operate as open and closed vectors to the circulation of knowledge about film, and thus are productive of particular cultural values that secure routes of distribution and exhibition. In order to explore this, I return to journalism as both the representation (and interpretation) of festival activities, and in itself a significant mediation and production of the event. Retaining a focus on the Berlin festival of 2000, journalistic reports read the relocation of the event in interesting terms: that of a wider ideological shift (from communism to capitalism). The move is represented as a metaphoric shift from a socialist-style, comfortless location, to a new commercial centre. Writing in *The Times*, James Christopher interprets the move: 'The symbolism is unambiguous. The Cold War wasteland . . . is now dominated by shiny glass monuments to the city's commercial future. Veteran filmmakers might be dismayed by the conference-centre atmosphere and lack of shabby bars. But the new screens are magnificent . . .' (2000: 40). The new venue represents a shift into a new age, departing from the divided city, and ideologies, of the Cold War period, entering a space of merged ideological forces; the quality of art cinema on new screens is facilitated by the shiny new commercial culture characteristic of twenty-first-century Berlin. Andrew O'Hagan, writing in the *Daily Telegraph*, makes the same connection between the architecture and the values of the festival; noting the new venue he comments: 'There's a heavy scent of the Free West. And the modern film festival itself has embraced much of that culture: Potsdamerplatz looks like a bust dream of Houston, Texas' (2000: 25). The regeneration of European cities as commercial centres threatens a slippage of identity into its putative opposite, America.

If the physical features of a city are read as ideological, that is, as signifying a set of semi-conscious political values, the reading of location extends to a logic of the exhibitionary venues and the films themselves. Noting that the reputation of the FFB (Berlin Film Festival) is 'a bit intellectual', O'Hagan goes on to draw a series of linkages between the FFB festival audience, the venue and the films themselves: 'The people who go there tend to be genuinely curious about, say, the films of the Nepalese underground, and most are happy – no, eager – to spend their afternoons in a makeshift bunker, watching solid, grey, 15-hour movies about half-starved *babushkas* with no teeth washing the dishes.' What this commentary conveys, disparagingly and problematically, is the corollary between an intellectual position, physical surroundings and filmic content. The figure of the festival attendee is ascribed through the association of a set of puritanical practices: the material harshness of the venue ('makeshift bunker'), the longevity of the film ('15-hour movies') and the politics of the representation ('half-starved *babushkas* with no teeth'). The aesthetic of the site creates a homology with the content of the film: the culture here is of a materially empoverished yet politically worthy cinematic subject, sacrificing comfort, spectacle and beauty for cultural interest. Implicit to this description is the racialization of non-Western cinema cultures, and non-Western societies, as impoverished, primitive and aesthetically lacking. Indeed, corporally lacking. The choice of metaphor here (orality) is interestingly poignant, for whilst the redevelopment of Berlin is associated with 'hamburger venues' for the consuming Western subject, non-Western subjects, it appears, have no 'bite'.

divisions and enclaves

The discourse of journalism reads the contemporary festival as a conflict of interests – commerce versus art, the worthy versus glamour – an interpretation that reproduces the assumptions of an historical division between economics and culture, between everyday life and art. There is a sense in which the festival has been a disinterested space of filmic judgement and appreciation, accruing a type of nobility in the sacrificial (and puritanical) comfortlessness of a film culture focused on the text. The contemporary registers here as a recent mixing of film and commerce, evidencing a tension that is culturally and aesthetically symbolic. Yet, to take some distance from these accounts, journalism needs to be seen as a particular discourse creating its own effects on the meaning of the festival, contributing to the 'live' experience of the event and to the 'insider' status of knowledge. It is no accident that festivals (unlike the Oscars ceremony) are not televised. Journalism is the main mediating function of festivals to the general public. The accounts represent first-hand experience, instilling a type of authenticity to the event, a personalized diary of the experience rather than simply reviewing films. In so doing, journalistic discourse reproduces the bounded field of the festival, an occurrence both spatially and temporally removed from everyday life. Festivals are a specific, intense and fleeting happening which generates expectation through its narrative of prize winning and creates a managed site of specialized knowledges.[6] Festivals invoke the presence of experience, which is then mediated through journalism as a type of authenticity.

If I have emphasized the significance of the spatial for understanding festival events, then the temporal is equally deserving of attention. Where first-hand experience is the premium value of the festival experience, this sense of originality is instilled in the structure of the festival through the notion of the film premiere. The majority of festivals stipulate as selection criteria that the film must be a national première in that country. Further, the IFB, Cannes and the Venice Biennale demand that films screened in or out of competition at other international festivals will automatically be excluded from selection. Such a stipulation automatically places the festivals in competition with each other as sites of cultural significance, and confirms their status in the register of importance. The festivals of Edinburgh and Rotterdam command less authority than Cannes and Berlin, for example; the selection criteria states that the festival organizers are 'particularly interested' in world or international premières, rather than demanding 'first rights'. But in addition to intra-festival competition, the notion of the première constructs a hierarchy of viewing through a temporal axis, securing the originality of the moment of festival viewing as a first. The boundaries that restrict access to film are both spatial and temporal. Festivals effectively enclave a film, seal it off from general release and, further, restrict its circulation among and between festivals.

The threatened imbrication of film and tourism in the redeveloped sites of festivals, of film slipping into the ordinary practices of everyday life, is countered by the organization of première-viewing as enclaved, circumscribed by admission to the festival event. This represents only a transitional stage in the life of the film

as commodity before it enters the flow of more dispersed channels of dissemination. The importance of the festival in terms of the value of film is that the early
phase of exhibition secures, to a large extent, the value of the text as product.
As Arjun Appadurai argues, the principal 'use' of luxury goods (the majority of
culture) is rhetorical and social (Appadurai, 1986). The level of value, he states,
relies on the features of the product itself and the management of its circulation.
Here, he identifies five signs of a register of symbolic value. First, the acquisition
of prizes; second, a complexity of acquisition, for example through managed
scarcity; third, semiotic virtuosity, a product that signals complex social messages;
fourth, specialized knowledge is a prerequisite for 'appropriate' consumption; and
fifth, a high degree of linkage in consuming the goods to the body or personality.
The relationship between these components can be seen to be accumulative:
if a product such as a film is prize-winning, is managed in terms of enclaving
and restricted access, it is likely that it contains a level of semiotic virtuosity
thus requiring specialized knowledge at the point of reception. Finally, the
accumulative value of each of these phases is the conferring of value on the
consumer.

Appadurai, in the same essay, uses the image of knowledge and ignorance as a
'turnstile', blocking and facilitating entrance to a cultural sphere. The properties
of knowledge, information and ignorance, he argues, are not restricted to the
spheres of production and consumption of culture, but characterize the process
of circulation and exchange. There is a traffic in criteria, a knowledge about commodities which is itself increasingly commodified. Advertising may represent a
'capitalist realism', but it does not render all products equivalent; indeed, advertising for festival films occurs at the moment of general release rather than during
its festival life. The festival generates forms of knowledge prior to the marketing
texts of general release, the 'mythologies of commodity flow' emanating from its
première exhibition. But whilst Appadurai's account remains at a general level of
explication, the festival provides insight into the types of knowledge produced as
mythology and other kinds of knowledge that remain opaque.

The accounts of festivals that are reported in the general press focus largely
on stories of personal festival experience, made up of reviews of films, rumours
of production controversies (the conflict between Lars von Trier and Björk in
the making of *Dancer in the Dark* dominated press reviews of Cannes 2000), and
personal encounters with film makers and stars. Significantly less attention is
offered to the marketing dimension of the festival, the sale of distribution rights
to various companies. These 'stories' of economic exchange also determine the
future circulation of films, and it is perhaps partly in a disavowal of the afterlife
of the film (which may detract from the intensity of the festival moment) that
such information is only thinly represented. Perhaps more convincingly, the

economic features of the festival are a further reproduction of the division between commerce and cultural value. Information of 'deals' and acquisition of rights circulate in the pages of trades publications, such as *Screen International*, but are separated from the evaluation of film in the popular press. The disjunction between the festival as marketplace and as a forum of aesthetic evaluation is not, however, permanent. The 'success' of a film is judged at a later stage in terms of financial reward; box-office takings function as both a triumph of business acumen and the formal merits of the film.

The organization of festivals represents a management of cultural resources in the divisions and demarcations of spheres: of the market, exhibition venues, the criteria of entry, the categories of award and the press office. Yet this separation of different functions, and discourses, is not complete. The cross-over, or collision, occurs in (at least) two areas, of those who attend and participate in the festival as viewers, and in the field of distribution. To take the former point first, of who attends the festival, the increased presence of 'stars' has attracted attention: 'Berlin's 50th film festival, bigger than Cannes and boasting more American films and stars than the French Riviera event has seen for some time . . .' (Malcom, 2000: 9) 'The arrival of Bono, George Clooney, Jeanne Moreau, Matt Damon and Gwyneth Paltrow has given the event a layer of icing' (Christopher, 2000: 40); and again 'I'd say there was a war going on – between the small and worthy, on the one hand, and the glamour of Hollywood on the other' (O'Hagan, 2000: 25). The threatened collision of 'worlds', the collapse of spatial territories of mainstream and restricted production, is rendered a more visible conflict of values through the presence of stars. The star phenomenon, as King argues, is predicated on a transnational media flow, whereby stars are signs within an international system of exchanges, recognized in different spatial sites yet remaining distant (King, 1985; for an alternative account see Geraghty, 2000). In terms of the festival event, stars transport the universalized culture of international commodity flows into the space of the festival, forging a hybridity. Similarly, the majority of films showcased move out of the context of the festival and into the commodity flow of major distributors. The traffic between these two discursive spaces is suggestive of a more complex relation than polarized fields.

If stars overtly signal the presence of a culture of international commodity flow, the marketing function of the festival is the nexus of apparently different cultures, of the multinational and national, of commerce and art. At the level of global infrastructure, the major multinational companies such as UIP, Buena Vista, Fox and Warner Brothers, claim ownership.[7] Whilst distribution channels may retain brand names as an index of an alternative culture, 'independent' film has become appropriated as a niche market by major companies (Sony Pictures Classics, Miramax, New Line). This acquisition of the 'alternative' market by the majors poses problems of distinction; when is a minor subsidiary a major? This is a problem that arises not only in relation to distributors appropriating completed films and marketing them through subsidiary companies, but of the eligibility of films produced under a subsidiary. The Sundance Festival in the United States, for example, attempts to define the boundary by stating that films produced, financed or initiated by a 'major' are excluded; alternatively, a film that is produced, financed or acquired by an independent division of a studio is acceptable. Thus, if a major studio acquires or acts *as if* it were an 'independent' producer, its performance is acceptable; the ruse is that it is the appearance of authenticity that renders the term 'independence'.

In response to the merging of corporate and independent cultures is the dialectical repositioning of the independent sector through the reinstatement of boundaries; as the mainstream shifts, other positions in the field move relationally. As festivals are perceived by film makers in the independent sector to have become commercial markets at the expense of advancing a heterogeneous film culture, the resulting shift in positions of distinction occurs. In a number of festivals, breakaway groups have splintered from the main event, organizing parallel forums and threatening the integrity and authenticity of the main festival: in Venice, the 'Giornate del cinema Italiano', in Berlin, the 'International Forum of Young Cinema' and in Cannes the Director's Fortnight. The oppositional movement is a rebellion against both standardization and cultural imperialism. The introduction to the catalogue for the Director's Fortnight event in 2000 asserts: 'When 85% of the world's filmgoers flock to pictures from a single national film industry, when we are headed toward a monoculture developed by powerful industrial groups to whom cinema is nothing more than a simple loss leader, it is vital that we continue to make room for forms of expression from around the world.' The statement ends 'the challenge of the world's film industries versus all attempts at standardization' (Quinzaine des Realisateurs, 2000: 2). In a further act of repositioning, however, the main festivals have absorbed the 'alternative' rebellion into their own programme.

The phenomenon of dissent is not restricted to the European context. The circulation of independent film in the United States at the Sundance Festival provides a similar polarization of art and commerce. Following the commercial success of the film *sex, lies and videotape* after being picked up by a distributor at the 1989 Sundance Festival, Soderbergh complained of the 'encroachment of commerce . . . suddenly this festival became this feeding frenzy, and it was no longer about art' (in Smith, 1999). In a continuation of what Rodowick has called the discourse of political modernism, the focus falls on aesthetics, leading critical attention to the site of production rather than systems of circulation. For what this binary of art and commerce eclipses is the infrastructure of dissemination, of circuits of distribution and exhibition which throw into relief not only ownership and control, but the creation of specific and oppositional cultures. Questions of formal strategy, of the potency of cinematic representation are not occluded by the infrastructure, but need to be thought through within the discursive paradigms that constitute opposing cultures of engagement.

fixity and flow: nation states

Where, in this account of conflicted conceptualizations of what the festival is and can be, does the nation enter the frame? If the emergence of festivals historically was closely aligned to a project of national, and more broadly European, redevelopment, does the nation disappear with the rise of the global circulation of media and a corporate control of infrastructure? For Julian Stringer, in an essay that argues for the 'spatial logics' of the festival circuit to matter as much as the films themselves, 'it is cities which now act as the nodal points on this circuit, not national film industries' (2001: 138). This suggests that the significant relationship in the system of cultural flow is the local–global, surpassing the nation. Yet, as Annabell Srebernny has pointed out, global discourse is effective in eliding the local and the national; the task then may be to separate out the different positions within the spatial logic.

There is no doubt that film continues to be a significant cultural product for the nation in terms of representation, a production economy, tourism and as a symbolic asset. Indeed, film continues to sustain a presence at the centre of national and international debates on cultural policy (see Chapter 5 for a discussion of GATT and WTO talks). The report carried out by the National Heritage Committee in Britain in 1995, 'The British Film Industry', cites the claim 'To the extent that audiovisual material made in Britain continues to raise the profile of Britain as an attractive, interesting location to visit, there is a clear economic as well as a cultural benefit to delivering that result' (Second Report, 1995: xxii). The assumption here is that British film will reflect, and mirror positively, the national 'body' (inferred in this document as landscape).[8] Film also remains central to the economy of a nation, not only in terms of films about a country, but in the provision of facilities of production and post-production; the 'creative industries' have both an economic role and symbolic charge that European nations attempt to harness through the measures of tax exemptions, subsidized infrastructure and the expedited processing of work permits relating to film production.[9] Within this context, the festival remains a crucial showcase for the symbolic capital of the nation; the local specificity is contextualized by this broader infrastructure of subsidy and policy framing, remaining connected to the nation. Against this context of national affiliations is the argument that film production and exhibition exceeds the bounds of nations; the increased practice of co-productions, where often multiple nations have an involvement, mitigates against a clear distinction of the location of national 'origins'. Paul Swann argues this point cogently:

> Ascribing national origin to either product or consumer, and perhaps the very label 'British film', ought perhaps to be abandoned as national and other boundaries collapse and disappear. Corporate media culture has internalized these changes, and the distinction elicited by the term 'British film' has been commodified and survives as a label on video store shelves or in film reviews. The label no longer 'belongs' in any simple way to Britain . . . (2000: 42)

Certainly the classification of films as national in origin is a complex task, but one that remains crucial to national representation (as the debate on the national definition of *Notting Hill* or *Sense and Sensibility* attests). Swann may be right in his assertion that the label of 'British film' is a commodity sign rather than a reflection of national origin in a way that is similar to the label of 'independent film'. Yet film, I would argue, does not float freely above national borders, but attains part of its value and meaning from its perceived origin and the paths of its circulation. These paths are located within as well as cutting across national borders; to conceive of global flows as outside of the nation omits the tension between national and global economies, the force-field in which film circulates.

An interdependency of nation and film culture exists at the heart of the festival event. Festivals are not simply spaces of commerce free from the state, nor are they localities disconnected from the national context. Festivals in Europe remain committed to a range of activities and purposes; in addition to marketing and evaluating film are the components of training, education and a commitment to cultural diversity. The festival context relies on the subsidized infrastructure of the locality, the state-supported museums, libraries, archives and educational institutions that condition the location of festivals (echoing de Hadeln's comments on the relocation of the Berlin festival within walking distance of these institutions). Similarly the nation as a competitively positioned unit within the market for creative industries, acquires symbolic capital from the festivals within its borders.

To what extent are festivals independent sites for the production of critical discourse about film? For Stringer, the context of festivals presents 'a series of diverse, sometimes competing, sometimes cooperating, public spheres' (2001: 138). This argument leads us back to claims about the conditions of independence and autonomy that secure a separate, critically discursive space for culture (Garnham, 2000; Habermas, 1962). It also takes us back to the division of art and commerce that Kant was ready to prize as the space of disinterest. To be fair to Stringer, the emphasis of his statement is on the diverse and competing forces that permeate the festival site. My reading of these conflicting forces is that festivals play out certain historic narratives without resolution. The presence of modernism continues in both the redrawing of the national borders in the space of the festival, in the nation's claim to film culture as creative symbolic capital, and in the political modernism of the independent film sector, attempting to reassert the space of cultural practice as separate from (and against) a homogenizing commercial interest. In tension with this narrative is the fluidity of the decentred logic of global capitalism, of postmodernism. What is crucial to film festivals as an object of study, is the spatialization of these narratives. Regarded in many accounts (albeit controversially) as historical ruptures – as discrete epochs – the continued presence of modernism and postmodern continues to condition the manifestation of film cultures in particular sites.

Notes

1 This political division was clearly articulated in the speech of the Mayor's at the opening ceremony, who hailed Berlin as 'an oasis of liberty and independence, surrounded by a system of violence and oppression, which uses art for the purpose of propaganda', calling on the city to be 'a bastion which the totalitarian powers storm in vain' (quoted in Jacobsen, 2000: 23).

2 The American military authorities donated DM 35,000, the German state DM 40, 000. For further details of funding see Jacobsen (2000).

3 Wilson (1997).

4 The relationship between the Film Guild and *Close Up* can be found in a review 'This Montage Business', by R. Bond. The use of the term 'amateur' by inference positions the POOL collective as something more professional and knowing: 'The Film Guild of London, an amateur organization, is suffering from a bad attack of "this montage business". The phrase in quotes is not mine; one of the members of the Guild aptly but thoughtlessly employed it at their meeting last month when several recent productions of the Guild were screened . . . In case I be misunderstood, let me say that the members of the Film Guild are honestly endeavouring to do good work, but they are afflicted with an attitude which can best be described as posing. Everybody recognizes the difficult conditions under which the British amateurs have to work to-day. But these difficulties cannot always be used as an excuse for careless work. Carelessness is impermissible in amateur production' (in Donald *et al.*, 1998: 278–80).

5 Sassen specifies African-Americans and Latinos as those who labour in the undervalued sectors of the global economy. In Europe, the immigrant population has become profoundly influenced by the destabilized economies in former communist and

socialist countries, and the war-torn zone of the former Yugoslavia. The illegal status of pockets of these immigrants is exploited in the paying of wages less than the national minimum and in conditions outside union protection.

6 As John Hill (1998) argues, film authenticity is guaranteed by the intensity of the experience of cinema, a practice markedly different from the dispersed flow of television viewing in the context of the home.

7 In *Cinemagoing Europe*, Dodona Research articulate the difficulty of a European film culture dominated by American products and by systems of distribution: 'Taken individually, European countries produce a fraction of the number of films produced in the United States. European films also find more difficulty in export markets, including those of other European countries. They rarely find strong distributors and, in foreign markets, lose the advantage of speaking directly to a national audience. In their domestic markets, however, European films are often enormously successful' (1998: 3). This argument is contradicted, however, in other accounts of the relationship between European film and distribution. In *The State of European Cinema*, Finney announces: 'Nearly half of the 69 films involving a UK producer that were put into production in 1994 had yet to be screened at a UK cinema by May 1996. Of those unscreened films, two-thirds did not have release dates' (1996: 145). And more recently, the TSO report, *Creative Industries Mapping Document* (2001), states: 'there has been a decline in the proportion of UK films achieving wide release and an increase in the proportion remaining unreleased a year after production. In 1998 23% of UK films achieved wide release after production, 56% remaining unreleased' (2001: 7).

8 For debates on heritage and British film, see Higson (1996) and Monk (2001).

9 See 'A Bigger Picture', the report resulting from the lengthy consultation process of the National Heritage Committee, for details of the British government's plans to adapt the Home Office Immigration Rules to facilitate a fluidity of traffic in production personnel. In the context of an increase in barriers to immigrants into the UK, this provides an exemplary instance of the asymmetrical flow of people within the global economy. Section 2.48 states: 'A fast track system along the lines of that recommended by the Committee is already in place. Under this system, streamlined procedures apply to applications for internationally established directors, producers, "stars", and specialist technicians with unique skills. Where necessary, a permit for personnel in this category can be approved in a matter of days. There is no charge for this service' (1998: 30). For a fuller account of the problematic distinction of applying the term 'British' to films, see the Advisory Committee on Film Finance document, 'The Definition of a British film' (July 1996).

CHAPTER FOUR

Marketing films and audiences

The marketing of film is often perceived to be the mediation of texts and audiences, products and consumers, the bridging function between the commodity and its destination. Conceived in this way as an interface, marketing can be read in one of two ways. First – the more benign model – marketing is the provision of information about film, an increasingly important communication function in a saturated marketplace. Here, marketing may be highly designed, competitively aimed, seductive in its appeal, but 'underneath' this appearance it serves a role as provider in the information economy. This approach is related to the conceptualization of contemporary cultural production as post-Fordist, a diversified market in terms of the fragmented range of audience tastes and preferences, and an eclectic spectrum of cultural products. The second reading of marketing renders it as a type of duplicity, always promising more and offering less than expectation. It masks the intention to sell with the promise of personal gain: marketing appeals to the nuanced differences of multicultural, plural societies, but this is no more than a veneer for a product which fails to speak to social diversity.

I want to suggest that marketing, more than a mediation between two preconstituted and distinct parties, is a production. It produces a concept of individualism as the exercising of free will, and brings film into being as an experiential culture of pure 'choice'. The appeals to free will permeate advertising space, as Eve Sedgwick notes, advertising is a 'landscape so rubbled and defeatured by the twin hurricanes named Just Do It and Just Say No' (1994: 140).[1] The appeals to take action produce the individual as at once empowered and commanded. The emphatic appeal to human will, consumption as a conscious act of embrace or refusal, negates the socio-economic contexts in which choices are proposed, made available and taken up. How then does this debate of choice, of taste, manifest itself in relation to film?

This chapter approaches this question through two routes. The first is the model of genre, a concept that has been used variously to provide a link between production and consumption, the strategies of marketing with the knowledge of audiences. Second, this chapter is concerned with epistemologies of the audience, the archaeology of audience habits, lifestyles and spending power in market research. Empirical research of this kind is of course conditioned by the interests of the film marketing industry; as such, it illuminates the way that audiences are imaged and defined rather than simply providing material evidence of audience behaviour. At the heart of market research is a desire to maximize the life of a film in different markets. This cuts horizontally into the range of potential markets for any one film (defined in terms of age, social demographic and gender). It also conducts vertically in terms of identifying the various windows of release for a film over time (theatrical release, video/DVD release, satellite and terrestrial premiere). It provides insight into the types of information on consumer practices of use to the marketing industry. In the analysis of the material provided by market research, these twin features that I have referred to as the horizontal and vertical work to produce a pattern of consumption differentiated in terms of temporal moments of film consumption. Whilst the reception sites and practices of cinema, video and television viewing are acknowledged as specific cultures, social distinction underpins the differential temporal access to film, either as moments in the hub of public debate or significantly lagging behind public discourse.

genre: the perfect marriage?

One of the richest forms of enquiry into the marketing of film has taken genre as its point of focus. As Christine Gledhill, in a summative essay on the cyclical nature of genre's return in film studies, writes: 'To understand exactly how the social and films interact we need a concept of genre capable of exploring the wider contextual culture in relation to, rather than as an originating source of, aesthetic mutations and textual complications' (2000: 221). The concept of genre lies at the cusp of discourses of production and institutions, of aesthetics and classification, of audiences and cultural value. At the centre of these divergent domains and spheres of expertise, genre provides a starting point for the unravelling of marketing and audiences.

If, on the one hand, marketing purports to offer a filmic experience that is innovative, genre has been read critically as the classifying principle that provides stability to the system. The central text in recent decades for the defence of on-going stability of the classical narrative form is Bordwell, Staiger and Thompson's *The Classical Hollywood Cinema* (1985). Their argument depends on a reading of production processes and aesthetic practices as congruent, producing a mode of narrative film that is, according to their claims, enduring. Characterized by certain forms of script, narrative structure and camera operation, the classical style creates a formal unity or equilibrium of these parts, which is read as the construction of an historically dominant concept of film. Despite its historical detail, the enduring nature of this mode of classicism tends to transcend the historical circumstances of its production, particularly where the authors argue that such a normative process continues through the decades of the latter part of the twentieth century. *The Classical Hollywood Cinema* presents a type of modernist argument, whereby rules, modes of practice, continue to carry authority beyond the studio system that initially provides the infrastructure for its development.

For some critics, the argument has been continued in terms of style, disputing the coherence of the classical period within the studio system itself (Alloway, 1971), or more recently arguing that the systems of production, distribution and consumption have radically affected the aesthetics and form of the film text. What is discernible in this debate is the persistent dialectic between stability and change, the endurance of certain modernist features of film and the practices of mixity, appropriation and bricolage of a more postmodernist account. The particular period of the late 1960s is cited as a critical point of eclipse of classicism, when Hollywood's appropriation of arthouse culture produced a less narratively driven and unified film text in the work of Altman, Scorsese and Lucas (Elsaesser, 1975). Yet for Thomas Schatz, this point of seeming rupture provides a starting point for a series of changes in a process of destabilization that has seen the return of genre and narrative at a hyperbolic level (1983a, 1983b). Schatz refers to film making from this time onwards as neoclassicism, characterized by a distinct break from European arthouse in the scale of budgets, the harnessing of new technologies to produce a spectacular form of visual display and an increase in marketing budgets.

In Schatz's work marketing is seen to impact on the text itself: scale of finance in marketing is not simply an indicator of a proliferation of promotional materials but a shift in the terms of address to the audience. This in turn is inflected by the repositioning of the film text as one product among many ancillaries, with two consequences. First, film is recontextualized by its related products as a lifestyle choice. Second, the film text itself is related intertextually to its life forms in other media and merchandise, and thus is transformed through those relations. Justin Wyatt presents an argument more forcefully still that generic, large budget feature films have structurally changed as a result of the development of ancillary markets and the repositioning of the film text as one among multiple components (Wyatt, 1994). Wyatt describes a modular aesthetic, a fragmented sequential series of filmic moments as the result, bound together by the twin aspects of stylization and music. Here Wyatt locates the influences of MTV, advertising and celebrity on the structural properties of the text. The influences are both aesthetically determined (audience expectation of sophisticated stylization borrowed from advertising and music video) and economically driven (the segmented film text facilitates a certain autonomy to its related products).

Within this reconfigured landscape, film emerges as a type of hypertext, narratively linked in sequence yet offering tangential paths, alleyways and flights of passage that will suture back into the main narrative at any point. The description of fragmentation endemic to the modular aesthetic points to a stability and necessity of narrative as a partially known format. Thus one of the the implications of Wyatt's reading, as for Schatz, is that genre continues to be a central feature of mainstream film production. The known properties of the text, situated in an evolving history of those constituent parts as a genre, are imperative to the success of the modular aesthetic. In effect, genre creates the unifying principle of the hyper-text, facilitating the role of marketing in pre-selling audiences to a film; genre presents overarching continuity for the audience and the historically proven formula for the production company.

This concept of genre is strongly contested by Altman in a recent historically informed study (1999). For Altman, the wielding of the term 'genre' in film theory as a conscious, instrumental 'tool' appropriated to industry intention and audience taste denies the existence of genre as a discursive strategy. This reworking of an understanding of genre situates its meaning in the context of the utterance, thus the insistence on 'the discursive status of all generic claims'. Altman continues: 'Pronounced *by* someone and addressed *to* someone, statements about genre are always informed by the identity of the speaker and audience. Hollywood studios are not single entities, speaking a uniform discourse. On the contrary, studios speak with multiple voices' (1999: 102). In this work, four groups of speakers are primary users of the term: producers, exhibitors, viewers and critics. Each of these groups uses and understands the term differently, thus the context of use becomes a site of investigation. In the first instance Altman appears to be making an argument against the reductive concept of studios as determining film product through a successful formula, yet there is a twist in the narrative. In returning to promotional materials of films in the 1920s, Altman argues that production studios avoided the term genre, appealing instead to individualism. The advertising materials of this era focus on studio names for coherence and appeals to quality and type of product, and to stars and characters moving across various films. There are several points of suggestion to take here. The first is that studios as early as the 1920s were engaged in what is thought of as the contemporary practice of branding, emphasizing the signature of a studio across various types of film rather than particular generic features. The individual nature of the studio identity, over and above competitors, was paramount. Second, that studios sought to offer a range of film texts that were dissimilar, offering choice rather than sameness. Third, the profitable enduring image of a studio and its products was founded on the continuity of specific characters, techniques, thematics and devices that have greater value than the particular films in which they appear. Fourth, the studios' relationship to genre was conditional on the access to distribution; studios with exhibition deals self-presented individualistically, whilst smaller production units with less secure access to exhibition presented films in terms of genre to clarify the film's meaning. Lacking a known brand, genre became a fall-back position, used unevenly across the film sector.

Whilst Altman's description of the facets of studio branding appears at moments to be poignantly similar to some critical understandings of genre, his central argument reverses the image of studios as complacent, and supports this theory with the issue of copyright. Whilst genres cannot be claimed, studio branding in the form of characters and serial films can. Thus, Altman moves from the early part of the century to examples such as the James Bond series, where copyrighted characters provide continuity rather than generic formulas. Which leaves open the question of who deploys the term 'genre' if not the marketing executives. For Altman, genre is primarily a term used by critics and audiences, in relation to practices of archival organization and shared cultural communities respectively. As critical discourse is concerned with the broad historical overview of film, genre becomes a retrospective term that organizes film historically into segments, accessible for analysis. In audience use, genre is invoked by particular constellated communities sharing filmic tastes as a way of providing forms of commonality across disparate national spaces. Importantly for Altman, constellated communities emerge in shared response to the text, in opposition to the notion that the studio formulates the genre, which then constitutes a community of viewers.

A conceptualization of genre as a term produced within particular discursive formations usefully locates genre within specific sites of discourse. Yet, whilst Altman's account separates out the diverse parties and interests in each domain, the model disregards the reconnection of genre to broader narratives of production, consumption and the individual. To take the issue of consumption first, Altman's reading of genre theory and its attention to audiences is a shift from a neoclassical to a postmodern position. Wholly embracing the postmodernist concept of audience fragmentation as empowerment, theory, 'with support from a commodified culture', moves 'towards increased sensitivity to audience needs and influence'. What becomes apparent in this reading is that Altman perceives the 'problem' of genre, a narrowly conceived and homogenizing model, as an effect of criticism rather than a condition of commodification. Indeed, film theorists (as a generic group if you like) are the bad object of Altman's text; addressing the question of whether the notion of genre has changed over the centuries, he remarks the enormity and impossibility of the task of unravelling this, adding testily 'especially given the paucity of assistance provided by previous genre theorists'. If commodity culture has been framed by academic writing as the bad object, in Altman's reading it is the theorists who have put it there.

For Altman, the diversified products and practices of commodity culture are presented as part of the solution to the (spectre of) homogenization; under post-modernism, the audience is now conceived as a wide range of narrowly defined target groups, in turn pressurizing demand for more nuanced films. This paves the way for Altman's claim that there is a larger social function at the centre of newly constituted niche audiences; culturally specific debate as emergent public spheres. Disseminated audiences, facilitated by the Internet, are making 'genres and genre texts essential to communication among members of constellated communities'. The claim here is of a grand order. In discussion of Hegel's newspaper and Habermassian thinking on the public sphere, Altman proposes that the critical discursive role of the public sphere is no longer contained by national affiliations or singular texts such as newspapers.[2] In its place, thematic clusters, imaged as 'scores of separate rubrics, separate styles and separate genres' will be the vehicles of discursive formations. He goes on to claim 'genres are simply the heirs apparent of the public sphere and imagined communities, the next in a logical series'. Yet, there is a fundamental problem with this evocation of discursive domains, such as fan sites and chat rooms, as a public sphere. For Habermas's model of publicness depends not only on the independence of reasoned debate from the influences of state and commerce, but on a forum in which the effects of such debate are brought into play with other interests and positions; the outcome of this presentation of conflicting ideas produces the situation of democracy. The concept of the public sphere cannot be applied to spaces of discussion that have no connection to the infrastructure of social and political power. Indeed, I would argue that Altman's constellated communities function as subcultures, satellites to the centres of power, with no obvious mode of correspondence.[3]

The second point of difficulty with Altman's account refers to the relationship of marketing to production. Building on the argument that studios have histori-cally avoided marketing films in terms of genre, Altman argues that the current concept of niche markets forces producers to think of films as a multiplicity of genres. The marketing of film is currently characterized by the concept of the multivalent text. Thus, in a reading of the marketing strategy for the film *Cocktail*, the genre of the film can be framed differently according to perceived market segments. According to Altman, strategists drew up four alternative conceptual-izations of the film, emphasizing different aspects of the narrative: romantic story, boy in the city, conflict of love and financial success, sibling/mentor story. A variety of marketing campaigns placed the emphasis differently, targeting the specific segments of the audience in a range of media forums associated with particular audience tastes. To this end, the multivalent text becomes the exemplar of a more sophisticated knowledge of audiences, reflected in the multiple strategies of marketing a film at diverse audience strains.

However, what remains unclear in Altman's account is whether the film product itself is transformed by the concept of multivalence (in the stages of conceptualization and development), or merely the final presentation (marketing) of the film. Certainly, the description of marketing traces an historical shift: 'When cinema was born, products determined publicity strategy; a century later, publicity determines product design' (1999: 132). The crucial word here is 'design', which retains a level of ambivalence – do we read this as design of the product from its moment of inception, or design as the packaging? Altman cites four techniques of production that facilitate the multivalent text: the processes of multifocalization, fertile juxtaposition, excess material and multiple framings. It would appear from this taxonomy of multivalent signifiers that the production process is a significant facilitator of diverse readings. Yet Altman stops short of the claims made by Wyatt that the mainstream commercial film has been fundamentally altered in terms of narrative structure, as it has become embedded in a culture of ancillary products and displaced or extended across various media formats. For Altman, the multivalent text and the practice of genre mixing are not new (clearly a reasonable claim), but have shifted in degree. The factors motivating this shift in degree are perceptions of the audience, the purported complexifying of demographic measurement: in a summative statement he argues, 'Recent stylistic developments – connected to changes in the conception and measurement of audience demographics – have led to still greater dependence on and self-consciousness about genre mixing.' The difference between the perceptions of Wyatt and Altman is not then an argument concerning change, but a disagreement about where pressure for change originates. For Altman it is the field of demographics, a shifting perception of audiences; for Wyatt, the heightened economic imperatives of a system of production, which situates film within a paradigm of related products.

If Altman's re-reading of marketing strategies in diverse historical contexts foregrounds the openness of the text to different audiences, the logic of this reading suggests that marketing discourse has come to imagine the audience in all of their complex diversity. Yet this account omits to take into account the shift from marketing the film text as singular form, to the current practice of marketing film as the primary product in a range of related commodities. Here, genre might be rethought as the cohering factor in a range of lifestyle products; and whilst a film may exist as a multivalent text for different audience segments, such fragmentation is recuperated at the level of lifestyle marketing. A new coherence exists in the clustering of taste formations for related products rather than clusters of audiences for filmic genres. I turn in the next section to the strategies of market research, which trawls a range of cultural forms and practices and cross-references this information to social demographics. This analysis will suggest that the shift   to lifestyle marketing, identified in various accounts of contemporary marketing as a complexifying of identity obfuscating social difference, in fact reinvokes social distinction. I will argue that distinction emerges through the marketing of film as a marked temporal effect, segregating audiences through lifestyle practices of film consumption conducted at different times and connecting audiences to different discursive circuits. Where, in the previous chapter, the emphasis on spatial practices of consumption traced socially demarcated spaces, through diversified marketing practices related to windows of release, the temporal crosses the axis of the spatial.

epistemologies of the audience

Marketing and promotional activities are underpinned by forms of knowledge about audiences, extracted from empirical research of a qualitative and quantitative nature. The activity of research, as academic analysis has ruminated widely in methodological debate, is implicated in the construction of knowledge rather than the reporting of it. Market research generates its own systems of classification, priorities, emphases, so that any enquiry into the findings of market research is also an exercise in how marketing executives are framing audiences. Part of Altman's polemic against the ahistorical understandings of 'genre' challenges the determining dynamic of research. Multiple choice questions enquiring why a particular film has been chosen readily supply 'genre' as a possible response. 'Suppose,' he asks us, 'a survey were to be conducted in a more open-ended manner, asking such questions as "What effect does genre have on your choice of movies?" Would such a study produce different results?' Such self-reflexivity about the research process is not, however, limited to academic ruminations. The research company Dodona in the introduction to their report *Cinemagoing 9* remark:

> Cinema audience research data is, however, notoriously unreliable. Over-claiming of visits by interviewees wishing to give the impression of a more lively social and cultural life than they actually lead is more or less universal. For example, if the 24% of the population in 1999 who claimed to visit the cinema once a month or more had actually done so, total admissions for that year would have been a minimum of 170 million rather less than the 140 million actually recorded. (2001: 35)

Market research entails its own level of fictionalization, constructed through the situation of the interview and the narrative of the questionnaire. What is of interest here is not a purported 'truth' about cinema audiences so much as the image of the audience constructed through this encounter. How does market research on cinema audiences elucidate the issue of niche markets versus homogeneity?

Recent academic writing on market research as a general practice traces the shift from the apparent postmodern segmentation of audience in a number of ways, but predominantly by considering shifts in advertising towards more emotive and design-led forms, supported by the results of market research into the fragmented nature of the population of consumers. In the text book, *The Production of Culture/ Cultures of Production*, Sean Nixon argues that advertising has been marked by a shift away from utility-based, rational explication of products towards the construction of an elaborate imaginary landscape into which consumers are invited. Nixon points to the complexity of consumer identification. No longer dependent on class-based allegiances, consumers are encouraged to think of themselves as individuals inhabiting a particularly nuanced symbolic, ethical and social world, the micro detail of which is lifestyle. Complicit with shifts in advertising is the practice of market research; no longer confined to demographics (favouring class-based classifications), research utilizes 'psychographics' to account for 'the most pertinent differences between groups of consumers which cut across social class' (Nixon, 1997: 203).

Nixon's account of lifestyle and psychographic marketing draws attention to two fundamental shifts in emphasis from demographics. First is the attempt to classify taste clusters according to a range of what are perceived to be personal attributes rather than the consumer's occupation. Second, the means of defining the self according to research is through cultural rather than economic or vocational definitions. Thus, Nixon argues, 'lifestyles and psychographics tended to produce both a more intense individualization of consumers than demographics and emphasized the differences between groups of consumers in more explicitly cultural terms' (1997: 203). In drawing on a lifestyle study of women conducted by a marketing company 'McCanns', Nixon suggests that the results, producing a profile of eight different female consumers, offers a more complex picture of consumer identity. Yet, on closer inspection, the study clusters the information into a set of new stereotypes as limited in scope as those of demographics. The survey, based on a range of attitude questions, is written up as a series of charac-ters, illustrated as animals. Thus, for example, the 'Lady Righteous' appears as a horse, drawing on the cultural associations of the bourgeoisie, the 'Down-Trodden' as a rabbit, confined to an underground warren (the home, the private sphere). Class is not absent from the account, but dressed as something else, recon-figured as 'fun like' tropes.[4] It might be more accurate an analysis to comment that the term 'class' has become erased from the lexicon of marketing whilst its effects continue to structure knowledge of consumers; demographics enters by the back door.

It is perhaps not the case that market research reveals a greater complexity in the lifestyle patterns of consumers, but rather that companies are making the links between various patterns of consumption, taste and social difference. The information that the survey solicits is, in fact, reminiscent of Bourdieu's account of taste, albeit geared towards a different outcome. Lifestyle research describes precisely the habitus, a set of dispositions that inform, at a conscious and un-conscious level, choices in cultural taste. More pertinent to the focus of this book, market research into cinema audiences in the United Kingdom deploys a mix of conventional demographics and lifestyle consumption. A major resource of market research into cinema audiences is commissioned by the Cinema and Video Industry Audience Research Consortium (CAVIAR), and conducted by BMRB International, producing an annual report for the industry.[5] The demographic model is utilized by the survey and analysis, producing information on consumers in terms of social grade, sex and age. The shift toward lifestyle research is evidenced in the range of topics surveyed. In addition to questions concerning the regularity of cinema-going and type of film viewed, respondents are asked about their ownership of forms of technology ('leisure equipment'), viewing patterns of terrestrial, satellite and cable television, video rental and purchase, and print media (magazines and newspapers).

There are two significant points to make about the structure of the survey. The first concerns synergy. The report is clearly focused on aspects of media con-sumption that extend beyond the choice of film text itself. Given the extent of cross-media ownership, and the predicted trend towards home-based consumption facilitated by digital forms of delivery and media format, the report offers information on a range of markets that companies are likely to be providing for, now and/or in the near future. Second, the survey produces a body of informa-tion on the lifestyle patterns of audiences, connecting consumption across the areas of shopping, leisure, information and culture (in its narrowest sense). Thus data is gathered on specific media forms and sources of information leading respondents to these practices, cross-referenced by factors of age, social grade and sex. What emerges is a composite image of consumers emphasizing differences of age, social class and gender. In addition, genre is consistently used to classify filmic taste, whilst a selection of specific top box-office films are monitored individually.

The findings of the survey elucidate key differences of film consumption according to social class (or social grade, in line with the statistical discourse of the research). The social grades A/B and C1 are regular cinema goers, 29 per cent attending once a month or more, and 37 per cent attending at least twice annually. These social classes tend to watch and buy film on video less, and watch film on television (particularly satellite and cable) least of all. The most popular genres for this group are drama and thrillers, with a particularly low preference for science fiction and musicals. Non-filmic video purchase is particularly high for subjects of health and fitness, and low for sport and music. The reverse is the case for the lower classes, grades C2, D and E. Home-based consumption is high (as noted in Chapter 2), with watching film on forms of television (terrestrial, cable and satellite) far exceeding video rental. Video purchase occurs mostly in supermarkets (Asda and Tesco feature prominently). The most popular non-film video purchase categories are sport and music video. Particular films confirm the genre preference in linking social grade and taste. Out of the ten films profiled for 1998, the drama *Sliding Doors* attracted 72 per cent of its audience from social grades ABC1, and 28 per cent from C2DE, whilst the high concept, action-adventure film *Armageddon* attained a 45 per cent share of grades C2DE. In 1999, the audience for the drama *Shakespeare in Love* was constituted by 76 per cent of social grades ABC1 and 24 per cent grades C2DE; similarly *Notting Hill* drew 69 per cent of its audience from the ABC1 groups and 31 per cent from C2DE. The most popular films at the cinema for the lower social classes were the comedies/spoof horror *The Mummy* (51 per cent) and *I Know What You Did Last Summer* (50 per cent).

It would be tempting simply to read these statistical results as empirical evidence of taste cultures. Yet, it is important to recognize the discursive domain in which the reports are operating, domains that condition the terms of analysis. Commissioned by the industry, the research aims to provide a broad but accurate picture of the audience, and within that, to be able to highlight key trends, enabling companies to maximize areas of growth and profit for future targeting. The 'prompted' questions peppering the survey encourage respondents to select from the given menu, where recognition of film or magazine titles is likely to blur into a positive response of use. Thus, the resulting reports announce high levels of film going (a continual year-on increase since the reports began, the only downturn relating to video rental, which is ameliorated by the increased viewing of film on satellite and cable). Another example of such prompting concerns the categories of 'favourite leisure activities'; offered a limited choice, the responses to these categories far exceed the percentages of other categories of use where questions were more embedded in the respondent's everyday practices. The 1998 statistics present the activities in terms of overall audience preference: cinema going (78 per cent), videos (73 per cent), playing sport (63 per cent), computer games (63 per cent) and theme parks (53 per cent). The favourite leisure activities, other than sport, are all related to film or video in some manner, suggesting that narrative rather than genre or media format is the most pertinent feature of the film text.

Such statistical information does not purport to explicate what audiences think of film, the value judgements they make in front of the text, or their various engagements with it. But what it does provide is a mapping of the contours of consumption in terms of time and space. The social grade analysis applied to the various sites of film viewing throws into relief the disparate practices of film viewing in cinema, home rental and television. The information suggests that the initial filmic release window at the cinema is a culture supported by the higher grade classes, with a declining social grade correspondence to the practices of rental and television premiere respectively.[6] This difference points not only to spatial practices of film viewing but to the temporal differentiation of film cultures. If we consider that film, as a dematerialized commodity, provides forms of symbolic capital in terms of its 'originality' and 'newness', the acquisition of this capital relies on accessing the film at the time of its release. The notion of the media 'event' to describe the practices of promotional culture orchestrated throughout the media has attracted comment in terms of the pervasive nature of promotion (Wernick, 1991). Yet, equally significant is the temporal management of film which reverses the problem of short life expectancy, returning as a positive in the promotional moment; release is the filmic moment which underscores and capitalizes on the ephemerality of the medium.[7]

The marketing of film constructs a momentary presence through a circuit of promotional materials and restricted screenings. The press screening secures a professional audience for the film in advance of its wider release, reviewing as a form of preparation for the event. Preview screenings again restrict access and create a notion of 'insider' knowledge. Often supplemented by the presence of 'celebrities' in addition to the standard cast and crew, preview screenings blur the fictional and factual signifiers of texts and the institutions of production.[8] In addition to preview screenings, print and televisual media produce interviews with stars and, occasionally, directors. Promotional material simultaneously permeates other consumer spheres, such as food, clothing or music, combining sponsorship with promotion, as well as the standard advertisements for film in posters and trailers in various media formats. What this orchestration of materials effects is a symbolic profile for a film within a particular moment. The debate of filmic value, interest and innovation occurs in the public domain at this time as a shared social network of exchanges. The 'premium' moment of filmic consumption in terms of social and symbolic capital is, then, the initial release. Further windows of release and consumption are, in contrast, detached from the collective debate of film and the sense of public 'happening'. Home view as a temporally disparate practice, whether video rental or televisual, is relatively disconnected from public circuits of debate and evaluation.[9]

The relationship of public and private spheres is a complex debate, where the distinction between two separate domains has been questioned from a number of quarters (Livingstone and Lunt, 1992; Tolson, 1991). Indeed, the Habermassian emphasis on the rational as the characteristic quality that secures the operation of democratic interaction has rightly been critiqued (Mouffe, 1993). Research into the sense-making activities of subcultural groupings has provided insight into the diverse modes of interaction that characterize debate in less legitimate forums, such as fanzines, in an argument for a model of filmic consumption as historical poeticism, to take but one example (Jenkins, 1992, 1995). Yet, acknowledging that subcultural enclaves produce distinct paradigms of discursivity, the question of how these domains attain social legitimacy remains unclear. Whilst statistical 'evidence' provides a crude overview of cultural practices, qualitative academic research provides the counter-detail in micro-focus. Between these two approaches lies the infrastructure of circulation, the flows of information between differentially marked spaces. The moment of filmic release, as media event, sets out the temporal and spatial management of such flows and points of interchange.

film, lifestyle and individualism

Marketing resides at the nexus of debates in cultural theory that become polarized in the claims for commodity culture as either pluralized or homogenized, and of audiences as fragmented or socially demarcated. Frank Mort speaks as a proponent of the pluralized model:

> There was a time when culture came clearly labelled. If there was no consensus about cultural values, then at least it was clear what we were getting . . . These certainties are fast disappearing. Late 20th-century culture scrambles styles, publics and patterns of taste to an unprecedented degree. Popular forms collide with high art genres and postmodernism celebrates the clash, while leisure industries re-think their markets for everything from concert-going to cycling. (1990: 32)

The market research of the film-advertising industry forges together these two opposing positions in its enquiry into related lifestyle products and practices, and in the cross-referencing of this material with a demographic model of social difference; the 'clash' and scramble of styles and tastes features as the postmodern, leaving the structures of class and other social difference as the modern. How then do we come to understand the offerings of culture as both individual choice and part of a competitive act of social distinction? And what is there specific to the nature of film that provides for its position at the centre of lifestyle consumption?

At the heart of lifestyle consumption runs the faultline separating the postmodern and the modern, a failure of the two terms to meet. The concept of lifestyle purports to shed itself of the old affinities of class, identifications exceed the traditional lines demarcating social distinction. Lifestyle consumption appears to offer the individual the opportunity to compose taste as a personal, idiosyncratic bricolage of eclectic elements. Yet it also suggests a conceptual coherence, an identifiable style that threads the diverse parts. And as these strands of style become stitched together in a fabric of taste, the old patterns of social distinction re-emerge. The marketing of film suggests linkages for us, not only in terms of extending the narrative into other media, but through product placement and sponsorship. The film text becomes a lifestyle advertisement in itself to the extent that major film companies employ product placement executives to consult with companies seeking to place brands in films. In turn, large-scale manufacturers employ a pool of script readers whose task it is to review scripts for product placement potential. An example from the 1980s testifies to the duration of this practice: in 1987 Adidas placed their product in 60 films.[10] In addition to the linkage of products and lifestyle within the film text, the connection is also made in the relocation of characters from films into the texts of advertising for other products. The 'character' of Bridget Jones, for example, appeared in women's magazines during the period of the film's release to advertise Diet Pepsi. In the hybridity of culture and commerce – the world of the film and the external world – products take on the significance of characters, and conversely characters are potential products. The film text then involves us in a intertextual space of commodity association reconfigured as style and taste rather than social distinction.[11]

Film, I would argue, is a form of media peculiarly positioned as a privileged vehicle for lifestyle consumption. Although it is possible to buy film as an object, either video or DVD, the majority of film viewing is a culture based on an experience rather than the acquisition of an object. Thus, film escapes the paradox identified by Dittmar (1992), who argues that the concept of lifestyle consumption presents us with a difficulty figured by the conjunction of the terms idealism–materialism. Here the notion of lifestyle plays simultaneously into the historical tradition of positivism, that identity is self-willed, present, autonomous, free of the constraints of socio-political environments, and at the same time reminds us that consumption is dependent on exchange with others, goods manufactured elsewhere, and on forms of ownership. Thus the object of consumption cleaves open the gap between subject and object, revealing a form of dependency on social context which problematizes consumption as self-will. For Dittmar, the middle classes have acquired a particular solution in the parodic practices of cultural play, denying the seriousness or meaning of the encounter between subjects and objects. However, if we consider the shift in consumption from the acquisition of material objects to experiences, which film as a dematerialized form offers, the idealist–materialist paradox is resolved in a different way.

If idealism and materialism are binary terms whereby idealism is the positive pole, film escapes the paradox by offering an experience rather than a commodity. 'Experience' then resonates as the opposite to possession and materialism (Lee, 1993). Thus, the reframing of consumption as experience converges with Anthony Giddens's writing on modern identity shifting from emancipatory politics to life politics (Giddens, 1991, 1992). Giddens locates a positive movement towards an ethical basis for identity, characterized by reflexivity, self-determination and responsibility in place of collective identification; consumer culture provides in part the resources for such a transition.[12] Whilst this model partially describes the movement towards a politics of global awareness, there is also a contradiction in the wielding of consumption as the facilitator of such movements; global awareness is fundamentally a movement in opposition to surplus consumption and the exploitative practices on which the system of multinational production and consumption depends. Self-reflexivity, I would argue, is both an ethical re-thinking of identity, and complicit with a culture of experientiality that is sharply distinguished in terms of social hierarchies and difference. To echo Sedgwick's remarks at the beginning of this chapter, the culture of experience produces the subject precisely as wilful, responsible and individual, eliminating the social infrastructure within which reflexivity is brought into being.

Film as a dematerialized, exhibitionary media lends itself to the present demand for experiential culture. Firmly embedded in the mesh of associated products and sponsorship, it leads us to a range of commodities through a media of the imaginary. The experiential in film is, of course, conceived of differently in what I have called the historical production of film cultures. In mainstream film culture, the experiential is played out in terms of an enhanced corporal experience of the cinematic in the development of technologies of production and exhibition: special effects, surround-sound, wide-screen and the Imax cinema format of three-dimensional viewing. Mainstream film culture elides the experience of everyday life with the corporal experience of the senses, imbricating the aestheticized world of the film with everyday life. In contrast, the arthouse and the art gallery remain focused on the image of the text. There is an historic irony to this development. Recalling the early development of cinema, part of the project of the avant-garde, such as the surrealists, was to reduce the distinction between art and life, to reduce the autonomy of art as a specialized domain. As Habermas notes, this project failed: 'These experiments have served to bring back to life, and to illuminate all the more glaringly, exactly those structures of art which they were meant to dissolve.' For Habermas, one of the outcomes of this failure has been the predominance of 'special cognitive judgments of taste' (1983: 11). The practice of cultural engagement is individualized at the level of the aesthetic. Ironically, the levelling of art and life has taken place through the process of commodification, where the aesthetic, in a design-led market, connects our practices of film, shopping and leisure.

Notes

1 Sedgwick's point in this essay, 'Epidemics of the Will', is that commodity culture provides both the cause and the resolution of consumption; whilst it produces excess, it renames its own symptom as addiction of various sorts (food, alcohol, drugs, shopping).

2 Altman extends this argument to claim that genres operate 'like nations and other complex communities', as 'regulatory schemes facilitating the integration of diverse factions into a single unified social fabric' (1999: Chapter 12). For Altman, the nation state is in the process of extinction: 'The nation-state environment has lasted long enough to convince us that the processes that once contributed to the constitution of existing nations are now extinct.' Whilst I would agree that nation states are in a process of demise, there is also a counter-movement for the production of nationhood in relation to the global economy (see Chapter 5).

3 In a discussion of television and the public sphere, Peter Dahlgren connects the question of discursivity with political competence, questioning the significance of 'interaction' alone: 'There are many topics which can be raised in regard to the discursive aspects of interaction; perhaps most relevant for the public sphere is the question of discursive resources and repertoires: what are the ways of meaning-making at work within given sectors of the populace and what bearing do they have on political competence? . . . regardless of possible inherent suppressive aspects of the dominant modes of political communication, if one does not have access to them or at least to their translatable equivalence, one is excluded from the processes of democratic participation' (1995: 19). It is also interesting to compare Altman's proposals for film as a public sphere with the examples provided by both Negt and Kluge (1972/1993) and Hansen (1991).

4 This practice has become common to marketing agencies; other consumer tropes include fruits, plants and weather systems. Tropes are by necessity drawn from the 'natural' world ensuring that commodities (objects such as cars) do not become imbricated with the consumer, the subject of discourse.

5 The research is conducted as face-to-face interviews with a sample of 3000 individuals including children from four years of age. A computer-assisted personal interviewing (CAPI) system was used to allow respondents to shift between relevant sections according to age, etc.

6 In the category of those who never attend the cinema, 21 per cent of respondents were cited as social category of AB, whilst twice that number, 44 per cent of the respondents were from social group DE.

7 The release windows for a film are often commented on in terms of an extension of economic potential, and/or in relation to the fundamental versatility of a film narrative. James Paul Roberts, in an analysis of the British film industry and marketing strategies, comments: 'Today, a film product, aimed at mass market, must now not only have the appeal and "legs" to be a success in the domestic theatrical market, its form and content must allow it to be exploitable in numerous other geographic and product markets. It must be easy to promote, have significant merchandising potential, be transferable and exploitable in the video sell-through and rental markets, suitable for TV syndication and so on' (1992: 108). Also see Hoskins *et al.* (1997).

8 In *The Film Marketing Handbook: a practical guide to marketing strategies for independent film,* the notion of celebrity extends to royalty, somewhat confusing the 'how to' approach of the book with such observations. The authors note: 'In Spain, the UK and certain other major European countries, a common practice is to invite royalty to major premieres, boosting the media profile of the event' (1993: 155).

9 The CAVIAR research supports this argument in many of its analyses, but particularly in the survey of how information about film is acquired. Lower social grades rely more on commercials than higher social grades, whilst higher social grades show a preference for specialist magazines and television review formats at the time of release, such as 'Film 95'. There is also a difference in the degree of connection with national and international formats; higher social grades tend to utilize national information media, whilst lower social grades tend to refer to the more internationally circulated 'MTV at the Movies', and 'Movies, Games and Videos'.

10 Alex Abraham argues that the relationship between product placement and film production is more complex still. Using the example of the film *Cast Away*, which featured Tom Hanks as a FedEx worker washed up on a desert island, he notes that the CEO of the company FedEx, Fred Smith, is an investor in the film's production company (from the online magazine *Feed*, www.feedmag.com, January 2001).

11 This shift from the film text as the object of value to the notion of characters as asset coincides with the emphasis of trade turning from products to copyright. This transition is addressed in a discussion of TRIPS in Chapter 5.

12 For Giddens, the present system offers both opportunities and constraints for individual reflexivity. As Lury notes, Giddens does not consider the social variegations of participation: 'But is this reflexive relation the same for all individuals? Do we all have access to the same freedoms and suffer from the same responsibilities?' (1996: 241).

CHAPTER FIVE

Postmodern praxes: production on the national and global stage

Does postmodernism, with its total permeation of the lifeworld and formidable global web, suggest that it is all over for the nation state? If the authority of the nation is perceived to be in demise, have taste cultures become severed from their mooring in social hierarchy, given over to a form of individualized eclecticism? And by some feats of critical connectivity, hasn't film come to stand for, become metonymic of, a postmodern condition? Take Fredric Jameson's famous account of late capitalism:

> It seems to me exceedingly symptomatic to find the very style of nostalgia films invading and colonizing even those movies today which have contemporary settings: as though, for some reason, we were unable today to focus our own present, as though we have become incapable of achieving aesthetic representations of our own current experience. (1985: 117)

For Jameson postmodern film is culpable of scrambling the teleological order of history, removing the referents of social markers and reducing the text of history to a one-dimensional surface play of style. In contradistinction to Benjamin's angel of history dragged backwards into the present, splitting open a dialectical relation of past and present, Jameson argues for a different backward pull – that of nostalgia. Complexity gives way to sentimental recognition, which is also a misrecognition; the past that film has come to represent bears no relation to any discernible period or location. Postmodern film condemns us to live in a perpetual melancholy for a life lost (although never having existed), displacing attention from the present; '[the subject] can no longer look directly out of its eyes at the real world for the referent but must, as in Plato's cave, trace its mental images of the world on its confining walls' (Jameson, 1985: 118). Where for Jameson the postmodern inflicts a kind of cataract, inhibiting perception of anything other than the 'thin' images of film on the cave wall, Marxist geographer David Harvey evokes a whole tradition of literary criticism when he proclaims film to be a mirror to society: 'Both *Wings of Desire* and *Blade Runner*,' he argues, 'hold up to us, as in a mirror, many of the essential features of the condition of postmodernity' (1989: 323). In accounts of the postmodern, film is both witness to and perpetrator of the crime.[1]

The problem with these accounts concerns both the treatment of film and that of postmodernism. First, the textual analysis of film relies on a concept of culture as mimetic, reproducing the image of society without any attention to its production. Further, if we read Jameson's account of the retro literally, it infers that film indisputably has particular effects of temporal dislocation; this claim is at best generalized. Less literally, I think that Jameson is actually referring to film as a symptom of a larger condition, but with such a diagnostic reading the causes remain obtuse. Second, the concept of postmodernism proffered here implies a radical epochal shift; for Jameson into late capitalism, for Harvey a condition of space–time compression. Whilst this 'condition' characterizes part of the present, it appears as a new horizon that we have crossed into. The old territory of modernism, I would argue in contrast, remains the ground from which post-modernism attempts, but never quite manages, to lift off.

Before examining the institutional domains in which film culture is produced I take a slightly circuitous route to unravel what I am referring to as post-modernism and modernism. Painting with a broad historical brush, a Western narrative of postmodernism has been eloquently argued in the work of Jameson (1991), Lyotard (1984) and Baudrillard (1981, 1988) to suggest that the post-war period represents a significant break with the past on a number of key terrains. Representation is no longer separate from the real (the excitement of Baudrillard); the grand recit of religion, Marxism, history, science and progress are now stories separated from the referent of belief; history is lost to us as a knowable reality (White, 1978), and thus we are left with the debris of a past age with no real resources to access a lineage of social change (the melancholy of Jameson). Described by some as a critique that leads to political abandon (the fury of Callinicos, 1990), the postmodern condition threatens to make us immobile witnesses, powerless in the face of new forms of global division and devastation. Yet, this is but one projection of where the postmodern leads us. Other critical accounts take a more optimistic sojourn into the spaces of unfixity, of celebration in the loosened structures and practices of free-fall. If postmodernism describes a collapse of official structures, this reading suggests such a transformation facilitates new forms of identity less adhered to the formations of nation states and fixed forms of identity (Fukuyama, 1992; Owens, 1984). Here consumption has become a central focus for the dispersed practices of identity formation. The plethora of images, texts and cultural practices lends itself to a form of bricolage and appropriation where cultural sense is made rather than received. A significant body of work has excavated the practices of cross identifications located in subcultures (Hebdige, 1986, 1988), the result not only of disorganized capital but of migratory, diasporic movements. Perhaps most significant of all is the critique of postmodernism as the appropriation of a discourse of displacement and hybridity for a Western culture in post-imperialist crisis. In contrast, it has been argued, the experience of displacement is geographically and historically widespread, the effect of Western colonial and imperialist practices producing social and subjective fragmentation in periods prior to the 'official' parameters of the postmodern (Appiah, 1993; Gilroy, 1993).

In response to these assertions, I would argue that modernism continues in certain institutions and forms of government, and is mobilized with recourse to a system of binary structures underpinning discourses of economy and culture. This understanding of modernism borrows from various theoretical accounts rooted in the history of European modernity. It draws in part on Foucault's project of reading the characteristic traces of modernity through the production of specialized discourses located in institutional formations. Where, for Foucault, the school, the asylum, the hospital and prison served variously as the locus of power, the institutions of culture have an integral part to play in the construction of social relations. Habermas is also at work here, influenced by Weber's reading of the process of discursive separation and reformation in the eighteenth century. All of these accounts of modernity, giving rise to modernism in the late nineteenth century, trace a process of splitting occurring in the eighteenth century as a defining moment for European culture. For Weber (1930), such a process is motivated by the loss of a unified world view as it had been expressed in the discourses of religion and metaphysics. Incompatibility or contradiction gives rise to a necessary separation of perspectives into the domains of science, morality and art, producing specific claims of legitimacy in the pursuit of knowledge, justice and taste respectively. This in turn generated a meta-discourse of experts within each domain, and in Foucaldian style, a body of institutions within which each discourse existed within its own autonomy.

For Habermas this is, of course, the moment in which the lifeworld becomes divided from the domains of expertise, each with their own forms of rationalization. It is also the historical process that enabled Kant's formulation of art as a separate sphere from commerce (outlined in Chapter 1). For Habermas, one of the consequences of the division of specialized knowledge from the hermeneutics of everyday communication has been a reaction against the expert: 'This splitting off is the problem that has given rise to efforts to "negate" the culture of expertise.' He warns ominously 'the problem won't go away' (1983: 9). Indeed, for Habermas the solution is a reintegration of the discourses of expertise and the lifeworld, a solution that he attributes to the original intentions of the Enlightenment project. In my reading of the cultural discourses and institutions that materialize film cultures in the present, however, such a reintegration does not take place. Where globalization has brought about a culturalization of the lifeworld, culture and the lifeworld are so thoroughly elided that a redivision may be more desirable.

This chapter approaches the production of film cultures as a struggle between a discourse of global economy characterized by a process of boundary erosion (of spatial boundaries as well as conceptual boundaries of culture and economy), and the modernist institutions of the state which attempt to demarcate categories of definition. Within this struggle the interests materialized are not simply those of a pre-given nation and those of the multinational corporation. Rather, the effort to influence how and what kind of film is produced and distributed is also, at another level, a production of the terms the 'nation', the 'people' and 'culture'. Thus, what Bourdieu calls the dynamic of the cultural field, characterized by flux and a parallel restratification of culture and social status, refers not only to the structure of social hierarchy within the nation, but to the field of international struggle for position. Indeed, I would argue that it is not possible to think socio-cultural divisions of a nation without recourse to the global processes that traverse and permeate its domain.

Coming back to the questions that open this chapter, the production of taste and 'the nation' occur in the institutional sites of film production and policy; indeed, policy remains a key area for the production of symbolic meanings (McGuigan, 1996; Moran, 1996). The analysis here examines first the infra-structure of film production as it is spatially located. Second, the institutions of film policy situated in the forum of global discussion of trade agreements (GATT and, subsequently, the WTO), the European Union and British national institutions of film policy (the Department of Culture, Media and Sport, and the Film Council). Finally, the discourse of journalism provides a visible, public representation of issues of policy, bearing on and reproducing discourses of aesthetics and taste. More than a metonym for postmodernism, film culture is produced at the conjuncture of the modern and postmodern in moments of dialogue, confrontation and repositioning.

vertically (and virtually) disintegrating

Where Hollywood has been characterized as the dominant institutional form of film production at least until the 1960s, accounts of film production since that period have argued, in a postmodernist vein, that production processes have undergone a fragmentation and decentring, raising questions about whether we can think of film as having an institutional base (Smith, 1998[2]). The structure and organization of the film industry has received critical attention as an almost iconic semblance of a shift from a studio production line to a flexibly organized set of practices orchestrated by major studios. The focus of such accounts has varied; in some accounts the emphasis has been the spatial reorganization of cultural production, with the film industry providing an exemplary instance. For others, the question driving the account has been whether such reorganization produces a set of differentiated films, broadening the genre-format films of the studio age into an array of filmic styles. The former focus is represented here by the seminal essay by Christopherson and Storper, 'The City as Studio; The World as Back Lot: The Impact of Vertical Disintegration on the Location of the Motion Picture Industry'. First published in the journal *Environment and Planning D: Society and Space*, the article connects the reconfiguration of the film industry with patterns of urban regeneration and development. The spatial is, ostensibly at least, the focus of this account of change. In this essay, the authors map the historical development of the film industry from the decline of the studio system, and the system of Fordist production, through to the current post-Fordist model. Where one might expect the decentralization of production to signify a dispersal of practice across locations, Christopherson and Storper trace a recentralization spatially n key areas. Thus, as the title of their article suggests, what initially appears as a fragmentation of production, both economically and spatially, is in fact a re-agglomeration, which returns the present system of production and distribution to its former state of American dominance; the world exists as the receptor of film products from a centralized imperial source.

The historical overview that the article provides takes production as its point of focus, tracing the economic, technological and social determinants that impact on and produce epochal change in the system. The significant historical markers set out by the authors as provoking the shift from studio production to flexible specialization are twofold. First, the ruling against Paramount in 1948 that the company could no longer retain ownership of distribution outlets, thus ending a monopoly and assured circuit of production and exhibition. Second, the competition for consumer income and leisure time from television. Both of these events, it is argued, opened the market to wider forces of competition, from other film markets and from new forms of cultural consumption. In terms of television this represented a tidal shift away from public towards domestic forms of consumption. According to Christopherson and Storper, these forces exerted a pressure on the studios to differentiate products in a number of ways. The star system provided one means by which films became readily identifiable, and desirable, not least through the extra-textual knowledge about 'stars' that has become an integral part of the marketing of film. Another response to the demand to differentiate products was manifested in the cinematic experience itself; from the 1950s onwards, special effects became a key mechanism for heightening the dramatic experience of cinema-going, gaining impetus in the development of production and exhibition technology such as wide-screen formats and the Imax experience. A third response was the industry seeking out new markets, both in terms of films for television, and in an international domain.

The transformations that occurred in response to a context of increased competition affected not only the product itself, but the structure of production. Having lost economic security in terms of a market, the American film industry shifted the investment in its production base to the sphere of distribution and circulation. As a result, production became the domain of independent producers as work was contracted out; specialized units of production became, and have become, the practice of film production, eliminating the risk of sustaining a large industrial base. Small-scale specialized units clustered in urban centres, trading not only in film, but in a range of products for the entertainment industry became the norm. Thus, flexible specialization represents the shift from a product-based industry to a process-based practice, a movement facilitated by the synergy of productive technologies. Companies specializing in editing, lighting and sound design offer a service to a range of industries, spreading their own financial risk.

Christopherson and Storper's point about the geographic implications of this development is precisely the re-agglomeration of production in certain key areas. As they note, the reassembly of the entertainment industry necessitated a spatial proximity of companies trading among each other, leading once again to a centralized core of production, and a powerful nexus of economic, cultural and social interaction. What appears on the surface as an unravelling spool, on closer inspection is revealed as a tight-knit fabric of integrated working relationships, practices and technologies. This reconfiguration of a centralized production base replays more than the geographic centralization, it also reproduces the division of labour; cultural workers in small industries pay the price of job insecurity and its concomitant negativity in the lack of pensions and redundancy pay. Large companies relocate the risk of production at the lowest level of involvement (Beck, 1992).

The local, however, represents only one half of the transformation of cultural production. As flexible specialization demanded the creation of a base of small companies, so competition and control of distribution demanded a global system of dissemination; in a series of mergers and takeovers, multinational corporations were formed. By divesting themselves of economic liability in production, multinational operators have repositioned themselves as institutional investors, refocusing critical power in a more profitable area, that of film circulation. This development, above all others, represents the idiom of cultural production in the postwar period and into the present moment. With the proliferation of distribution channels and outlets, the control of cultural products (and the concomittant tracking of copyright) has become the most profitable point of the commodity circuit. As gatekeepers of product dissemination, major corporations perform a role closer to that of editor than manufacturer, as Garnham notes. In managing the afterlife of a film, companies are able to control cultural flows, creating scarcity when required, timing the release of films with a range of tie-in products, saturating the market at the appropriate moment. Significantly, the terms of trade have shifted from the ownership of a prestigious production base to the less visible but highly lucrative ownership of cultural property rights.

Whilst Christopherson and Storper argue that the film industry typifies changes in production generally in the late twentieth century, moving from assembly-line techniques to a situation of vertical disintegration, their critique remains undeveloped at the level of distribution (Aksoy and Robins, 1992). The critical point of the article is that the reorganization of production appears as vertical disintegration, a dissembling of the film industry as monolith. The point of interest for Christopherson and Storper is the spatial disintegration of production practices and their subsequent reintegration in specific urban sites, with implications for labour flexibility and insecurity. Yet, as Aksoy and Robins argue, the distinct nature of film, the 'particular economies of the film product and film business', are absent from an account that is ultimately interested in spatial reorganization of industry per se. For Aksoy and Robins, the nature of film production is peculiar in terms of its high capital outlay and risk of return, a situation that demands that film financiers devise strategies to minimize risk and secure returns. The point of fixity in the system of production is then in controlling the level of market demand, or audience, if the success of a film is dependent on how well 'the cultural and aesthetic preferences of the consumer are anticipated, nurtured and channelled'.

The securing of audiences is conducted through various strategies affecting production scale and aesthetics, distribution and exhibition control, and horizontal reach into ancillary markets. To take each of these separately, control of distribution, despite the Paramount decree, has remained a monopoly. As Petley (1992) has argued, five distribution companies in Britain were responsible for 18 out of 20 top grossing films in 1992; a system of 'alignments' ensures that certain distributors obtain first refusal for films from certain companies (Rank has first choice on Columbia, Fox, Disney and United Artists). Thus, major distributors co-exist rather than compete. The situation is further monopolized by the ability of distributors to block book theatres, denying space to other films from 'minor' companies. Despite the increase of screens through the development of multiplexes, the possibility of securing a booking for an 'independent' film is severely limited; exhibitors demand that a film reach a 'break figure' within the first week, ensuring the exhibitor's fee at a certain level (based on percentage). This monopoly on distribution is reproduced at the level of television sales and satellite channels. Whilst television rights produce the greatest level of return, the major companies have moved into ownership of broadcast and digital media. Thus, each window of possible return feeds back to the majors; in the process, other forms of filmic competition, or diversity, are eliminated or severely curtailed. As Wasko has argued, Christopherson and Storper's account fails to address the further reintegration of the film industry at the level of distribution and exhibition in various media forms, or what Richard Maltby has named 'the unnoticed return of vertical integration' (Maltby, 1997: 39; Wasko, 1994). The situation is further compounded with the selling of rights to film-related merchandise, and with Disney shops peppering the new malls, goods become a business in their own right and within the control of majors.

If the fragmenting effects of flexible specialization have been recouped at the level of distribution and exhibition, how has this affected the product of film, the aesthetic dimension of texts? As Aksoy and Robins note, there are two dimensions to the development of films themselves: the development of a distribution network for independent films and the move to high concept film within the mainstream. In terms of distribution, a form of corporate appropriation characterizes the structural development of an independent film culture. The examples of New Line and Miramax serve as an indication of the relationship between the independent sector and the mainstream. Both companies originated in a specific site, targeting a particular audience of college students as a sector whose tastes were not addressed by the mainstream. Film screenings were, in the case of New Line, combined with lecture series (Wyatt, 1998) featuring talks by Norman Mailer, William Burroughs and R. D. Laing among others, producing a discursive space for film within an intellectual environment. Both companies operated by advancing finance to production companies in pre-production deals, acquiring the rights for distribution. New Line, for example, forged a three-year deal with the British company Working Title in 1989 for all North American rights to features, and home video rights.

The success of New Line enabled the distributor to invest in larger productions, such as the *Nightmare on Elm Street* series, which enabled the division of the company into mainstream and speciality divisions by 1983. The success of Miramax resided in the ability of the company to seize relatively avant-garde products such as *sex, lies and videotape* and *The Crying Game*, pushing films over into the mainstream through successful marketing campaigns trading on notions of transgression and controversy (Wyatt, 1998: 81). Yet the movement towards oligopolistic control through mergers, incorporating competition, characterizes the independent sector in addition to other ancillary markets. In 1993 Disney acquired Miramax, and Turner Broadcasting Corporation merged with New Line. Whilst the major studios had attempted to develop a niche market in independent film in the early 1980s, for example Triumph Films developed by Columbia, and Twentieth Century Fox International Classics, the specialized divisions had lacked knowledge of the audience and suffered unsuccessful marketing campaigns. Thus, the incorporation of independent distributors within the mainstream signifies the buying in of cultural capital, further strengthening the presence of such distributors within the marketplace. As Wyatt notes, the effect of corporate take-over of the independent distribution sector has significantly destabilized the field, forcing 'a contraction of the market for independent film' (1998: 87). In terms of the aesthetic and political possibility of the sector, the notion of independence becomes nominal, filtered through the corporate body of major studios.

If the major studios effectively secured dominance of the independent sector, the development of mainstream films is marked by a key shift away from the proliferation of genres towards a more epic cinema in the high concept film. According to recent accounts of film production, the outcome of the series of mergers between studios and other cultural producers, forming synergies, is not the proliferation of film in terms of quantity or varied formats. Indeed, Tino Balio (1998) argues that Hollywood's response to globalization has been the reduction in the number of films produced, and a concentration of resources on an innovative format, the high concept film. Characterized by an enormity of budget, special effects and particular stars, the high concept film eliminates the possibility of smaller production units competing in the same market. Justin Wyatt (1994) describes this format as 'post-generic' film making dependent on the simplification of character and narrative, and a symbiosis of image and sound-track, resulting in montage sequences which are readily reconfigured in other media windows. For Wyatt, the high concept film configures a type of excess, a hyperbolic performance of spectacle in terms of the characterization and the bodies of stars, and the foregrounding of music: 'In place of this [conventional] identification with narrative, the viewer becomes sewn into the "surface" of the film, contemplating the style of the narrative and the production. The excess created through such channels as the production design, stars, music, and promotional apparatus enhances this appreciation of the films' surface qualities.' The terms of Wyatt's analysis here suggest that identification is replaced by a spectatorial distance, and that in place of a 'depth' of understanding or connection, the relationship between the spectator and film is located on the surface. Arguably, the high concept film emerged with the release of *Star Wars* (1977), a film that expanded both the perceptual scale of vision within the texts and the presence of film in spaces external to the cinema: 'while the effects of the film extended what cinema could do, and while the first shot promised an expansion beyond the parameters of human scale, the film itself extended outside the cinema into a multimedia, global consciousness' (Bukatman, 1998: 249).

The high concept film has readily identifiable economic and aesthetic effects. Economically, the format precludes the possibility of rivalry, and whilst the scale of funding represents a potential loss on unprecedented scale, the potential return is also magnified. Thus, one economically successful high concept film supports a range of less successful features. Aesthetically the film text is dependent on a formula both knowable to and successful with audiences, but suggesting a series of formal shifts from previous Hollywood products. The significant point here is that the formal characteristics of the film text do not appear as an intellectual issue in the discourse of critics, but as determined by the economic context of circulation (Wyatt, 1994). The economic risk of the film is lessened by the range of associated tie-in products, and ancillary markets such as theme parks, television spin offs and video, which in turn inflect and condition the aesthetics of the text. Yet, to ascribe the development of the format purely to economics produces a reductive case, for the high concept film continues a style of cinematic experience present from film's inception in what Gunning has called the cinema of attractions. Defying the rational, linear narrative structure of a literary model, the cinema of attractions is located instead in a bodily response to the image, a cinema of theatre and spectacle conditioned in part by the earlier forms of vaudeville and music halls, within which cinema first emerged in the form of short films within a hybrid programme of theatre. The high concept film resonates that history of embodied spectatorship, but one which is enabled and constrained by media conglomerates; the root of the word 'corporate' (*corporatus*), meaning to form into a body, nicely elides the aesthetic and economic dimensions of the film experience.

The shift in production practices towards flexible specialization is not a simple causal trajectory determining the aesthetics of the text, but is connected to and conditioned by the relationships between production, circulation and consumption. Production practices themselves depend on the possibilities of film technology (special effects, wide-screen format, surround-sound), in addition to budgets. The high concept film is also dependent on, and transformative of, the practices of distribution and marketing. Designed to market a range of associated goods, the release of mainstream film has become by necessity an event (Balio, 1998; Wasko, 1994). As Balio and other critics point out, the marketing budget of a mainstream film is often in excess of its production costs. The creation of a media event is in part the media saturation of a market, but within a temporal limit; scarcity needs also to appear within the dynamic of supply and demand (Appadurai, 1986). Yet the media event of a film's release is also, I would argue, dependent on the visceral promise of high concept film. The event is desirable not simply through its excess presence in media space, nor the need to acquire contemporous cultural knowledge, but the notion of a peculiarly cinematic experience of the sublime spectacle.

In summary, and returning to the question of whether film has suffered a fragmentation within the terms of a postmodern discourse, the effects of flexible specialization on film production and distribution are suggestive of a shift in strategy incurring a recentralization of economic power in key sites and corporate structures. Transformations of this order have facilitated and contained the development of mainstream film as hyper-text, and appropriated and curtailed the market for (and thus the feasibility of) independent film. The analysis leads us to conclude that filmic tastes are produced simply through a global cultural and economic imperialism. The problem with this economic analysis as a free-standing cartography of film cultures is that it absents the complex inter-relationship of nation states and multinational entertainment companies, and the local cultures of taste that drive consumption from a series of sedimented histories not formally recognized in the economic model. In the following section the global negotiations of cultural rights and responsibilities are considered through the prism of the GATT talks where the notion of cultural territories and frontiers is both produced and resisted.

global discourses

Aksoy and Robins end their analysis 'Hollywood for the 21st Century' (1992) with the question: 'Hollywood is ubiquitous. What does this now mean for the development of alternative spaces of film production and culture?' Five years later in a paper entitled 'From Cultural Defence to Political Culture', Philip Schlesinger argues, 'I would suggest that official worrying about "American-ization" should not obscure a critical analysis of what is presently meant by the "Europeanization" of audiovisual culture' (1997: 374). Between the space of these two papers the GATT talks in Uruguay had occurred in 1993, finalized in a legally binding Marrakech Final Act in 1994 (Miller, 1996). If the GATT discussions were an initiative to facilitate the free exchange of goods, and to establish a legal procedural agreement, European nation states emerge as the residual blockage to this network of flows. The significant outcomes of this dispute concern conceptions of space and culture. Space returns as specific iden-tities of place, albeit internally divided and contested; in addition, the production of a second unifying spatial entity emerges beyond that of individual states in the form of 'Europe', signifying an ambiguity that Schlesinger remarks upon. The

European manoeuvre of removing audiovisual products from the trade agreement in 1993, facilitated by the French representatives, was heralded as a 'victory'; yet this needs to be viewed as more than an act of resistance. At another level it is a production of European identity, defined in opposition. The consequences of this production continue to be played out in the institutional framings of European cultural policy.[3]

The 'resolution' of the discussions established a spatial distinction through the differentiated comprehension of 'culture'. Laden with the critical history of complexity, whereby culture is understood as both a way of life and a series of valued objects (Williams, 1961), a series of symbolic representations and a commodity in an economy of exchange, 'culture' is further complexified by its mutation into the culture industries (McIntyre, 1996; McRobbie, 1999; Pisters, 2001). If the agreement forged at Marrakech attempted to retain both of the historical meanings of this term in a European act of distinction, of culture as both symbolic and economic, the difference between an apparently homogeneous America and a unified Europe needs to be regarded as more than a resistance to cultural imperialism. As Schlesinger argues, such frameworks of perception are themselves the product of fundamental constitutional differences inscribed in law and its institutional habitus. Schlesinger traces the difference of approach to the different discourses of rights. Whereas the official concept of Americanness is a juridico-political collectivity, the constitution places the priority on the equality of citizens' rights and freedom of expression. The right of expression extends to free trade, a notion of autonomy of expression and choice symbolized by the free-play of the market; restrictions therefore appear as an inhibition of individual rights. The European position in contrast places emphasis on collective culture, cohered under the sign of the nation; a more defensive position, the European conceptualization defines culture as more than commerce, its meaning located in the various cultural practices within the bounds of the nation state. The difference is significant, the former supporting the individual and the market, the latter reinforcing the collective national body.

Schlesinger critiques the European defence of national culture on two fronts. First as 'distinctly Third Worldist' in tone (1997: 376), presenting an argument from a position of relative disadvantage; second, the European argument invokes a 'simplistic counterposition' of European and American culture. Whilst I share Schlesinger's disquiet concerning the presentation of a unified European culture, based on the model of unified national cultures, his characterization of the oppositions within the debate replay academic oppositions as much as political conceptualizations. I would argue that what is at stake in the debates on trade is not simply caricatures of national (or, more correctly, continental) differences, but an issue of the visibility of cultural flows and centres of power. The call to further liberalize trade is simultaneously the facilitation of the flow of goods through global paths of dissemination. The position ascribed to 'America' in the discussion of trade is not an historical national referent. Where Schlesinger argues for a less homogeneous conceptualization of America, as internally divided by questions of multiculturalism, political correctness and educational curriculum, his analysis is founded on the national culture of the USA. In contrast, I would argue that opposition to 'America' at GATT is in dialogue with a different conceptualization, a notion of 'America' as the representation of multinationally based corporate empires. Whilst the multinational company pursues interests external to particular national affiliations, its corporate ownership resides largely within the domain of the USA. From this perspective, resistance to the liberalization of trade is a resistance to multinational corporate power.

As Castells argues, the 1990s in the West represent a decade characterized by the accelerated process of international networks of production, distribution and management of trade and services (1996: 116). For Castells, the formation has been facilitated by the development of technologies of communication and information, mobilizing capital and goods in dematerialized flows. As Saskia Sassen notes, the global infrastructure is increasingly privately owned.[4] Within this context, the assertion of a European position is not simply an invocation of traditional national cultures, but an assertion of place into the space of flows. Viewed from this perspective, the 'American' call to liberalize trade barriers and exemptions is a demand for the facilitation of capital to manoeuvre globally; in denying this complete liberalization, the paths of flows are thrown into relief at the points of blockage and national resistance. In this context, the nation state comes to represent an embodied form of material culture where the multinational company exists in practices largely dematerialized in its operations, secured by private networks of circulation and exchange, operating in a different language and codification. As an example of this somewhat abstract claim that GATT represents a shift towards dematerialization and abstraction of the economy, the legacy of GATS, the WTO obliges. Set up in 1995 to offer a structure and framework to the Marrakesh agreement, the WTO organized three specialized councils: the Council for Trade in Goods (GATT), the Council for Trade in Services (GATS) and the Council for Trade-related Aspects of Intellectual Property Rights (TRIPS). The separation of these different aspects of 'trade' illuminates the direction in which trade agreements are moving, from the concept of goods as material objects of exchange (GATT) towards the notion of trade as rights, abstract properties of ownership (TRIPS).

The functions of the WTO are those of trade dispute settlement, management of specialized councils and trade policy review. For Castells, the WTO operates as more than a global mediator; the outcome of its management has been the facilitation of the global economy:

In the late 1990s, on the initiative of the United States government, the WTO focused its activity on liberalizing trade in services, and on reaching an agreement on trade-related aspects of intellectual property rights (TRIPS). On both grounds, it signalled the strategic connection between the new stage of globalization and the informational economy. (Castells, 1996: 114)

The WTO as a global institution represents a shift away from regulation as a national process largely conducted informally between government and the regulated towards a culture of corporate legal 'rights', rights relating to procedure and ownership. As Toby Miller argues, the WTO replaces the conventional notion of trade debate involving collective discussion with a practice of multinational companies lobbying national countries individually:

This new machinery will make it easier for multinational corporations (MNCs) to dominate trade via the diplomatic services of their home government's representatives, to the exclusion of environmental and other matters of public interest, which will no longer have the entree that GATT gave via recognition of non-governmental organizations. (1996: 74)

The effect of the WTO is not a representation of the preconstituted interests of multinational companies; rather, it forges a coherence through on global commerce through its jurisdiction. The multinational company is characterized by both strategic alliances and more tactical operations, connecting up smaller enterprises where local knowledge is in demand. What the WTO presents is an institutional body of representation for the largely immaterial, dispersed activities of multinational companies.

If the trade discussions at GATT and the WTO are forged through a concept of 'trade', then culture is the ghost in the machine that returns to trouble the negotiations at Uruguay. In a reversal of Kant's separation of the disinterested space of art, demarcated from the contaminating sphere of commerce, in global negotiations it is culture that is perceived to be the polluting influence. The oppositional positions however effect the same separation of culture and commerce, art and economy. In contrast, the forums of policy making within the European Union attempt to hold culture and economy together in a project to facilitate cultural diversity within the sphere of European unity, and to reinvigorate national film industries. The internal divisions and asymmetries of Europe are addressed in various ways. A series of conferences between European–Mediterranean partners has considered the possible collaboration between nations in terms of training, marketing strategy and intra-European distribution. The three areas of focus for debate have been how to organize and regulate the audiovisual market, how to maximize public–private initiatives and how to utilize new technologies. In a finely balanced act of keeping in play the individual nation and the collective supranational union, public infrastructure and private finance, the institution of the EU presents a performative calling into being of 'Europe'.

In constituting a collective European audiovisual space within the talks, the issues of diversity and technology, as Schlesinger notes, feature as both problems and solutions. On the one hand, cultural, ethnic and linguistic differences provide a rich resource of specialist cultural products, whilst on the other, they act as barriers to cross-national distribution. Similarly, technology is proposed as a solution to the oligopolies of theatrical distribution of film, potentially offering nations a new vehicle to distribute film. Yet distribution technologies return the debate to the hybrid relations of public–private partnerships; new technologies of dissemination have conversely increased the inward flow of audio-visual products from outside Europe. The situation of European policy in the post-GATT period for film (strategy papers from the European Parliament, Media 95, Media 2000, Media Plus) attempts to address the necessarily complex interplay of national protection, intra-national trade, national economies and productivity, and citizens' rights and consumer cultures through a series of mea-sures – training, co-production strategies, strengthening transnational distribution and the profiling of European film. The initiatives also address imbalances between member states and promote structural adjustments to economic and cultural development (Evans and Ford, 1999). The measures provide a hybrid response to the imperative to stimulate European film production and audiences, drawing on both American notions of commercial, genre-based film and on an unspecified indigenous film culture.

In 1997, Schlesinger wrote of the failure of the European media programme, asserting that European films remained confined to the national audience, the European star system had collapsed and that deregulation of television and video distribution had strengthened the major conglomerates. Whilst the latter two points may be conceded, the issue of films crossing national borders is an uneven practice. Britain remains fairly resistant to foreign-language film, with the majority of screenings occurring within London and a few other cities (Dodona, 2001: 36), yet Italy imports 40 per cent of films from other EU members, and France 30 per cent (OECD, 1998). The more critical underlying tension within the EU is whether an emphasis on European film culture is appropriate to the mix of ethnic identities that constitute the shifting formation of the continent. As Schlesinger notes, the concept of 'Europeanness' is itself fraught with tensions of diversity. Such diversity is manifest within nations in the movement towards decentralization and the disjunction between ethnic identity and national affiliation. And as Colin MacCabe argues, the legacy of Europe's imperial past further fractures any simple sense of historical linearity and national cohesion; 'In the movement from the sixteenth to the twentieth century we pass from a

European to a global perspective which demands that we analyse contemporary culture in terms of an imperialist imposition of authoritative norms which are then contested, negotiated, mimicked in the crucial emphases of our post-modernity' (1992: 191–2). Here MacCabe rightly extends the concept of postmodernity from global flows of capital to that of a transient and migratory populace.[5]

British film: national (re)solutions

If the EU represents an attempt to reunite commerce and culture, to bring together the complex understanding of culture as a way of life with the contemporary inflection of culture as industry, within the British context the oppositions are again set in play. I want to argue this through three facets of policy and review – the government review and forecast for the film industry (published in an initial slim-line report 'The British Film Industry', 1995, and further elaborated in the report 'A Bigger Picture', 1998), the inauguration of the Film Council and the press response to Lottery funding of films. The argument returns us first, to the juncture at which the 'internal' taste formations within a nation meet global discourse, or the national habitus (Hedetoft, 2000) and, second, to a particular representational or aesthetic definition of British film.

In the 1990s, the government undertook a review of the British film industry. The National Heritage Committee issued 'The British Film Industry' in 1995 under a Conservative government, the product of a long consultation with various representatives of aspects of production, distribution and exhibition. The title of the report is significant, for what it effects is a shift of the notion of a national film industry based predominantly on indigenous production (production by British directors and creative teams along with the remit of cultural diversity), towards a British film industry offering production services and location.[6] There are two related features of the report that provide an emphasis for policy and position. On the one hand is the foregrounding of location, a reconfiguring of the discourse of heritage within a familiar rhetoric of economic regeneration. The rhetorical appeal to the 'meaning' of the landscape of cities, or more specifically London, punctuates the narrative: 'London is the jewel in the crown of the UK's locations', and 'Film makers know that when their audiences think of Britain, they think of Big Ben and Tower Bridge'. The planning for future productions is then focused on the attraction of foreign investment to Britain as an historic location, and the creation of the London Film Commission is set up to improve Britain's competitiveness. On the other hand, the review of indigenous production shifts the notion of British film from a representation of cultural diversity to that of commercially competitive industry. The report reiterates the necessity of 'popular' film. Here, in a discussion of the monopoly of distribution and exhibition, an interesting transition takes place in the logic of the narrative. For whilst the diagnosis of an industry in crisis is clearly related to the statistics cited in the report relating to ownership of distribution and exhibition, and further, the report states that a monopoly and mergers investigation concluded that a monopoly situation exists, there is retreat from confronting the situation. The commission recommends certain measures restricting minimum exhibition periods, but states that the monopoly is the result of 'US studios . . . skilled in producing and promoting films that the UK public want to see'. The adjustments to restrict exhibition runs, if implemented, 'might facilitate the showing of British films, in so far as the British film makers produce popular film' (1995: 14).

In 1998, under a Labour government and the newly formed Department of Culture, Media and Sport, the Film Policy Review Group published the report 'A Bigger Picture'. This lengthier document on the film industry is the more significant of the two in that it sets out plans for specific review groups and proposals for further action. Whilst the report clearly identifies areas of distribution and marketing as key sites for intervention, suggesting centralized agencies as a way of pooling resources, the main overview of the report confirms the former emphasis of 'The British Film Industry' in terms of production and the conceptualization of film. A central component of the report is the concern to develop relationships between the public and private spheres (the City of London in particular), and the provision of tax incentives for foreign investment. Capitalizing perhaps on the indistinct definition of 'Britishness', which in most areas of public debate has concerned questions of ethnicity and representation, the problems of defining a British film are reduced to percentages of finance, production, crew and post-production being of national origin. The Middleton Committee's proposal that 75 per cent of production spend should be within Britain is accepted by the report, but also reduced to 60 per cent in some cases, particularly if postproduction takes place within the national boundaries. Whilst co-productions present a problem of national definition, the policies proposed in the report and its definition of the 'industry' emphasizes the importance of Britain as a facilities house for film production from 'other countries'. This term becomes more specific in the detail of a decision to open a British industry office in Los Angeles, 'to help attract more productions to the UK and to build links between the UK industry and Hollywood' (1998: Summary).

The policy emphasis on attracting private finance and encouraging links with other industries is not in itself problematic, but in the context of the report generally there are two related problems that arise. The first concerns the framing of film production by British creatives. The report places emphasis on providing support for larger production companies in Britain who can sustain a slate of work and have a proven track record of commercially successful films. And whilst training is schematically placed in the plan as a necessary mechanism, the tasks of training are off-loaded onto Skillset and higher education more generally. The emphasis on commercial success is the determining factor of production. This criteria of commercial viability leads to the second problem, which is that of perceived audience taste for film. The report cites research conducted into audience tastes and attitudes to film. The findings presented offer an image of cinema-goers as 'conservative' and 'anxious to avoid films they might not enjoy' (Annex 3). Whilst Hollywood product scores highly overall, and particularly in terms of glamour, spectacle and family appeal, British film draws both negative and positive responses. The criticism of British film is of 'depressing, gritty realism'; the positive facets are 'cool appeal' for the youth market, and 'humour' and 'carefully crafted classics' more generally. These findings allow the report to announce in summary that *The Full Monty* and *Four Weddings and a Funeral* are 'quintessentially British, [and] have universal appeal' (1998: 33).

These aspects of the report represent the overriding problem of this imaging of the British film industry. The unproblematic emphasis on commercially viable films and audience demand detaches culture, in the sense of culture as a representative medium concerned with and historically driven by the need for diversity, from the commercial world. Between the national iconography of landscape as an asset, and the perceptions of popular cultural film judged singularly through commercial success, the image of a British film culture is mired in a hackneyed discourse of nationalism. From images of Big Ben through to the bleached white tones of *Four Weddings and a Funeral*, the concept of Britishness excludes the majority of the population, and certainly refuses to engage with Britain as a complex ethnic mix of identities and tastes. Here, film policy carries forward the historical split between market and art, commerce and culture, in refusing the interplay of culture and commerce as a negotiation of diverse audience tastes and social functions. This premise is unfolded further in the institutional support that is set up in the Film Council and then in the administration of funds from the National Lottery.

The Film Council was set up in Britain in May 2000. Its remit has been to produce fewer, more commercially successful films. The introductory statement from the chairperson, Alan Parker, states 'Essentially our intention is to use public money to make better, more popular and more profitable films in real partnership with the private sector, which drives our industry and largely creates our film culture.' This is an important statement for its description of the relationship of public and private finance. In place of the European emphasis on public–private *partnership*, within the Film Council the balance has shifted in weight to the private sector to 'largely' determine 'our film culture'. Parker continues in his analysis, 'The overall aim is well-targeted assistance rather than scatter-gun subsidy' (Film Council, 2000a: 1). Thus, the role of public finance is in assisting the private sector rather than building a film culture from the diverse and multicultural resources that constitute Britain (the measures to promote cultural diversity remain at odds with a broader British film culture celebrated).

These policy documents represent the last wave of a tidal shift away from the postwar European model of a mixed economy, represented as a market-based model regulated and shaped by a 'benign' national government tailoring the market to the needs of citizens and curtailing its excesses. In its place, the state embraces the logic of the market (Danan, 2000). The dysfunction of the mixed economy model was recognized in the 1980s, as Garnham's paper for the Greater London Council reported; the market clearly provides for the needs of the majority of citizens, whilst state-subsidized culture provides predominantly for the educated middle classes (Garnham, 1983). Where in the 1980s the problem of minority state-funded culture was perceived to be solved through widening access and attracting larger audiences, the situation is now reversed: the audience is no longer the problem or solution, but the culture itself. If film does not attract audiences then it is 'the product' that needs to change; the problems presented by a globalized infrastructure remain peripheral.

There will, of course, be proponents of the move towards a market model who may argue that the forms of subsidized culture have produced an élitist minority culture, in effect an enclaving of 'inaccessible art'. Whilst I would agree that the mixed economy model has reproduced social difference and inequality through the naturalization of oppositional tastes in particular sites and practices, the solution is not to shift the balance in favour of culture as an industry, given over to market forces alone. What needs to happen is a reintegration of the terms 'culture' and 'commerce'. The current conditions of film culture reproduce the historical split which, in the eighteenth century (as I have argued in Chapter 1), legitimated a separate sphere of disinterested bourgeois art. Today, the division enacts different privileges; the separation of culture and commerce legitimates the market forces of a global capitalism, which overrides the specificity and diversity of local cultures. Certainly, a reintegration of culture and commerce needs to attend to the complexity of culture in a climate in which traditional nation states cease to represent the range of interests and identities within their bounds. But without such a project, 'national' cultures embracing the market become internationalized, and specific local cultures remain subcultural, detached from the wider systems of representation and communication, insulating diversity in pockets of parallel existence.[7]

I am aware that I am speaking generally of the term 'culture' in this argument around policy, yet there is a particular importance for film in the present moment that so far I may have sublimated. I would argue that film is both a major export industry (for the USA it is the second largest export product) and a cultural resource within the nation. As policy documents have evidenced, film is perceived to be a crucial symbol of the nation, an advertisement for tourism, heritage and national status. Film 'speaks' a language of national representation more than other cultural forms such as music and art. This rests partly on its mimetic function, its re-presentation of 'real' locations, and in part its qualities of narration. British film need not, and is not, singularly a reproduction of national heritage, of the symbols of London's tourist economy. Indeed, a counter-argument could be made in response to the perceived crisis of national audiences and the lack of support for British film: British film does not represent the diverse interests of the population. The policy appeal to the 'popular' misreads the situation.[8]

The culmination of this disjunction between commerce and culture occurred publicly in the journalistic debate over National Lottery funding and film in the British press. To clarify the context of this particular form of funding, the National Lottery was set up in 1994 to contribute more than £250 million a year to arts funding in Britain. The Lottery funding is distinct from traditional subsidies by its remit; funding cannot be used to finance production but can only contribute to capital projects, such as buildings and equipment. However the rules for film are exceptional as expenditure on film production is treated as capital expenditure by the Treasury as the outcome of production is an asset that can be sold. If these are the rules that condition how the Lottery functions, there is more to be said about the perceived source of this subsidy. As the title 'National' Lottery implies, the money is linked explicitly to the nation. The Lottery itself has been widely criticized as a 'tax on the poor', an additional form of income tax that the government has established through a popular form of entertainment. The situation of Lottery funding, unlike previous forms of subsidy, makes explicit the source of income (the pockets of 'the people') and also the uses to which it is put. Whereas previous forms of subsidy have derived from a central source of government finance, characterized by the opacity of how taxes are spent in general, the Lottery represents a direct channel from the source of income to the recipient. The effect of this is that Lottery funding remains, in journalistic discourse at least, a property of 'the people', a concept produced by this discourse.

The public press debate on Lottery funding of film reveals the complex and volatile fusion of class, culture and commerce – in short, taste cultures. Boundaries are drawn, other cultures expelled in the name of the 'people', an ill-defined concept used similarly to the term 'popular' in film policy documents. What emerges in press discourse on Lottery funding is the reduction of debate on culture to a binary opposition, of miserabilism versus entertainment, arthouse versus commercial film. In January 2001, the film critic for the London paper the *Evening Standard*, Alexander Walker, cited 11 British films to have received Lottery funding, which had failed to attain box-office success. In 'Ten film turkeys, one juicy plum', Walker listed the films with the comment 'Below are the films that took our money', a share of a £92 million Lottery grant. In another diatribe Walker asserts that National Lottery funding, amounting to £100 million since 1995, was invested in more than 130 films, 'most of which the British public shunned at the box office'. Prior to Walker's 'exposé' of film failures, the *Independent* newspaper had published a feature 'Millions spent on British films no one wants to see' (April 2000), in which an interview with producer Stephen Woolley is the story. Woolley's criticism of the quality of British films again makes the same connections between particular sources of funding and audiences: 'new European grants and lottery money have been used to pay for British films that no one wants to watch'. Again the *Independent*, in June 2001, reported that Britain had a phantom film industry as many films produced failed to find a distributor: more than half of 103 films made in the Uk in 1999 had failed to find exhibition in 2001. The journalistic framing of the debate on Lottery funding refuses the complexity of why films may fail, for example through low marketing budgets, and monopolies of distribution and exhibition. In the 'naming and shaming' lists of film 'failures', which vary from paper to paper, British films that are unsuccessful commercially become the *bête noires* of the crisis in the film industry, both symptom and cause. Muddled with the perception of Lottery funding as explicitly 'the people's money', the oppositional forces of taste culture become an incendiary device.

There are different issues raised in relation to quality that open up yet another dimension of film culture. There are arguments to counter the criticism of quality in some of these films; for example, it is argued that many first features for directors are necessary training grounds, and it is only the collapsed state of the film industry that is unable to sustain the procedure of development. Second, the comparative gesture towards a singularly successful American film industry is erroneous: the majority of films made for the largest companies fail, but one success on the scale of high concept film recovers the loss. Third, the practice of measuring commercial success on initial box-office takings is a misleading calculation, as the majority of films generate income through various release windows and over a longer period of time. However, my focus here is not the particular (good or bad) qualities of films, but the paradigm in which this debate operates. What has occurred in this debate is the complete separation of culture from commerce, which operate in opposition. The single criterion for a film's success is box-office takings (indeed, Walker cites the critically acclaimed film

Ratcatcher in his list of turkeys, as though any amount of acclaim for cultural values does not shift the definition of success as economic). Further, commercial success proves a form of popularity, which in turn reinforces the sense that commercial films are unproblematically the films of 'the people', who are, after all, those to be served because they have provided the finance. The homogenized and mythical term of 'the people' produces a notion of consensus that belies the interests and diversity of the 'actual' population. The discourse, in effect, divides culture from commerce, popular from critical, working class from middle class. The class divisions historically in place within the modernist nation state come full circle to serve the global disjunction of specific cultures and generalized commerce. The nation state, in its peculiarly modern condition, continues its narrative by repressing the knowledge that transnational corporate power (in marketing, distribution and exhibition) punctures the national body; the nation blocks its ears and whistles its own tune.

genres for the nation

The effects of these debates on film policy from the mid-1990s can be seen in the types of film that have been produced and presented emblematically as representations of Britishness in the present. In part embedded in a political moment of the return of a left-wing government in Britain, film is part of the cultural symbolism mobilized by that event. The Labour government swept into office with a sense of a new generation taking position, harnessing the image of youthfulness by inviting key figures of the cultural industries (such as the band Oasis) to Downing Street. But just as the moment of Brit pop derived its radicalness with reference to an earlier moment of the 1960s, so the social imaginary is more generally coloured by the reliving of an earlier radicalism. The period of the late 1990s capitalized on this nostalgia for 'swinging London', a narrative of Britishness located in street culture, an energized, expressive, youthful national culture – also explicitly white (Alexander, 2000). And whilst heritage film was perceived to be a discourse of a white British past in the 1980s (Church Gibson, 2000; Higson, 1996), a different historical moment is evoked in the recent genre developments of British film. The genres of the gangster film and youth/club culture have become key thematized accounts of the present, often returning to the 1950s and 1960s to restate the connection.

Both the gangster film and the youth/club genre promote a sense of Britishness through explicitly urban thematics. Cities provide the location for excitement, danger and energy, whether for gang warfare or for partying. The success of films such as *Mojo, Lock, Stock and Two Smoking Barrells, Snatch, Trainspotting* and *Human*

Traffic generate an image of a nation in industrial decline but finding revelry in that moment, and turning that revelry to some personal gain. Schematically, the films utilize music to enforce the myth of creativity, producing soundtrack ancillary products. These films both work to the remit of the Film Council's vision of creating generic films, but also produce something more meaningful in terms of national identity. The nostalgic return to a rural past is overwritten with an explosion of working-class urban life, of small stories testifying to the greatness of national expression; despite working in a dead-end job for a multinational company, British youth locate their identity in the musical scenes of urban club culture (*Human Traffic*). The opportunistic underdog, the backbone of the national character, finds a means of self-expression.[9]

Whilst these films are not clearly defined genres, they represent a shift in production in accord with the imaging of Britishness in national policy documents. We have yet to witness the main products of Film Council endorsement. Such a vision of film, imaged as commercial in the name of a cultural populism, radically reduces what film can offer, that is a culturally eclectic, ethnically diverse and differentiated film culture that might speak to the most pressing national issue that Britain faces: the fraught relationship between different social, ethnic and cultural groups within its own bounds.

Notes

1   The textual representation of postmodernism in film has, in many accounts, come to stand metonymically for the condition of loss: of centred subjectivity, teleology and spatial orientation. Films like *Blade Runner* (1982) have become canonical texts in the readings of postmodern effects, of the post-industrial city in ruins, space–time compression, and representation and identity as simulacra (Bruno, 1987; Doel and Clarke, 1997; Harvey, 1989; Wakefield, 1990).

2   Murray Smith provides an insightful overview of the accounts of change that characterize academic attempts to define eras, shifts in practice, fundamental breaks with previous modes of film production and filmic aesthetics.

3   'This is a great and beautiful victory for Europe and for French culture' (Alain Carignon, French Minister for Communications, quoted in *Facts*, 1993: 931).

4   Sassen asserts, in a paper concerned largely with the current privatization of the stock market, that at least two-thirds of the trade in finances is conducted in privatized networks (paper for the conference 'Cultural Studies at the Crossroads', University of Birmingham, June 2000).

5   For a discussion of the ways in which global film cultures are embedded in historical contexts, see Shohat and Stam (1996).

6   The 'up beat' tone of the report largely endorses the culture of the relationship with multinational companies. Statistics evidencing growth in cinematic attendance are attributed largely to the development of the multiplex phenomena. Production is separated into two tiers: that of foreign production based in Britain, 'high budget, star-driven pictures financed almost entirely by the large vertically integrated American companies', who have succeeded in establishing 'a close and sophisticated relation-ship' with audiences; and indigenous production of film, low budget productions 'frequently mainly financed by television' (1995: 9). Distribution is noted to be problematic, with difficulties experienced by British companies in securing distribution and exhibition deals with multiplex cinemas. The problem is apparently alleviated by technology and British television: digital channels of dissemination (Channel 4's distribution outlet Film Four) are to supply the perceived specialized product of British film.

7   Concepts of cultural diversity are abandoned to the sphere of television, in particular Channel 4. Funded by advertising that was part guaranteed from the established commercial channel, the company worked to a remit of innovation and multiculturalism (McGuigan, 1996: 93). A hybrid of commercial and state-interested forces, Channel 4 facilitated the workshop system for many non-profitmaking cultural collectives, including Sankofa, Retake, Ceddo and Black Audio Film Collective.

8   The BFI's research into ethnic minority audiences supports this view. In addition to the general dis-identification with 'British' film, respondents expressed criticism of the stereotyped representation of ethnicity in *East is East*.

9   For a slightly different reading of contemporary British genre see Toby Miller (2000), 'The Film Industry and the Government: "Endless Mr Beans and Mr Bonds?"'.

CHAPTER SIX

Aesthetic encounters

It might be argued that a significant absence of this argument is the subject of aesthetics; that is, aesthetics both as a discourse describing or evaluating textual features and as a theory of the subject's relation to aesthetics. This is in part a deliberate absence in an attempt to deflect critical attention momentarily away from particular texts and specific audiences to consider the circulation of film as the construction of cultures. Our access to film is situated, I have argued, in networks of time (release windows, festival circuits) and space (diverse exhibitionary sites, home view), which connect us to particular discursive practices of film culture and diverse histories of cultural value. This failure to address aesthetics, should it be read as such, leaves the argument vulnerable to two further (mis)readings. First, that the description of film cultures presented here as relational can be mapped onto a difference of aesthetic practice in different domains. In other words, that each film culture purports an aesthetics exclusive to its own domain (art gallery, arthouse cinema, multiplex, home view). A type of essentialism would apply to the argument, whereby systems of production and distribution collude to create mutually exclusive aesthetic cultures. There is a type of slippage that occurs in the arguments about a functional aesthetic and effect: in identifying and essentializing the properties of certain texts (for example, the 'popular' genre of romance-comedy), the impact on audiences becomes a proscribed and predictable encounter. The film text becomes the site of particular aesthetic properties, and the audience become defined by their relationship to the aesthetic in an overly reductive account. A second broader criticism may find the neglect of aesthetics a political opportunity lost. Isobel Armstrong makes this case with characteristic forcefulness: 'I would regard with dismay a politics which subtracts the aesthetic and refuses it cultural meaning and possibility' (2000: 30). In neglecting the aesthetic for its Kantian political disinterest, argues Armstrong, critical discourse abandons the aesthetic to precisely that conservative practice of abstract evaluation.[1]

With both of these dangers (of essentialism and abandonment) in mind, I want to pursue the possibilities of aesthetics in relation to film cultures to clarify what I see as the limits to a sociological account. It is perhaps necessary to state at the beginning of this enterprise that I am not retreading the extensive terrain of debate in film studies given over to the analysis of particular readings of aesthetics as the features of historical periods, genres, or semiotic effect. This work has produced a rich body of writing relating to particular films and the methodology of interpretation. In contrast to theories of spectatorship that have proposed the apparatus of cinema as the guarantor of certain effects, I am concerned with the phenomenological possibilities of film, of 'affect', of how film 'acts', and its function within what I have set up as diverse film cultures. The critical focus therefore is more broadly positioned by the two charges above – how is aesthetic 'affect' related to diverse film cultures? Do aesthetic traditions accrue to class-based cultures and historical eras? Second, what, beyond the abandonment of aesthetics to a Kantian reading (or Bourdieu's reduction of aesthetics to forms of capital), does aesthetics offer the film spectator? In neglecting the aesthetic in an analysis of film cultures, do we risk, as Armstrong argues, abandoning the attempt to find a language for, and a comprehension of, the complex yet elusive appeal of film cultures?

aesthetics: anti, post or returning?

Why, we may ask, has the aesthetic suffered an abandonment, or at least an eclipse in cultural theory? Is the problem endemic to the study of aesthetics or to the socio-historical contexts in which aesthetic discourse takes root? Any consideration of aesthetics in the present is necessarily engaged with the history of its application, the legacy of Kantian thought confronted by a twentieth-century Marxism, played out most poignantly in the work of Benjamin and Adorno.[2] Further, a theory of aesthetics predicated on the relations between subjects and objects necessarily meets the overwhelming saturation of aesthetics in everyday life; expanded from its base in the arts, the aesthetic as a 'furnishment of reality' permeates our experience of the environment. 'We are,' asserts Wolfgang Welsch, 'without doubt experiencing an aesthetics boom' (1997: 1). The first part of the chapter will stake out the oppositional arguments against continuing to think the aesthetic as a conceptually and politically useful category, and the attendant responses, before moving on to the specific relationship between film cultures and aesthetics.

Welsch's description of an increasingly aestheticized world appears at once a seemingly banal observation and the description of a profoundly historical phenomenon. Welsch's work testifies to the extensive practices of design, packaging and presentation that characterize experience of the social in the Western world, taking in academic practice along the way: '[aesthetics] extends from individual styling, urban planning and the economy through to theory' (1997: 1). Theory, then, offers no sanctuary from the permeation of a design-led culture, it cannot be thought to stand outside this practice but is complicit with it. Theory is subject to the same critique levelled at cultural representation: it has lost access to the real, and further, in a thoroughly commercialized context its autonomy is denied. Theory cannot stand outside or against, any more than aesthetics can. The analogous fate of aesthetics and theory converges again in Hal Foster's 1983 edited collection of essays. Published under the title *The Anti-aesthetic* in America, and interestingly retitled the more anodyne *Postmodern Culture* in Britain, the editorial connects this sense of loss of critical leverage to the loss of a narrative of political modernism. Foster's introduction is significant in that it prefaces essays by 'key' twentieth-century critical thinkers (Habermas, Baudrillard, Jameson, Said). Whilst these names represent a heterogeneous post-modern grouping, Foster's perspective on aesthetics is certainly underwritten by a number of these writers. Foster's refusal of the aesthetic as subversive appears derivative of Baudrillard's thesis (or prognosis) on the disappearance of the real into the simulacra: representational practices are but one discourse constructing an account of the social, yet bearing no relation to it. 'Reality' and 'representation' are both representational structures claiming legitimacy through a difference that ceases to exist (if, as Foster notes, it ever did).

An engagement with aesthetics as a critical practice suggests for Foster a type of romanticism, but one for which he expresses some regret. To linger over aesthetics is merely to extend the nostalgic notion that cultural representation, or a critique of it, can influence social change. Foster comments: 'The adventures of the aesthetic make up one of the great narratives of modernity: from the time of its autonomy through art-for-art's-sake to its status as a necessary negative category, a critique of the world as it is' (1983: xv). Yet the loss of the 'real' has also implicated a disorientation of critical purpose. 'It is this last moment,' Foster continues, '(figured brilliantly in the writings of Theodor Adorno) that is hard to relinquish: the notion of the aesthetic as subversive, a critical interstice in an otherwise instrumental world' (1983: xv). If critical thought can no longer rely on a critique of the aesthetic, or an investment in the aesthetic as a site of change, as ideological, what does its purpose become? In the summative paragraphs of the introduction, Foster invokes a strategy of resistance for criticism as reinscrip-tion, 'a critique which destructures the order of representations in order to reinscribe them' (1983: xv). He is keen to present the argument of the anti-aesthetic as precisely not another modernist version of negation, yet the project of reinscription remains fairly opaque (on what grounds and pertaining to what kind of authority?); at best, critical reinscription is gestured towards as a local affair, less assured of its status, contingent perhaps, 'rooted in a vernacular'.

This approach to the aesthetic, an *anti*-aesthetic, accedes much of the ground to a postmodernist dissolution of macro narratives into micro formations, the movement from revolutionary politics to clusters of responses and interventions. Foster's anti-aesthetic is also, significantly, an approach implicitly in dialogue with a political modernism. It marks the end of an investment in aesthetics as the fighting ground for social resistance, of the assumption that textual aesthetics condition audience readings and spectatorial response. The historical juncture between modernism and aesthetic critique is explored extensively by Rodowick (1988), who traces the particular strain of critical practice and political film making in the 1970s to the modernist aspirations of the avant-garde. Here, in the discourse of what Rodowick names political modernism, the aesthetic features as both symptom and cure: the aesthetic is at once the manifestation of ideology in the mainstream culture of film production (interpellating spectators into a system of narrative illusion) and the solution in the manufacture of an alternative film practice working against normative aesthetics. For Rodowick, the project of political modernism seals over a paradox that emerges in its treatment of the spectator. Whilst this political practice relies on a poststructural notion of de-centred subjectivity, its need to read ideology as determining returns the subject as unproblematically centred by the text; contradiction, excess and contingency disappear in the desire to establish the textual aesthetic as the site of intervention: 'Despite the insistence within the discourse of political modernism on the centrality of a theory of the subject,' writes Rodowick, 'it is the centrality of questions of the aesthetic text and of aesthetic form that have predominated' (1988: 287). The unviability of making the aesthetic the centre of political critique and redress leads Rodowick to argue that the intertextual paradigm within which a text takes on meaning is the site of a critical enquiry of a different kind, a political economy of film culture which 'intervenes in the institutional sites of the production of knowledge' (1988: 297). Whilst this is clearly consistent with the development of critical theory (and in its turn with extra-textual knowledges, contexts of viewing and modes of circulation), the aesthetics, now dethroned, is left in hiatus.

If the anti-aesthetic and the critique of political modernism represent a with-drawal of investment in the category of the aesthetic as a critical enterprise, a more Marxist engagement is squarely in opposition to the aesthetic. And where the anti-aesthetic and political modernism are seen to be in dialogue with a recuperated form of modernism, of cultural critique, the Marxist positioning of the aesthetic takes its point of departure from the earlier moment of Kantian aesthetics. Here, aesthetics is a discourse emanating from, and in turn reproducing, social hierarchy. Terry Eagleton's *The Ideology of the Aesthetic* (1990) provides the most lucid and representative account of a critique of aesthetics from a materialist viewpoint. For Eagleton, the aesthetic is complicit in reproducing the worst manifestations of the Enlightenment project. In the Kantian appeal to distanced contemplation, the act of aesthetic judgement produces the individual, rational subject. In the pronouncement of evaluative judgement, the particular contexts of aesthetic practices and their value are rendered universal. In its abstraction and elevation of value to a spiritual form, it disguises the relations of property and exchange. In short, for Eagleton, the aesthetic is both everywhere and no-where, constantly disguised as something else, performing the work of a bourgeois ideology.

Isobel Armstrong takes Eagleton to task for the 'intellectual slapstick' and 'carking ironies' of what she also describes as an impressive work. Most pointedly, Armstrong is critical of Eagleton's reading of Kant: 'Thus to remind oneself that Kant's was one of the earliest attempts to see the political and cultural problems around the changed relations between the new civic individual and the modern state, for instance, or the problems around rationality and representation, would be to confuse the genre of [his] discussion' (2000: 32). She continues, exasperated, 'why does Kant have to mean this in Eagleton's text?' Armstrong's recourse to Kant is carefully, historically located, in line with other readings of the Kantian project as a treatise on the possibility of knowledge within experience and the impossibility of knowledge outside of experience. Clearly, Kant can appear as both good and bad object, according to the critical enterprise (the traditions of disciplines). Without detouring into a further reading of Kant, what is significant here is the affinity of critical approaches, otherwise at odds with each other, in a reading of Kant. Along with Eagleton, both Bourdieu and Derrida are masters of a similar repudiation, although within different traditions and to diverse ends.

For both Derrida and Bourdieu, the philosopher and the sociologist, the aesthetic incurs a refusal of difference, an expulsion of the other, which effectively institutes the binary division that separates the subject from its other. For Derrida (1981), this is the work of the narcissist, unable to leave the maternal body, caught in the trap that the aesthetic sets, for an expulsion is at the same time a production. The aesthetic facilitates the replay of a necessary psychic manoeuvre. Bourdieu, perhaps surprisingly coming from a sociological rather than a poststructuralist perspective, refuses to make this expulsion purely an act located within the social symbolic. The naturalization of taste, aesthetic predilection, is effective precisely for its presence within the unconscious. Here, the unconscious is not a causal force but the seat of predispositions, schemata. Further, the subject has not introjected schemata as an alien other, but has come to know the self through its terms. In Scott Lash's description, 'unthought categories are also ontological foundations of practical consciousness' (Beck *et al.*, 1994: 154). Bourdieu's reading of the aesthetic in *Distinction* unravels the naturalized disposition by tracing the consistency of taste within class fractions. The aesthetic, with its semantic elision of biological and cultural referents, shores up the cultural as the natural. Aesthetics places us, and places us relationally ('it's not for me'), yet it masquerades as an expression of an arbitrary preference.

From Welsch's assertion that the aesthetic is everywhere in everyday life, in critical thought it is nowhere – the disappeared of theory. Such emptying out, as Armstrong would have it, demonstrates the work of two different traditions in critical thought and two different emotional responses to the demise of the aesthetic. On the one hand is a mourning for the loss; the failure of the aesthetic is an inevitable effect of the failure of the modernist project whose promise it was to transform the social fabric through aesthetic means. Such a project, as Foster wistfully notes, appears now as distant and ethereal as a day-dream. On the other hand, the demise of the aesthetic is to be celebrated (should it have actually occurred); here, in the ranks of the neo-Marxist fraternity, the aesthetic is that which has colluded with dominant forms of hierarchy, in part sealing the hegemony of the dominant class through its naturalization of status.

How then can aesthetics be recovered without abandoning social analysis? Isobel Armstrong, in *The Radical Aesthetic*, attempts a retrieval of the aesthetic from the mire of ideological critique by claiming the opposite, the democratic potential of the aesthetic. Armstrong's project is a refutation of the binaries that have marked the critique of aesthetics, binaries that with some irony reinvoke the oppositions attributed to the Kantian position. Armstrong's thesis is largely phenomenological, a reading of emotion within the space of the rational. Attacking the poststructuralist project of deconstruction, Armstrong's metaphor (again) takes a visceral edge: 'If the imagination is cut through to the bone, a state in which to *think* the aesthetic is renounced, one is confronted with conceptual emptiness' (2000: 55–6). The choice of language is appropriate to the task: Armstrong's challenge to deconstructive thought is the return to, and reproduction of, binary divisions such as culture/thought, subject/object. In a move to address the relations between these terms as a dialectic, key processes or tropes are proffered, drawn largely from philosophy and psychoanalysis; play, mediation (and the broken middle), affect and cultural dreaming. In an impressive tour of a range of work, Armstrong draws on Hegel's assertion that thought enters the world as experience, and from Gillian Rose that as philosophers we are already in the middle, not thinking from the outside in. Thus the broken middle offers a route out of the subject/object division in which aesthetic debate has become mired: either as the affect of the object for the subject, or the subjective interpretation of the object. The central argument of this text is a reassertion of the significance of aesthetics both for an understanding of culture, and the part that cultural relationships play in the formations of democracy, and the importance of rescuing aesthetics from a conservative domain.

These are pressing issues for any study of culture which, arguably, a Marxist emphasis on social reproduction, detached from the belief in the necessary rupture caused by capitalism's endemic contradiction, leaves in abeyance at its peril. Central to Armstrong's argument, and to what I propose for film here, is a fluidity between the terms of a binary system, a complexity to both film aesthetics and the engagement with films. Within aesthetics, as elsewhere, we move between the fixed terms of the modernist structure and the postmodern flux that cuts across those predictable positions. As spectators we are both constrained and enabled, by our histories, the contexts of our engagement, the time-based form of film and the particular text itself. We move between proximity/distance, content/form, familiar/unfamiliar, distracted/concentrated gaze, routine/shock. The constraints of critical thought have been to set up the binary terms and argue for the higher value of one over the other. And yet distance cannot be conceived as resolutely positive (Brecht), and neither can proximity (Bourdieu). A more demanding question is how we might move between them, and what kind of aesthetic we might begin to describe in relation to film as a time-based media.

In order to understand the particular constraints that trouble thinking about filmic aesthetics, and the enabling factors that push thought elsewhere, we need to return to two related terms – mimesis and presence. The nature of film as a mimetic form is essential to its (denigrated) value in relation to other products in the art–culture system; it merely reproduces the 'real'. Similarly, film is a fleeting, transient media, a rehearsal of acts past, an absence rather than a presence, for the acts and characters are no longer with us. Thus film is a mimicry of the real, but it is fake, for the real is not summonsed for us. Moreover, it can be returned to, replayed, repeated – a rehearsal of the rehearsal of the real; yet in so doing it moves us no closer to the presence of the art object or the artifact in the 'real' world. In fact, its repeatability remarks its absence; we are merely caught in a loop. These readings of mimesis and presence reproduce the binary's unrelenting terms and the value judgements endemic to such polarization. In the following sections I want to suggest a different way of reading mimesis and presence.

mimesis, replay, reiteration

Film and photography have long suffered a cultural devaluation for their mimetic relationship to the 'real'. One of the most forceful representations of this view is cited by Armstrong in the introduction to her book on aesthetics, the work of Roger Scruton in *The Aesthetic Understanding: Essays in the Philosophy of Art and Culture* (1983). Scruton's argument in this text is extreme: photography, and by implication film, is pornographic in its re-presentation of the empirical world. The rationalization for the term 'pornography' becomes evident in the staging of the argument. Photography, argues Scruton, reproduces one moment from time, captures the arbitrary object or scene with no act of translation but merely as reproduction. In so doing, it fails to achieve what painting can – a synthesis of different moments of temporality. For Scruton, the object of the photograph in the 'real' world can substitute the image, like a reversible garment that takes the same shape inside out. The qualities of reproduction eliminate thought and emotion from the process of creativity. There is no sign of translation in the photographic, of working on the empirical; an object remains beautiful, radiant or ugly as we perceive it to be outside the photographic image. Painting, in contrast, presents the subject in the picture, not its referent in the world; indeed there may be no recognition of an object in empirical time and space. There is no arbitrary effect in painting as there is in photography, for the painted image offers an understanding of the subject, it makes it so and produces its own originality in that process.

This is a familiar and tiresome argument for theorists of film and media, which has been rebutted to great effect elsewhere. What I want to pursue in Scruton's argument is the notion of cultures of reproduction as pornographic. Scruton builds his argument around the notion that art operates through a language, conventions which are passed on, necessitate training and enhance a community of viewers; as Armstrong notes of Scruton, 'We have to be socialized to recognize conventions, and conventions themselves are socializing' (2000: 7). In the counter-position, the reproductive arts are marked by their lack of language, for their re-presentation provides no separation between the image and the world. Echoing a Lacanian model of accession into language, the reproductive arts fall into the preoedipal, outside language. This enables Scruton to argue that photographic images are a substitute for the real, a fetish, a fantasy of possessing the object in its immediacy. We are back then with Kant's division between the distanced contemplation of icy, solemn thought, and the contrasting proximity of gratification.

Whilst this argument of mimetic reproduction appears in critical discourse in the denigration of photography, film and television, its binary terms can also operate in defence of such cultural forms. In an attempt to refute, or at least expose, the process of social legitimization of various cultural forms through arguments such as Scruton's, Bourdieu invokes the same terms but in reverse. In a description of the popular gaze, Bourdieu asserts the value of the working-class primacy of connection, the immediate gratifications that are found in cultural engagement. In the much vaulted extract 'Everything takes place as if the "popular aesthetic" were based on the affirmation of continuity between art and life', Bourdieu effectively seals the popular audience into this space of immediacy and reifies it. The mimesis that art performs of life facilitates a further binary opposition, this time of form and content. In the 'subordination of form to function', cultural engagement becomes a pursuit of the use of culture, a use predicated on the extraction of content from form. Form remains the remit of the distanced aristocratic subject, whilst content is voraciously swallowed up by the popular audience. In Bourdieu's reading, form blurs into the formal, and subsequently formal refinement.

The argument is developed a stage further in a consideration of which particular cultural forms might facilitate such immediacy. Drawn to both festivity and spectacle, the working-class audience, Bourdieu suggests almost as an aside, has a propensity for certain genres: 'circus and melodrama' he cites, and further down the same paragraph, '(I am thinking also of the music-hall, light opera or the big feature film) – fabulous sets, glittering costumes, exciting music, lively action, enthusiastic actors – like all forms of the comic . . .' (1979: 34). For Bourdieu, such revelry in the immediacy of cultural form suggests investing oneself, giving oneself over to 'easy seduction and collective enthusiasm'[3] (1979: 35). This account of particular genres retaining a specifically popular appeal has been argued in many redemptive accounts of popular culture. What it proposes, I would suggest, is a reversal of a binary, an emphasis on the positive appreciation of a culture that is immediate, gratifying, Bacchanalian. What it leaves in place is the division between form and content, distance and proximity, contemplation and gratification.

At this point it is worth pausing momentarily before pursuing the implications of this argument for film cultures. For what is at stake here is also a reading of difference and similarity. In following Bourdieu's replay of the terms of Kant's thesis, the popular engagement with certain genres enacts a mimicry of the real: life is inseparable from art, therefore the hearty laughter of the audience of comic film merges with the laughter of humorous events in life. Audience identification with the film replays the paradigm of comprehension, the schemata, applied to empirical situations. Thus, cultural engagement reproduces the experience of life (just as film reproduces the empirical for Scruton). Caught in a cycle of 'what you know', the popular audience is destined to rework its own assumptions and positions, to choose the familiar, the similar – to mistake art for life. The implications of this argument echo Derrida's reading of aesthetic taste as a culture of narcissism. In the repudiation of other tastes, Derrida in 'Economimesis' finds that such distaste (producing nausea) is grounded in the refusal of heterogeneity, the expulsion of the other from the body of the subject. In Derrida's essay it is the work of the hysterical narcissist, fearing the merging of categorization, the collapse of borders, repudiating everything that is not the same. Aesthetic engagement becomes a form of defence, either in attempting to transform difference into sameness, or expelling it from the self. Mimesis is the trope of self–identity, a process that validates the identical.

In reading together these two positions on mimesis – Scruton's art historical discrimination against photography and film as a mimesis of the real, and Bourdieu's sociologist account of 'popular' cultural engagement as a mimesis of the text (as content) – the aesthetic possibilities of an encounter of film are severely delimited. For Scruton the camera pretends to the real and fetishizes its product, whilst for Bourdieu popular culture draws us into a symbiotic relationship to the text which pretends to (blurs with) everyday life (the real).[4] Yet, are there ways of reading film against its relation to art (the pretender to a legitimate sovereign), and other paradigms for thinking spectatorship against practices of identification? In other words, can mimesis, an effect of filmic and spectatorial practice, signify more than replication? Judith Butler's reading of mimesis as reiteration, a necessary and necessarily open process of performance, offers a way of rewriting the encounter of cultural forms and the real, and cultural forms and the subject (Butler, 1997). Butler uses the term 'performativity' rather than mimesis, but I would argue that the two concepts are connected, and it is worth tracing this connection.[5] At first sight Butler's notion of performativity is quite removed from mimesis, derived from Austin's linguistic account of the illocutionary effects of the speech act, the bringing into being of what is pronounced. The subject is constituted at this point of utterance in the context of the speech situation. Language is attributed the power of naming and bringing into being in a way that shares some conceptual phrasing with Althusser's notion of interpellation. However, for Butler the question becomes not one of assured reproduction of social relations, conditioned by the authority or legitimacy of the speaker, but the possibilities of misfiring, of speech acts taking on a disruptive, dissident effect.

Butler is at pains to point out that such misfiring is never the result of a conscious, willed act but is dependent on two further considerations. The first of these is the context of utterance. For Butler, the context of an utterance, or performative act, cannot be circumscribed as contexts of radical disruption or consolidation; indeed, some of the most authoritarian and normative contexts of utterances, such as the law court witnessing the military invocation of homosexuality as contagion, are the spaces where the repetition of language performs its undoing. The repeated calls for homosexuality to be pronounced on and legislated against descend into a pantomime of hysterical speech that fractures the logic of the discourse, even turning it against itself in what becomes a questioning of the persistent interest in the replay of 'homosexuality'. Second, Butler argues, harnessing Derrida's argument on reiteration from *Writing and Difference* (1978b), that iteration is a structural foundation of language, a need for repetition in written texts as in spoken language: 'for a mark to be a mark, it must be repeatable, and have that repeatability as a necessary and constitutive feature of itself' (1997: 149). As language is dependent on this structural repetition, it contains the seeds of its own potential undoing, the vulnerability of its own existence as a claim. The authority of language does not reside in its essential qualities or structural properties, but in its re-enactment; thus, the moment of the reproduction of linguistic authority is also the moment of its own potential misfiring.

The Derridian emphasis on the structural properties of linguistic reiteration enable Butler to distinguish this model of performativity from Bourdieu's description of authoritative speech acts in *Language and Symbolic Power* (1991). Where Bourdieu ascribes the effects of the utterance to the social power of the speaker, Derrida and Butler locate the instability of the linguistic effect in the structure of language itself, 'a structural status that appears separable from any consideration of the social'. The difference is a significant one that concerns functionality. For whilst Butler's invocation of a structural principle separable from the social may appear a utopian gesture to locate dissent outside the realms of power, what in fact this argument facilitates is a concept of linguistic effect that is socially mobile, an unpredictable effect of language that can misfire at any time in a range of contexts, articulated by speakers of diverse social status. Where Bourdieu's account of linguistic effect is circumscribed by the status of the speaker, with the subject invested with legitimate power making language act, Butler's reading offers a model of effectiveness that is altogether unpredictable. Neither the context nor the status of the speaker can assure the performative effect of language.

This is an important critique of Bourdieu, for it addresses the functionalist quality of his thesis, the dogged emphasis on reproduction which shadows the more dynamic account of how distinction operates. Butler argues the unpredictable effect of discourse in relation to spoken language, but I would argue that a reading of filmic language within the same terms is possible. If we consider the necessary replay of existing filmic culture, the authority with which film narrates and animates a story is dependent on historic precedence, its past success in defining film as cultural form, and its ability to continue to do so. Authority is located in ritual, naturalized in seating arrangements (the hierarchy of balconies elevated above the stalls), the theatrical curtain, the darkness of the auditorium, the appropriate responses of silence and laughter. Further, the certification of film exhibition (its submission to other, regulatory bodies), the studio logos of the roaring lion, the statue of liberty carrying the sparkling animated torch, are the icons of a past film age that speak of continuity and tradition. These are the ritual features of a culture in its performative gesture of authority (there is an echo of Hitchcock's frustrated demand to shut the auditorium once *Psycho* had started, the institution of a forced etiquette). These rituals are the performative rites of a culture coming into its own legitimacy in relation to other sanctioned cultural forms (art, music, literature, theatre). Whilst the rites of film culture are more or less standardized in the early part of the twentieth century, each ritual is specifically located, placed within networks of spatial relations, marked off against each other as centre or periphery, mainstream or arthouse, rural or cosmopolitan. Yet, does this performance guarantee the necessary effect of filmic language and authority? Is it possible to predict how certain filmic effects, conventions, generic flourishes will be understood?

The argument that I am making here is that although social distinction permeates the spatial and temporal circulation of culture, and subsequently impacts on the types of culture that we inhabit, it can never guarantee the effects of that encounter (Harvey, 1996). The relationship to film aesthetics remains more complex, and possibly less tangible than Bourdieu allows for. But the reference to Butler's work here is more than a critique of Bourdieu, for Butler's theory of performativity articulates a model of mimesis that allows a reading of filmic engagement as something more than a repetition of identificatory norms. Mimesis, read through the prism of performativity, is an act not only of repetition, but reiteration with all of its attendant indeterminacy. Filmic representation is precisely re-presentation, a fabrication, a replaying of stories, images and conventions; it is the replay of a language rather than a replay of the 'real'. Subsequently our engagement with this language, our interpellation by it, is never assured, but open to replay, performing differently, potentially rupturing the spaces of normative identification as much as shoring them up.

The concept of mimesis offers to shift the functionalism of Bourdieu's model, but also the paradigm of aesthetics and spectatorship that has dominated what Rodowick (1988) calls political modernism: the notion that the spectator's response can be deduced from an analysis of the formal properties of the text, and conversely that the aesthetics of the text can be constructed to produce responses. This is a concept that has permeated, driven with a missionary zeal, the discourses of avant-garde film making, journalism and theoretical critique, particularly during the decades of the 1960s and 1970s in Europe. To relinquish this model of aesthetic effect is to disinvest in the power of the aesthetic, in its ability to produce dissonance. However, to argue against political modernism is not to rule out dissonant effects, but to open out the process of aesthetic engagement as a space of potential replay and reiteration. Our particular engagement with a film may confirm all of our sentiments, ideas, affiliations and emotional landscapes – it may repeat what we know and confirm our differences. Or it may reiterate those positions precariously.

recovering presence

In order to inflect the concept of mimesis with the insurgent potential that Butler allows for, the question of filmic form, film as presence, and as effecting spectatorial presence, needs to be attended to. The reading of mimesis as presence echoes Benjamin's writings in the first half of the twentieth century. In place of a mimetic repetition of the real, film for Benjamin suggested a dialectical movement, an opening out of possibilities of aesthetic engagement. This argument can be found in Benjamin's work on the optical unconscious, the splitting open of history in the juxtaposition of images and objects. As Susan Buck-Morss comments on Benjamin's dialectic, 'The elements of past cultures were drawn together in new "constellations" which connected with the present as "dialectical" images' (1989: 56–7). Benjamin's writing on cinema and the dialectic connects with Vivian Sobchack's recent work on filmic presence, outlined in précis in the article 'The Scene of the Screen: Envisioning Cinematic and Electronic Presence' (1994).[6] Where Benjamin claimed a radical political potential implicit to the process of editing, so Sobchack claims that film fundamentally transforms temporal consciousness, although without an assured outcome. In comparison with photography, caught in the empirical realist mode of possessing time, film throws us into the fluctuation of the temporal, but not in a way that fundamentally undoes the subject with no return. On the contrary, film as a medium heightens our sense of time as accumulated, as passing, as returning, of the present as a composite of different lived moments, and also a negotiation of competing perspectives, particularly between an objective ordered notion of time and a subjective experience of disruption and partiality. Whilst the temporal features prominently in this account, the spatial is also present as the second axis, although perhaps less convincingly. For Sobchack, just as time roots the particular vision in that moment, so space materially grounds perspective, located and embodied in the concrete space of viewing. Yet, like time, the spatial is understood as a dialectic, a tension between what is present and that which is absent, the spaces represented and the discontiguous spaces outside the screen and of the viewing situation. The spatial is revealed as synthetically ordered, arranged for our viewing (both in terms of what we see and the context of our watching), and as exceeding this – space as an unfolding fabric of different places, landscapes and territories which butt up against the manufactured order of the filmic text and viewing context.

In contrast to photography, according to Sobchack, the cinema is a coming into being of life, a continual staging of time passing and the urgency of the present. Its emergence in the 1890s places its mode of aesthetics within modernism; it is a struggle between different modes of perception, the atomized experience of an industrial society in which alienation butts up against the experience of mass society, of cities and crowds. For Sobchack, this period is defined economically by monopolistic capital: the cinema offers up fragments, the cut and spliced particles of life, just as goods are assembled from parts and transported elsewhere. Vision is mobile, fragmented, synthesized through the processes of capital production. Sobchack, perhaps problematically, shifts between the vision of the camera and that of the spectating subject, the embodiment of on-screen presence and the embodied viewer, to argue that both stages and reproduces in its moment of exhibition, the experience of presence. For Sobchack this is a phenomenological understanding of presence, referencing Merleau-Ponty to claim 'images testify to a mobile, embodied and ethically invested subject of worldly space' (1994: 74). Film makes visible not just the 'objective' world as representation, but the structure of subjective, embodied vision which had, until the advent of cinema, been experienced as private.

In contrast to photography, which is characterized by an appropriation of objects, spaces and time, film throws us into the present by foregrounding the changing perspectives and limits of vision (through the camera), and the corporal limits that ground the spectator. Sobchack's thesis rests on a sense of film as a mimesis of psychic processes of perception, shot through by memory, punctured by detail. The process of editing, moving back and forwards in time, and the shifting perspective of shots, creates a sense of 'the reversible, dialectical and social nature of our own subjective vision' (1994: 75). Caught in time, yet also disrupted by the past and projections of the future, film creates a disjunction between the ordered, linear trajectory of history (as it is represented socially), and the subjective experience of time as fragmented. For the subject, despite the experience of discontinuity, time is synthesized in the lived body, just as film presents a synthesized text in tension with the disunity of its timescale. Thus for Sobchack, the experience of film creates a sense of presence, of being in the world, which defies the philosophically centred notion of presence as complete understanding of self; rather the experience of film foregrounds the dialectical tension between running time/the objective representation of time as progressive and the fragmented ephemeral, accumulated understanding of subjective time.

What does it mean to claim that film is intersubjective, to draw the experience of viewing into a space of phenomenology? What is being claimed here is the experience of film viewing as one in which the multiple forms of perspective offered through the camera's movement and the process of editing, disrupts the singularity of vision. The private sense of vision is thrown into turmoil by the shifts in perspective, opening up as a dialectic between what is seen and the seer, between the objective world and the subjective eye. Drawing on Merleau-Ponty's model of the intersubjective moment as the 'I' appearing to itself as both seen and seer, the notion echoes the misrecognition endemic to Lacan's mirror stage. But whereas a Lacanian reading holds the subject in the space of the other (the subject's knowledge of self mediated by the other's gaze), in a phenomenological framework, the subject sustains a fluidity between these perspectives, and is undone and remade in the fluctuation of subject positions. As Jan Campbell (2000) argues, a phenomenological understanding of spectatorship troubles both presence and absence, or rather that presence is predicated on both of these terms. In claiming an intersubjective reading of the experience of film, Sobchack in a sense rewrites the moment of modernism, reinscribing the alienated, fragmented model of subjectivity with a socially grounded, embodied self.[7]

For Sobchack, film reproduces the psychic and embodied experience of modernity, an experience also described as a form of presence by the philosopher and cultural geographer, Henri Lefebvre (1958). Lefebvre's work covers a range of interests that move in different directions and take various emphases, but central to his project is a rethinking of the significance of the subject's engagement with time, space and everyday life. For Lefebvre, the everyday is both the site of the banal, the insignificant, the laborious and the quotidian, the alienated subject. But within the everyday is the possibility of affect, of what Lefebvre terms moments of presence – when time appears to stand still and also to echo the past, a moment of déjà vu, a haunting. As Rob Shields comments, 'Presence, a pure exception in the undifferentiated, is temporalisation, and this is a remarkable indication of the centrality of time in Lefebvre's thought on space' (1999: 61). Less explicit than 'realization', which suggests a cognitive response, moments of presence puncture the banality of the real, collapsing knowledge, experience (history) and sensory effect into the moment.

The significance of Lefebvre's account of presence is first, that it does not depend on a formally designated object of culture (or art) but resides in the relationship between objects and subjects in everyday life. Moments of presence occur between things, people, terms; in the intensity of love, the momentum of collective social events, in the proximity to death. Second, presence is an embodied affect facilitating change which can be situated in opposition to Bourdieu's notion of embodied experience as a culmination of fixed individual histories. Presence moves perception, the teleological effects of history displaced by a new experience of time as possibility; it is Lefebvre's way of holding onto both the constraints of the model (Marxism) and the chance of transformation.[8] Thus, Lefebvre inserts a fluidity into the reproductive model of social capital. Within such admittedly enduring systems of social reproduction (detailed by Bourdieu), there is the possibility of change and movement, facilitated by an intersubjective presence, an awareness of others in relation to the self, and of the self in relation to time.

As utopian as Lefebvre's moments of presence may appear, there seems to me to be a resonance of this concept with film's potential to throw us into a space of temporal awareness. Read together, Lefebvre and Sobchack redress the 'emptying out' of the aesthetic in film by attending to presence as a particular relationship with time. For Sobchack, film as a time-based media has a privileged relationship to presence compared with other cultural forms. It is precisely the re-play of film, its fabrication manifest in certain production techniques, that strikes Sobchack as 'intimately bound to a structure not of possession, loss, pastness, and nostalgia, but of accumulation, ephemerality, and anticipation − to a "presence" in the present informed by its connection to a collective past and to a future' (1994: 77). Thus the speed of recording action, the splicing of events (and thus time) into non-linear sequences, the shifting of perspective and of focus, all construct a sense of time different from the onward flow of narrative, perhaps Lefebvre's moments within time. What Sobchack pays less attention to, and which I want to argue offers a different facet to the temporality of film, is the soundtrack, the realm of the audial. Where Sobchack focuses on vision and the scrambling of time through the disruption of linearity and speed, sound provides a layering of temporality, a different dimension of sensory affect.

aesthetics of the soundtrack

Aesthetic affect, or the puncturing of the real, is produced through the combination of image and sound in film. Whilst the film image attracts critical commentary, sound is an implicit partner, assumed to be at once sublimated to, and supporting, the image and narrative movement. Moreover, sound, when it is addressed, is often regarded as the most manipulative aspect of film, invisibly working on the audience, drawing them into close identifications, stitching them into the narrative flow.[9] As Richard Dyer (1977) argues, sound as music can unify the narrative image and moment into a utopian moment. But just as Sobchack points to the inconsistency of the temporal flow, music is not necessarily an adjunct to the narrative sequence, but can equally be distracting, disruptive and interventionist. In *Audio Vision: Sound on Screen*, Michael Chion (1994) describes the possibilities for sound as empathetic, working with the visual text, or anempathetic, working in discord. Yet, in an age of digital expansion of the soundtrack and the proliferation of recording channels, the possibilities for sound surely exceed the binary of working 'for or against' the image. Sound can perform more than one trick, deliver more than one effect, so that the juxta-position is not simply between sound and image, but between various sounds and the image. In this respect, sound exceeds the image in its potential to complexify the temporal; despite experiments to divide up the image (such as Mike Figgis's *Time Code*), the potential of 'layering' remains with sound rather than vision.

Chion points out that sound had a key historical function in the fixing of temporality, an act that has remained suppressed in the history of film devel-opment. The advent of sound imposed restrictions and standardization: 'Filmic time was no longer a flexible value, more or less transposable depending on the rhythm of projection. Time henceforth had a fixed value; sound cinema guaranteed that whatever lasted x seconds in the editing would still have this same exact duration in the screening' (1994: 119). Chion's comments resonate with Charles Musser's description of the standardization of cinema with the coming of sound, and the attendant shift of authority from exhibitor to producer. Certainly, sound stabilized the speed of film projection during exhibition, yet it did not necessarily tie sound to a supporting or even an antagonistic role. 'Sound' covers a potentially infinite array of audial effects, most recognizable in diegetic effects of dialogue and circumstantial sound, musical accompaniment and dramatic enhancement. Yet the multiple possibilities for the layering of sound suggests that time may not only be mixed up, but possibly moments of time collapsed or vying for primacy. Aesthetically, the layering of the audial track presents the possibility of experiencing time outside the onward march of narrative progress, offering potential pockets of presence in Lefebvre's terms.

In an insightful article on the use of sound in the *Batman* films, 'The Classical Film Score Forever?', K. J. Donnelly (1998) argues that the film scores of these films utilize various scores connected to different temporalities. An orchestrated soundtrack by Danny Elfman provides what Donnelly calls the conservative element of the musical weave, music characterized by a combination of brass instruments and an emphatic beat, which both compensates for dialogue and emphasizes the tension in key moments. This score plays on the slippage between Gotham and gothic; it renders a menacing yet sublime undercurrent, referencing earlier scores from horror films. It might also be argued that Elfman's score, in underlining this gothic dimension to the Batman films, fleshes out the adult dimension to the film; the reverse side to the laughing malevolent Joker is hysteria, and to the all-purposeful Batman, despair and loss.

Donnelly argues that Elfman's score works in a classical narrative fashion. It clarifies and emphasizes the distinctiveness of characters (each have their own theme in addition to their visual iconography), and it echoes the moments of tension and conflict; in short, orchestral music 'demonstrates film logic dictating music logic' (1998: 149). In contrast to this conventional usage, the music by

Prince provides a different experience and function. Few of the tracks from the album appear in the film. Instead, the music that Prince creates connects with the earlier televised moment of Batman by sampling the 'original' theme, as well as intercutting dialogue from the film, and extending the characterization by creating specific songs for characters. As Donnelly notes, the soundtrack from Prince proliferates the narrative possibilities of the film, and connects with other products: 'it manifests an *extension* of the text beyond its traditional boundaries to include intersecting aesthetic products' (1998: 144). In so doing, the album creates an intervention into the film's hermetic whole, taking on a life of its own, and, as with all film-related products, extends the reach of the film aesthetic beyond the realms of cinema. The mobility of sound allows it to permeate a range of spaces outside the cinema, not only the home but public spaces where radio is played, on the journeys of people carrying Walkmans scattered across various urban and rural spaces. It is the aesthetic, the affect of film, as excessive at some levels, scrambling time, as beyond the bounds of the cinematic moment, endlessly repeatable, and disrupting the spatial and temporal centrality of the moment of viewing.

This description of the filmic aesthetic as potentially enabling moments of engagement as 'presence' is not a prescriptive account; any aesthetic affect is highly contingent, depending on individual and collective, historical and located, contexts. Yet, this reading of filmic presence as a disjunction of the linearity of the temporal through both visual and audial means dislodges as much as it confirms Sobchack's claim for film as a proto-typically modernist media. If, for Sobchack, presence is dependent on an awareness of time as embodied, both objective and subjective, does the multiple scrambling of the temporal audially render the terms subjective and objective fundamentally redundant? Can we distinguish the 'objective' and 'subjective' audial features of a soundtrack? Is Sobchack in danger of essentializing film as a cultural form, and periodizing effect in an ironically linear way (realism is followed by modernism, to be superseded by the postmodern)? If this is so, she is not alone in the desire to delineate cultural effect within technologies and eras. Wolfgang Welsch argues in a related manner, but with a shift of focus, that the aesthetic 'revolution' of the present is the ascendancy of auditive culture over visual culture:

> A suspicion is circulating: our culture, which until now has been primarily determined by vision, is in the process of becoming an auditive culture; and that this is both desirable and necessary. Not only for reasons of equal treatment must hearing be emancipated following more than two thousand years of vision's dominance. Moreover, the person who hears is also the better person – one, that is, able to enter into something different and to respect instead of merely dominating it. (1997: 150)

The problem with Welsch's otherwise interesting account is the naturalized perspective of 'our culture' belying a history of Western dominance now in decline. It is a familiar narrative presented by postmodern philosophers, and duly critiqued, as the articulation of a partial perspective as a universal. The servile position of the 'listener' has indeed existed for centuries in relationships between colonial and colonized subjects.

Where does this leave an account of filmic aesthetics? Certainly, I would argue, aesthetic engagement with film can provide one of the potentially transformative features of culture, shifting perspective, denaturalizing time, confronting the viewer with differences. Yet it is not possible to state the conditions or contexts of this happening, nor to specify the textual form in advance. We can read the social value of certain aesthetic configurations in the form of genre, itself a shifting constellation; yet this does not allow a reading of the engagement between film and viewer that takes place. If the paths of filmic circulation and the contexts of viewing provide socially demarcated texts, the relationship between text and subject remains more obtuse, the fluidity within the model of structures, the possibility within the paradigm of constraint.

Notes

1 Although this is Armstrong's thesis throughout the book, the remark quoted is directed specifically at Terry Eagleton's 'emptying out' of the aesthetic in the name of a Marxist literary criticism. Armstrong's frustration is that, worse than a vacuum, aesthetics is handed over to that same tradition that has dominated it. Her response is to reclaim a radical aesthetic, a counter-tradition which asserts the potency and possibilities of aesthetic affect.

2 The caricatured re-presentation of this debate over the years has enacted a reduction of the complex nuances of the arguments of Adorno and Benjamin, focusing largely on Benjamin's essay on mechanical reproduction and Adorno and Horkheimer's essay on the cultural industries. For a re-reading of their entangled approaches, see Isobel Armstrong's restaging of the encounter in Chapter 6 of *The Radical Aesthetic* (2000).

3 Note Bourdieu's slip into gendered terms with the description of proximate popular culture as 'seduction'; popular culture is the easy, available, close-up. Crossed with the metaphors of temperature (see the end of Chapter 1), popular culture becomes the 'hot' against high culture's 'icy solemnity'. This less-than-subtle imaging of cultural forms in gendered terms perhaps goes some way in explicating the severity of condemnation or celebration, reproducing the very split Western concepts of femininity.

4 The mimetic appears in psychoanalytic and film theory in various guises, but largely in each of these as a deathly activity, a replay without distance. This is the fated melancholy of repeated trauma in Freud's texts that takes its visual equivalent in the

televisual grainy repeats of Kennedy's death, the bombing of the Gulf War, the twin towers collapsing; mediation, proximity, implosion. In theories of representation it is the position of Scruton's dismissal of a visual culture repeating the empirical with no interpretation. In theories of the spectator, it is the identification with the apparatus and the relay of looks that squares the circle of ideology and subjectivity. Mimesis boxes us in, sets us on a treadmill where the scenery changes but our position remains the same.

5 In *Excitable Speech*, Butler stages an encounter between Bourdieu and Derrida in a confrontation of questions of authority and change. Whilst Butler is engaging primarily with Bourdieu's work on language, his model of speech acts as either authorized or lacking authority according to the context and the status of the speaker, reworking his central thesis of *Distinction*, that social effects derive from the divisive forms of social sanctioning.

6 Sobchack's thesis (drawing explicitly on Jameson's periodization) provides a vertiginous journey through three different epochs and their manifestation in technological cultures of the photograph, the film, and electronic media (the computer). Whilst she reminds us that 'the essence of technology is nothing technological', there is an underlying residual of technological determinism here. The analysis of film and temporality is illuminating, but I find the reading of electronic media as 'surface' dismissive of the phenomenological potential of new media. This dismissal appears almost as a result of the model that is employed; each era produces a technology whose impact may not coincide with any other. This reading is at odds with the main argument of this book, that what have become known as epochal movements exist simultaneously, are overlapping, convergent and also competitive.

7 Sobchack's work is in many ways in opposition to Leo Charney's reading of film and modernity as a convergence of the loss of presence. For Charney, the early cinematic experience presents us with a knowledge that poststructuralism was to enforce decades later, that meaning is endlessly deferred to an elsewhere. It is absence parading as presence, a series of signs leading us to 'real' places endlessly out of reach. This is read by Charney as a positive process he names 'drift', an 'empty present taken forward'. He writes:

> More exactly, cinema formed a nexus of two characteristic elements of the culture of modernity: an ontology of representation and an epistemology of drift. The absence of tangible present moments gave rise to a culture of re-presentation in which experience was always already lost, accessible only through retrospective textualization. (1998: 7)

Drift is written as both the directionless passivity of modern experience against which the shocking effects of modernity are enacted, and a more positive space to manoeuvre within. Yet, the emptying out of the presence of the text and consequently the ontology of the spectator is, I would argue, a reductive move that merely extends the understanding of film as a mimesis of the real; as such, it fails in its mimicry, just as it fails to muster the lost object present. I would argue that the problem lies with Charney's passive imaging of the subject, a languid backdrop to modernity's events.

8 Lefebvre's work influenced the Situationist movement and was in turn affected by the encounter. Lefebvre's fluid movement between oppositional terms, the everyday and the transcendental, the trivial and the profound, found a resonance with the Situationist position. As Shields argues, what appears in Lefebvre as utopian appears in Situationist discourse as an urgent practical question (see Plant, 1992 and Shields, 1999).

9 In an interview, Lars von Trier, the Dogme film maker, comments on the manipulative quality of music in mainstream film as a reason for the manifesto's rule that non-diegetic sound is not allowed. He subsequently went on to make the non-Dogme musical, *Dancer in the Dark*.

CHAPTER SEVEN

Digitalization and its discontents

The questions of whether digital film has 'happened', or indeed whether there is a subject clearly distinguishable from analogue film, or of whether digital film irrevocably blurs the boundary between film and other forms of culture, are questions that move swiftly into the territory of polarized positions. 'Computer media redefine the very identity of cinema' writes Lev Manovich, in an analysis flushed with the energy of the *Zeitgeist* (2001: 293). In contrast, Julian Stallabrass writes more generally of digital technology, 'The rise of digital media has encouraged the propagation of a "theory" which lauds these very qualities of shallowness and dispersal as a new form of radicalism' (1996: 356).[1] His argument is a polemical attack on the claims of political democratization that digitaliza-tion, and the new media 'revolution', are forecast to bring about.[2] He continues, 'As the real world is left to decline, the air once again becomes full of phantoms, this time digital, promising at the last moment to pluck utopia from the apocalypse' (1996: 362). For Stallabrass, 'new' media unwittingly reworks old, tired stories of technologies facilitating political transformation and equality. The discourse of utopianism, it might be noted, is not limited to intellectual speculation on the potential of technologies. Policy documents from the European Council and planned communication and cultural infrastructures are equally invested in the potential of digitalization to unleash markets and recreate new forms of cultural affiliation.[3]

This chapter takes the position that there is no separate object that can be designated 'digital' film, but that digitalization exists within and across the activi-ties of production, distribution and consumption. The structure of the account here addresses the impact and reception of digitalization in these three areas of film. In terms of production, it has been argued that digitalization, in the form of special effects, has returned cinema to its earlier moment as the cinema of attractions and spectacle (Darley, 2000), and, in the rise of animation, a recentring of a tradition once marginalized by lens-based imaging (Manovich, 2001). For Manovich, this suggests a reconfiguration of filmic hierarchies. In response, the argument here is that digitalization is taken up differently in traditions of film culture that remain distinct. The discourse of policy documents of the EU conceptualize the potential effects of digitalization in similarly seismic terms; digital delivery of film is constructed as a solution both to the existing monopolies on terrestrial channels of distribution and exhibition, and the national fragmentation of the 'collective' audiovisual space. Whilst new channels of dissemination suggest new possibilities, old allegiances of ethnicity, nationality and class are the historical context that technology is mapped onto; as such, digitalization as the 'new' will be taken up in relation to these existing paradigms. Finally, in the space of the home, digitalization represents a potential shift in consumption practices from terrestrial and public forms of viewing film – perhaps a move towards the postmodern fragmentation suggested in many accounts of new technology. Yet this is met with practices of containment, such as the collection of and personal archiving of film, which reintroduce a type of fixing of meaning in terms of personal taste.

The filmic technologies of celluloid and digital lend themselves metaphorically to figuring this split between modernism and postmodernism, the bounded and the fluid, the fixed and the ephemeral. Celluloid film provides a bounded frame for the image, whilst digital film is a proliferate patterning of code; and whilst the digital code appears to function through a binary structure (zeros and ones), the structure is non-hierarchical. Code can be patterned in an infinite number of ways, and once live recording is digitized, it attains the same status as other digital information, therefore shifting the hierarchical claims of celluloid film to the indexical, the real (Manovich, 2001: 295). But whilst these descriptions purport an isomorphic relation between these narratives and the technologies associated with each, I am not suggesting that technologies exist squarely within each trajectory, nor that technologies are productive of either modernism or postmodernism. Rather, consistent with the usage of the terms 'modern' and 'postmodern' in this book, they appear as ways of describing processes and characteristic features of film cultures, impacting on the way in which digitalization is narrated as a history and a departure from that story.[4] The aim of this chapter, then, is to identify the areas where tension between the two discourses of modernism and postmodernism is most evident in what I have called film cultures and digitalization.

film production and the digital

Digitalization has entered the world of film largely through the back door. We have been witness to digital effects in the form of special effects introduced into film production with various levels of publicity and attention.[5] If there is no exact moment when digitalization entered film, there is a further lack of clarity about what digitalization offers that is different from previous forms of image manipulation. What we may consider a contemporary form of manipulation as digital production has developed out of prior forms of image play that extend as far back as Eisenstein – editing, montage and appropriation – traditions in which filmic images have been 'dressed', touched up and processed through practices that were not singled out as special effects but were part of the craft of film. Further back still, the notion of a 'pure' visual text is upended by the legacy of film production from its illusionistic heritage; trickery, magic and spectacle, as Burch (1990), Gunning (1991) and Hansen (1990b) note, are the antecedents of many forms of cinematic production in the present.

The tracing of the contemporary back to historic practices characterizes one approach to digital imaging: the new, it is argued, is in fact the continuity of particular traditions of film making, denying claims of rupture and periodization. Both Lev Manovich and Andrew Darley contextualize forms of digital film making within these earlier traditions, but in different ways. In *The Language of New Media*, Lev Manovich argues that new media needs to be understood through the historical and cultural paradigms that pre-exist it, and that to an extent determine its shape. Whilst this provides the architecture for his text, in the final section Manovich makes some significant claims for the impact of digitalization on film cultures, particularly the place of animation in film culture and avant-garde practice. Prior to considering these claims I will outline the main features of what Manovich prefers to call new media rather than digitalization, in order to clarify the distinction between digital and analogue film making, before attending to the dispute of ruptures and continuities.

The larger project of Manovich's book is to analyse the impact of cinema on computing, and conversely computing on cinema. 'How does computerization affect our very concept of the moving image?' asks Manovich. 'Does it offer new possibilities for film language? Has it led to the development of totally new forms of cinema?' (2001: 287). In order to pursue these interrogatives he lists the ways in which computerization has entered cinematic life. These are first in the area of film production: 3-D computer animation/digital compositing, digital painting, virtual sets, virtual actors/motion. The second list refers to the effects of computer imaging on cinema. Here the list broadens spatially: location-based entertainment (simulation rides/parks), films designed for distribution through the Internet (short film) and typographic cinema (title sequences that combine film, graphic design and typography). Manovich is fond of lists. He supplies another extensive list of the qualities of the computer-based image. The most significant features of this (at least for the context of the discussion here) are that the image is pixelated as a code rather than a representational practice, the image is layered (there is surface and code) and has depth and surface as either a window or a control panel; the image is an interface that we enter, yet it also has hyperlinks to a world outside itself. Thus meaning is endlessly deferred to elsewhere, other possible sites. In addition, the image is open to endless manipulation and reproduction, thus the single image is replaced by a databank of images.

Within this account, the digital reconfigures our cultural relationship to the real. The legacy of photography and natural life painting as replicas of an external reality are overturned by the ability to generate, to manufacture filmic scenes totally from the computer. Moreover, in the practice of mixing filmed sequences and digital imaging, once the material is digitized it becomes information, and treated with equivalence by the computer system itself. Thus, the distinction between an original and a computer-generated image is not recognized, losing its indexical relationship to reality. This process has had a profound impact on the way that we perceive images as veracity; for example, digital images are disallowed as evidence in a court of law in Britain precisely because of their potential to be manipulated and not disclose the signs of that process. For Manovich, the digitization of film returns us to the properties of animation, the plasticity of the moving image, its playful creative dimensions that refuse any mimetic relation to the real. This return of film to animation potentially eclipses the twentieth-century history of film culture and its most prevalent divisions and distinctions:

> From the perspective of a future historian of visual culture, the differences between classical Hollywood films, European art films and avant garde films (apart from abstract ones) may appear less significant than this common feature: that they relied on lens-based recordings of reality. (Manovich, 2001: 294)

For Manovich, the differences between existing film cultures, the differences that underpin the analysis of film as cultures in this book, are potentially about to be elided as a further distinction, that between lens-based mimetic film and animated film, becomes a new, defining classificatory division.

I want to extend this argument of what is in excess of technology (precisely the concept of film as culture) by pursuing Manovich's thinking about new technologies and the avant-garde. For Manovich, the avant-garde becomes historically recentred in the era of new media, for the practices characteristic of new media composition share an affinity with earlier avant-garde practices and film. The creative practices made available by the computer, such as painting the image, reproduce the work of avant-garde artists of the early twentieth century; Len Lye's practice in 1935 of painting on film, scratching and marking the image, is returned in computer commands, or even further back, the handmade images of the magic lantern slides. The image of digital cinema is recast within the tradition of the painterly rather than the photographic. Another shift in practice towards avant-garde techniques is from the rigidity of camera movements to the fluidity of multiplane animated perspective. In enabling such fluidity, the animated camera is able to enter the space in different ways, and in tandem with the layers of moving images in a virtual 3-D space: the singular perspective and surface features of analogue film are displaced. Different textual properties are combined in the image. The effect, according to Manovich, echoes the avant-garde practices of collage, working against the prescribed aesthetic and technological norms of film as it became institutionalized. 'One general effect of the digital revolution is that avant-garde aesthetic strategies came to be embedded in the commands and interface metaphors of computer software,' he writes in full revolutionary style, continuing, '*In short, the avant-garde became materialized in a computer*' (2001: 307, italics original). This is clearly creative thinking, forging connections between the common-place cut and paste commands of most computer interfaces today with the practices of earlier avant-garde practitioners. Yet there is a familiar ring to the revolutionary appeal of new technologies and aesthetic strategies, which bypasses the social embedding of those forms.

Before attending to the specific claims made by Manovich, I want to turn to another account of digital film that again traces current digital practice to earlier cinematic forms, although with a different emphasis. According to Andrew Darley, the 'new' forms of spectacle cinema offered by large budget mainstream film draw on a heritage of film making from the early part of the twentieth century. Modes of 'live' entertainment of circus, theatre, vaudeville, wax works and the amusement park which entered the early forms of film culture (most famously in the cinema of Méliès), argues Darley, suffered a repression at the hands of narrative film. In the last decades of the twentieth century, it is claimed, the cinema of the attractions, or more specifically spectacle, experienced a renaissance in a number of films that were produced to effect stimulation and astonishment (*Star Wars* is the canonized example).[6] Commenting on twentieth-century spectacle cinema, Darley opens up a distinction between content and form:

> Certainly, these images of preposterous actions, fantastic events and bizarre beings are staggering for *what* they depict. However, the astonishment involved here parallels that experienced by the early spectator insofar as it appears to turn on the question of *how* it is possible to produce such high degrees of surface accuracy in such patently unattainable scenes . . . Technology itself is the message. (2000: 53)

Clearly, for Darley the emphasis is on the reception of film and on the large budget feature, whereas for Manovich the significant import of digital film is the process of production and the avant-garde. What is common to both is an emphasis on the formal properties of film. In both accounts, digital film making has emphasized form over content.

Darley qualifies this claim through a detour of the work of theorists of the post-modern, namely Baudrillard, Eco and Jameson, to argue that the current propensity for spectacle is part of a broader cultural shift towards 'forms of seriality, repetition, self-referentiality and spectacle . . . rising on the back of sign proliferation and enabled by continuing developments in mass production techniques' (2000: 74). The manipulation of images is connected to practices of appropriation, bricolage, the recycling of images and pastiche, earmarked by postmodern theorists as signs of an era.[7] Darley leans towards the thesis of the image as simulacrum to understand digital film, a theoretical space where images are detached from the real. This is, of course, another way of framing Manovich's description of the creation of digital worlds separate from any referent in the real. The problem with the Baudrillarian thesis of the loss of the real, apart from the minor difficulty of its pretension to speak for all of humanity, is its dissociation of culture from its contexts of circulation and use.

In order to explore these theses – that formal properties of film texts have become pronounced over content and that digital film returns us to the avant-garde – I want to consider sequences from two films, one a high budget, high concept American film, *The Matrix*, and the other a relatively low budget German film, *Run Lola Run*. Both films employ digital technology, but the similarities run deeper than this one feature. In many ways both films characterize the sorts of shifts that Darley and Manovich have described (and which Justin Wyatt also speaks of in relation to high concept film); both are dependent on a form of serial structure, they also foreground action, and each are formed of hybrid qualities of live footage and animated/special effect sequences. Yet I would argue there are significant differences between the texts that locate them within different film cultures, an argument that problematizes the concept of digital culture as trans-forming film production in general terms. Technological transformations may be used across different contexts of production, but each context brings to bear the history of that paradigm. The argument that I want to make relating to an understanding of their difference relies on both textual structure and relationships to other textual forms. *The Matrix* I will describe as a hypertextual film, whilst *Run Lola Run* is intertextual. This is a difference that locates each film within different traditions of knowledge and taste, and connects each to different systems of circulation.

The opening sequence of *The Matrix* places us immediately at the interface of a computer screen. We hear a telephone conversation whilst reading on the screen that the call is being traced. The action cuts to follow police entering a derelict building cautiously with guns aimed ahead. As they kick down a door and enter a room, a reversal in expectation occurs with the realization that the danger is in fact a woman. The stylization is futuristic – she is androgynous, cropped hair slicked back, dressed in black PVC and operates a mobile phone (widely known to be modelled on a product from Nokia). Cut to an external scene and a car arrives carrying a different set of agents dressed in suits and dark glasses. An exchange takes place in which we hear the police lieutenant say 'Relax, I think we can handle one little girl.' Clearly the audience at this point is assumed to have fuller knowledge than the characters. Cut to the interior scene and we see the woman spring into action to defeat the police. The woman is a highly trained, skillful fighter who displays a dexterity borrowed from martial arts. She also has exceptional powers of mobility. In the shoot-out sequence she runs vertically up and along the walls, and swiftly deflects the fire from police weapons onto each other. This scene plays out the manoeuvres of a computer game, reminiscent of the combat sequences generic to the format, with the scene commandeering all of the command functions of jumps, pace and direction-defying gravity, and combat skills. The greatest spectacle of the scene, however, is the chase that follows. The character is pursued across rooftops, jumping an unfeasible distance between buildings, and finally leaping from a building and flying head first through a window and into another interior. The utilization of special effects is accompanied by a slowing of the action, creating a spectacle of the 'exceptional' qualities of character.

The opening sequence of *Run Lola Run*, which runs beyond the title sequence, cuts between a variety of media formats: animation, super 8 (or its emulation, run at a faster speed than 24 frames per second), grainy footage from (mock) CCTV, black and white film signifying flashback, the text of a map and written text. The film opens the title sequence with two quotes: 'We shall not cease from exploration, And the end of all our exploring will be to arrive where we started, And know the place for the first time', T. S. Eliot, 'Little Gidding', and 'After the game is before the game', S. Herberger. These texts overlay a swinging pendulum and the sound of a clock; the camera moves up over a clock face and through the mouth of a gargoyle above the face, opening out onto Super 8 or digital footage of a public space with passers by in fast forward. At this point a voice-over delivers a philosophical meditation on the nature of man, 'Man . . . probably the most mysterious species of our planet . . .'. The speed of filming slows as the camera focuses on a police man who throws a ball into the air. The camera takes the perspective of the ball and looks down on the scene below, where the crowd has assembled into what reads from this height as the title of the film. The text then cuts to a cartoon image of a woman running through an animation clock face, through a tunnel traversing various obstacles and dangers (knives cutting through the wall, a spider's web, jumping up to smash glass objects on the tunnel ceiling). It then cuts to still images of the actors shot in the style of criminal records. Finally, from an image of a map of a city, the camera performs a radical zoom into one area, which moves into a 'real' street location and enters an apartment by the window to focus on a ringing telephone.

Both films contain references to animation and comic book graphics in terms of extreme camera angles, abrupt shifts of focus and an emphasis of the super-properties of 'human' characters.[8] Beyond these common properties, however, there are differences of tradition. The process of cutting between different media formats in *Run Lola Run* remains visible, sharp cuts between animation and live action that expose the sequence almost as an exercise in versioning. In contrast, *The Matrix* ties its effects into the diegetic whole, suturing over differences with graphics that are embedded in the verisimilitude of the scene. It is a film that requires the audience to suspend disbelief in terms of its genre (futurist/science fiction), but within the genre it adheres to conventions of accepted realism. Digital effects are barely distinguishable from other forms of image production. Where *Run Lola Run* moves between different forms and layers the image with text, *The Matrix* retains a smooth surface of imagery that runs unbroken with the narrative thrust. The effect of these different strategies is that *Run Lola Run* refers the audience to texts beyond its bounds, to cartoon forms and the texts of poetry in an exercise of intertextual referencing, whilst *The Matrix* refers us to further texts connected to itself, extending its narrative and 'experience' in the form of commodities (product placement) and other versions of the narrative in computer games and soundtracks. Thus, the German film creates intertextual references to established pre-existing texts which are also canonized literary works; in so doing, it retains a singularity to the boundaries of its own form. In contrast, *The Matrix* offers itself as a hypertextual experience opening out onto other versions of the film in a model more closely aligned to the CD ROM and games. And as recent work has shown, the narrative of games once again does not depart from convention, despite the interactive nature of the format; according to Mingay (1996), the three-act structure of Aristotelian principles is the foundation of many games.

To be fair to Manovich, the focus of his text is the recentring of creative practices developed by the avant-garde in the current moment of film production; the ways in which those practices are embedded in socio-historical systems in the current moment receives less attention. There is, however, a moment towards the end of *The Language of New Media* where the difference of filmic traditions is seen to impact on *how* digitalization is incorporated. He comments, 'Commercial narrative cinema continues to hold on to the classical realist style in which images function as unretouched photographic records of events that took place in front of the camera' (2001: 309). Whilst this is clearly the case with films such as *Forrest Gump* and *Titanic*, it is also the case that narrative realism provides the naturalization of digital effects across genres. He continues, arguing that when Hollywood creates a 'fantastic reality, it is done through the introduction of various non human characters such as aliens, mutants, and robots' (2001: 308–9). Yet the distinction that this suggests between different contexts of production is elided immediately by a reference to Metz and the persistence of narrative form. Whilst Metz is noted to have pondered the possibility of the demise of narrative form bringing about the end of verisimilitude, Manovich readily asserts 'Electronic and digital media have already brought about this transformation' (2001: 309), and we are back to the general thesis of digital cinema. The persistence of narrative alongside digital forms troubles the larger thesis of the book. In an earlier passage, for example, Manovich has adapted Marc Auge's (1995) distinction between modernity and supermodernity as a scheme within which certain formal characteristics can be aligned oppositionally. Narrative is opposed to database and hypermedia, objective space opposed to navigable space, static architecture to liquid architecture. Yet, in attempting to apply this scheme to the two films cited, the films fail to adhere to one side of the binary. The hypertextual, supermodern text of *The Matrix* relies thoroughly on narrative, whilst *Run Lola Run* straddles the divide even less comfortably in its mix of liquid and static architecture, its representation of objective space and navigable space.

The different traditions of American commercial cinema and European independent film continue across other digitally inspired practices, whereby the former sutures digital effects into the narrative realist text and the latter presents their formal disruption. The use of miniature digital cameras, which facilitate a new mobility of use and therefore of perspective, appear in *Julien Donkeyboy* as a formal disruption. Attached to actors' bodies, the perspective shifts radically throughout the film, and acquires the unstable movement of a body. Similarly, in *Timecode*, the ability to record for lengthier periods of time with digital film than on celluloid is exploited to make a film in one take, albeit on four different cameras. Figgis uses this new facility to reconfigure audience experience of narrative and point of view. The film frames all four narratives within the one screen, thus miniaturizing the image of each, and filling in the spatial and temporal gaps of a film that moves between different narratives. Each runs simultaneously, with characters at moments moving in and out of the various frames. The effect is not a total 'openness' to each narrative, as sound directs and controls attention, directing perception, but it offers the possibility of moving across the different visual planes. Here again the effects of digital technology in film production are foregrounded, indeed they are the innovatory and thus 'new' commercial potential for a film within this tradition.

Part of the difficulty of mapping digitalization in relation to film is the void between the potential use of technology in various applications, and its take up in production practices and contexts of consumption. *The Language of New Media* provides a topography of computer and film media, suggesting their increasing imbrication in shared practices and applications. And certainly, Manovich presents a convincing account of how computer technology has developed through the influence of cinema and how the cinematic form has incorporated features of the computer; the relationship is mutual influence, moving towards convergence, rather than a dialectical exchange where each party is changed by the encounter but each retains a separate position. Yet technological convergence is not a force that eliminates historical tradition, as I have argued in relation to the two film texts above. Whilst the computer moves centre stage in postproduction as a facility for editing, providing new opportunities for organizing and manipulating text, the results of editing digitally are diverse, dependent on the contexts of that particular practice. The economy of digital production, the low cost of recording digitally as opposed to on celluloid, suggests that the amount of footage produced may increase, and creative focus may even relocate from the context of the shoot to the edit suite. These currently remain speculative claims. The point that I am making is that technological convergence is not paramount to the convergence of filmic cultures of production and consumption.

The different practices of digitalization within the domains of mainstream and avant-garde film are produced by and reproduce the socio-historical paradigms within which they are situated. The avant-garde lacks the economic capital of plural-related commodities, and so digitalization remains within the bounds of the text, located in symbolic forms of capital. The kernel of each film idea remains filmic, lacking the resources to exploit narrative form across media, whilst mainstream media pushes the narrative kernel across media formats and locations. These narratives of historical practice remain in tension, influencing each other but providing different filmic cultures. The notion that technology will collapse this distinction is, I think, excessive. 'What was once supplemental to cinema becomes its norm; what was at the periphery comes to the centre. Computer media returns to us the repressed of the cinema,' writes Manovich (2001: 308).[9] This may be true of certain technical practices, but it does not speak to the lived practices of film cultures as they are historically driven; repression suggests a cyclical model, a Foucauldian return to the centre of the aberrant culture, whereas what we experience as film culture, including digital culture, is an ongoing struggle between forces in the field.

The paradigm in which digital mainstream film operates forges relationships between economic, aesthetic and technological determinants and interests; in so doing, the aesthetic analogy creates links between films and computer games, or films and music videos, extending the life of the product in other versions. Each format retains its own software copyright (and demands that we purchase the hardware), and the singular narrative of the film is reformatted and versioned for optimum return. The economic imperative spreads the narrative and characters across formats and defines the domestic space as an area of multiple leisure activity. Where does this leave avant-garde practice? I would argue that digital media remains within the bounds of the film text itself, retaining the singularity of film culture that is characteristic of what I have called a modernist narrative. Here, digitalization facilitates formal experimentation, the questioning of cinematic premises of linear narrative, perspective and veracity through the dimensions of the text. In *Run Lola Run* the animated sequences serve to foreground the plastic properties of the text, which are then played out in the structure of the film. Rather than conforming to the three-act structure, one act (itself the miniaturization of the three acts) is played out three times, each sequence playing the narrative differently. In so doing, the film appears to mimic a computer game: the possible paths through a narrative sequence, the possibility of starting again, of shifting perspective. It plays with both the existential possibilities of being (the arbitrary factors that guide our journey, the possible intervention into our own narratives dependent on crucial decisions at particular moments), and with the game-like culture of virtual life where return, repetition and renewal are possible. Agency and structure, narrative and character are fleshed out as both philosophical questions and gaming pursuits. Where Vivian Sobchack announces the electronic age as the era where sequential narrative is in demise, and causality appears comic, we find these elements within film culture as well as computing. In contradistinction to both Sobchack's analysis of electronic media and the loss of presence, and Manovich's prioritizing of the shift from recording to animation, the divisions may not be simply between media forms, but the different usages in the various contexts of production.

circulating film in a digital age

If digitalization has created new opportunities for production which are none-theless embedded in socio-historical contexts, the same opportunities and constraints exist at the level of distribution affecting the circulation of film. Metaphorically, the fibre-optic networks that have enhanced cross-border flows of information and communication suggest a shift away from the confining boundaries of nation states towards a postmodern fluidity of exchange. The immediacy of exchange, of access, purchase and acquisition, that the Internet provides, coupled with a vast array of information without an overarching inventory, produces a sense of a limitless scope for our actions, of access to every subject 'under the sun'. The denial of visual mastery endemic to the Internet refocuses attention to navigation, the practicing of routes and pathways through what has been called a super-highway but is experienced more as a journey through back-alleyways. The lack of visual 'mastery' of the Internet is suggestive of larger 'blind spots' in the relationship between users and providers; legal, commercial, institutional, national and international infrastructures remain out of sight.

Digitalization enters the domain of distribution of film in various ways, from the creation of policy documents and strategies, the research and funding of compatible systems of delivery, market research on digital up-take and consumer habits, to the experience of receiving film through digital channels in the home. The space between production and consumption, the arena in which film is circulated, is fraught with tensions of choice and restriction, specialization and expansion, protection and liberalization. At a level of global discussion, the compromise reached in Uruguay (in 1994) in the GATT negotiations between American-led demands for the liberalization of markets and a European resistance produced an inconclusive outcome.[10] As a result audiovisual services are neither awarded a special status nor committed to the particular requirements of liberalization (Wheeler, 2000: 256). The definition of audiovisual services remains vague; it is unclear whether the term refers to a delimited concept of culture (music, film, television), or whether it incorporates on-line trading and multimedia. The multiple uses of the Internet blur distinctions of culture, commerce, information and communication. Attempts at the regulation of electronic media falls prey to questions of cultural value, of whether computer games merit protection in addition to film, which forms of 'culture' are part of a national representation and which are outside it. As Wheeler notes, a further problem arises with the attempt to separate transport and content; are national cultures merely the content or also the infrastructure of delivery?

Whilst digitalization in the form of distribution networks and the blurring of content and delivery have presented problems of definition (of goods and services, and of spatial borders), new forms of technology are recast with greater optimism in the policy discourse of the EU. The MEDIA Plus project, 'Development, Distribution and Promotion', running from 2001–2005, cites new/digital technologies in three of its six founding objectives. New technologies are to improve the competitiveness of the European audiovisual sector, enhance European audiovisual heritage, and to disseminate new types of audiovisual content (*Official Journal of the European Communities*, 2000). The drafting of policy within the EU attempts to manufacture a European constituency of media and cultural exchange supported by a network of digital dissemination.[11] Eligibility for subsidy from the EU is dependent on the promotion of non-domestic

European works. Thus co-productions and the distribution of films from other member states qualify for support. The document states the Council's provision of 'incentives to digitize works and create promotional and publicity material in digital form, so encouraging European companies (suppliers of on-line access, special interest channels etc.) to create catalogues of European works in digital format for exploitation via new media' (2000: 41). The intention here is clearly a mix of commercial speak and cultural address: the recognition of cataloguing and archiving which appears consistently in plans is both an ideological practice (the selection involved in the preservation of a past) and the ring-fencing of a resource (see McChesney, 1998[12]). The extent to which digital technology features in EU policy documents attests to the belief that technology can cure the crisis of European film cultures rarely exhibited outside their national borders (Hill, 1994). Digital distribution is commandeered into the project to create a European suprastate, whilst recognizing the cultural diversity that exists within its borders (subsidy is specifically targeted at projects promoting cultural diversity, and practices of translation and subtitling).

The tension in this discourse of European policy exceeds the matter of film distribution, and is more generally part of a debate on the maintenance of borders and conditions of cultural exchange and fluidity. Or, as Paul Hainsworth (1994) asks in relation to film policy, what kind of Europe is being produced? On the one hand, the EU appears as a site of resistance to a multinational domination of routes of cultural exchange, a redrawing of boundaries to create a sustainable infrastructure for indigenous forms of expression. On the other, the maintenance of boundaries belongs to an imperialist narrative of European nations well practised in the exclusion of others. For this reason, Ien Ang (1992) remains critical of the attempts to forge a European identity, urging the debate into the realm of the post-European. The threats wielded by the spectre of a European suprastate present two compelling needs: one is the possibilities of exchange with nations and cultures existing outside of its boundaries, as Said argues (1988); the second concerns the production of imaginary European identities as diverse, shifting, attached to cultures that are unattached to nation states or geographical terrain. Here lies the difficulty of audiovisual policy in Europe: Europe is composed of multiple linguistic and cultural groups, to be served by 'specialized' services delivered electronically. Yet the success of a European common network relies on cultural exchange, the circulation of products beyond niche markets. The focus of technology in such debate obscures larger questions of cultural translation; where and how films are circulated, discussed, promoted and exhibited become the most pressing issues for cultural policy. Indeed, if the difficulty of cultural exchange and translation is the historical obstacle to the success of diversity, the focus on technology rather than social relations between groups would appear to be misplaced. Commenting on ethics and digitalization in an American context, Stein argues for a different emphasis, suggesting that in place of investing federal funding in the US in CD ROMs, it would more beneficial 'to spend some of this money for story tellers in the community' (1999).[13]

Where policy focuses attention on dissemination to collective groups, digital distribution is represented to the consumer (largely by commercial companies) as the enhancement of individual identity. New distribution channels available through cable, satellite and the Internet are constructed around generic forms of film, defined for example by period or nationality. Here, the discourse of specialization takes us into more narrowly defined areas of interest, a process consolidated by information services available through the Internet and mobile phones. The marketing of digital services reproduces the discourse of individualism existing in other media, yet with 'value added' by the ability to personalize the service. The complexity of new technological software translates into the provision of tracking services, recording our practices/transactions and identifying our tastes. This record then provides an adjustable template that is used by a search facility to find a personalized range of information. The problem with the user interface of digital technology is that the provision channels us into narrower circuits of information based on what we know; in so doing, it effectively mitigates against the project of cultural diversity and the difficulties of cultural translation, of engagement with cultures that are different from our own.

'New' technologies have a double articulation in policy documents. They represent a solution to national fragmentation through the (potential) provision of a national or European network of distribution, yet they also threaten to compound the splintering of taste as it is manifest in differences of class, ethnicity, religion, age and sexuality. In addition, the commercial discourse that produces the concept of individualism, as unique and authentic, impacts on how technologies develop, the software of service provision. The tensions of liberalization and regulation produce a number of discourses that offer to interpellate the individual subject simultaneously as an actor in the global network, a citizen of a national/supranational state, and an individual consumer in the home. How then do these contradictions become embedded in filmic cultures of the home?

bringing it all back home

The instability and fragmentation of social relations at a global and national level impact on the conceptualization of an imaginary and material place that we call home. As David Morley argues, 'Certainly, traditional ideas of home, homeland and nation have been destabilised, both by new patterns of physical mobility and migration and by new communication technologies which routinely transgress the symbolic boundaries around both the private household and the nation state.' And if destabilization affects the spaces of home and the nation, it is also present in the electronic landscapes that we inhabit, which are 'haunted by all manner of cultural anxieties which arise from this destabilising flux' (Morley, 2000: 3). The micro unit of the home cannot be thought of as a retreat from this process, but is another site where such anxieties are played out. In this last section I want to draw out the ways in which our relationships to film are renegotiated through the effects of digitalization in the home, to understand in turn how film is part of our negotiation with larger processes of social instability.

Following Soja (1989), space (here the specific space of the home) is produced through material practices rather than being an inert property onto which effects are mapped. If practices create space, then the proliferation of home-based entertainment and leisure forms has to be seen as producing new kinds of space; the home becomes not a refuge from the world, but an extension of the pursuits of the outside. Technologies such as video, computer and Internet have opened up the home to a range of activities based around screens. These technologies have enhanced the practices of working from home, over-riding the division between work and the domestic as distinct spatial domains and temporal practices. Home then becomes a space of a renewed labour around leisure, purportedly more individuated than collective, more privatized than public. What are the ways in which we connect to film cultures in the home? What are the interfaces of public and private?

Whilst digital technologies render film culture, our choices for and engagement with film, less public or visible, Charlotte Brunsdon (1997) provides an analysis of visible manifestations of taste constructed through a relationship to networks of distribution. In the chapter 'Satellite Dishes and Landscapes of Taste', Brunsdon traces a series of debates about the construction of satellite dishes conducted in the media. As visible signs of taste attached to the home's exterior, satellite dishes are the target of a campaign for the conservation of property. Further still the class affiliations and judgements of taste spill over into concern with what type of media is consumed. Satellite dishes are perceived to be con-ductors of a media culture from 'elsewhere' beyond the bounds of the nation state, a sign of supranational affiliation or refusal of the national culture by the consumer. The debate reported in the media as Brunsdon presents it illustrates a class division in terms of those for and against, a positioning underscored by the information that the majority of satellite dishes rented or bought were by individuals from social classes C1, C2 and D. Furthermore, this opposition is played out asymmetrically in the reporting of the debate: those opposed to the construction of dishes attain a far larger representation, and articulate their concerns from positions of representation or symbolic power, such as councillors and representatives of trusts. Dish erectors in contrast are merely individuals. The layered meaning of the dishes draws together the discourses of the constructed environment, media policy, consumption and identification, status and social articulation. Brunsdon comments, 'in this one example we see condensed a complex set of issues, including a conflict of taste codes which is illustrative of the history and status of different taste formations in Britain', and is connected to national broadcasting policy (Brunsdon, 1991/1997: 151). Whilst our preferences for media are constructed as natural tastes, the debate about dishes exemplifies the paradigm of economic, cultural and symbolic power within which our discriminations are produced and manifested as individual preferences.

Since the writing of Brunsdon's paper in 1990, the situation of visibility, and of the social value of the culture received by satellite, has perhaps shifted. In place of dishes, cable has provided an alternative mode of connection, coupled with the multiple functioning of the computer as a media and cultural interface rather than simply an information vector. And at the time of writing in the early 1990s, the dishes in Brunsdon's account were clearly identifiable as transmitters of SkyTV; since that time, the extension of channels and programming has clouded the definition of what dishes and cable provide. However, the social antagonisms evident in the opposition of satellite versus terrestial television are reiterated in the opposition of home versus cinema viewing in the present moment. In the advertising industry's research of media consumption, the activities of cinema-going and home rental divide in terms of social class, the public form of viewing being the practice of viewers of a high social grade, and home viewing of film as video rental being the predominant film viewing experience of lower social grade viewers. Thus, parallel to the use of the public forum of the newspaper in Brundson's account, the groups with greater social and symbolic power are as film viewers more likely to occupy public spaces.

These examples illustrate the ways in which the consumption of media operates within fields of symbolic power, inculcating social difference across physical space. Home view and satellite reception does not simply signify a withdrawal from public collective viewing, but is representative of a withdrawal from the rituals of the television that offer to cohere viewers as a national collective (Silverstone, 1994). This is a feature noted mainly in relation to news programmes and national television, but it relates also to the viewing of films. In contrast to terrestrial formats, where film is organized in a viewing schedule around other strategic rhythms of national life (the news, regular soaps, serials and factual television), film view channels consolidate film as a media to be watched at any given time.[14] In Britain, terrestrial television provides two predominant routines of film viewing, one situated in the early afternoon – the favoured texts being reruns of old genre – whilst the late evening slot is reserved for premièrs and more recent films. The scheduling of national television suggests a ritual of viewing organized in relation to viewing intensity, structured around other televisual routines (such as news programming) and related programmes such as reviews and thematized evenings. Non-terrestial film channels are removed from this context of national ritual and domestic televisual routine, offering instead a particular branding of film taste through individual channels.

The viewing of film within the home cannot however be conceptualized as an activity on one side of a public–private binary (Light, 1999). The home is also the space of negotiating public discourse, and the forms of that engagement have been fundamentally altered by the presence of the Internet, with its provision of hyper- and intertextual information, extended range of film choice and immediate delivery.[15] Without the interface of a national apparatus, or the familiar locality of the video store, the downloading of film from specialist channels has produced a culture of film knowledge that directly connects the viewer with the producer. This is a phenomenon consistent with Appadurai's writing on the mythologies of commodity flow, 'Commodities and the Politics of Value' (1986). Here, Appadurai argues that the greater the distance between producer, trader and consumer, the greater necessity for commodity mythologies, the stories of production, biographies of directors and actors, and fan discourse. The circulation of commodities in Appadurai's model requires knowledges that are expert and authentic. Applying this criteria to the range of websites and chat-rooms for film, the notion of 'insider' information dominates the field. Accounts of production, budgets and special effects, what we might think of conventionally as 'demythologizing' of the production practice, create further mythologies as 'insider' knowledge. The demand for information has carried over into the format of DVD, film to buy and hire. The staple menu of films on DVD includes scenes cut from the final edit (some to view from a choice of camera positions, mimicking the director's role), production notes and interviews with cast. More recent editions intended for viewing on computer provide links to Internet sites, leading directly to commerce and further information.

Alain J.-J. Cohen argues that knowledge of the production process has been surpassed by a trade in knowledge of commerce and business acumen, of how films are performing at the box office and stories of industry rumour concerning studio executives. Cohen comments, '"Hollywood" has taken on the mantle of a simulacral business in which knowledge of (frequently illusory) profits and losses attests to the "insidership" of the film fan, who may, or may not, have any other expertise in film culture' (2001: 153). This connects with the more general trend of amateur stock market practice and the deprofessionalization of business practice that the Internet has facilitated. But what is significant here is the relationship between the terms of access and connoisseurship. Fundamentally, the relationship is one of paradox as the Internet is heralded by its proponents as the freeing up of access to information, the liberation of knowledge, yet at the same time, knowledge has the apparent status of the coveted and specialized; the gates are simultaneously wide open and slightly ajar. What the Internet offers for film culture, then, is a constructed sense of information as 'insider', positioning the consumer as connoisseur, in the same way that advertising provides us with an image of ourselves as discriminating.

This sense of connoisseurship pervades another aspect of digital information services, that of memory and storage. If one of the features of digital technology is a vastly expanded facility to store information (and with the broadening of band waves the ability to transmit), the practice of collection is technologically available in a new way. The discourse of the connoisseur surfaces again, a necessary component of a situation in which supply is excessive and taste produced as a way of inventing scarcity. In 'The Contemporary Cinephile', Barbara Klinger argues that media industries have played a significant role in generating a culture of film collection as a pervasive, routine activity. Klinger reads the new forms of film technology (DVD, laser disc) as shifting our relationship from one of abstraction to materiality, spectator to owner: 'This previously physically remote, transitory and public medium has thus attained the solidity and semi-permanent status of a household object, intimately and infinitely subject to manipulation in the private sphere' (2001: 2). Whilst this account emphasizes the manipulative quality of home technology as a way of personalizing film, there is also a sense of film as a domestic object, strewn casually on the coffee table or displayed in cabinets. The film collection becomes an object of taste alongside other interior furnishings reflecting the personality and attributes of the owner; film within the space of lifestyle.

Whilst Klinger argues that film production companies have 'explicitly targeted collectors as a niche audience', I would argue that the collector is precisely the construction of marketing discourses: despite the appeals to the connoisseur, that most distinguished character is all of us. Her analysis of audiovisual magazines locates such constructions in advertisements, appeals to 'Accessorize Your Evening' with the purchase of a particular DVD, and 'the perfect addition to your home video collection'. Perhaps the most overt appeal to the discerning collector is the label of 'classic'. As Klinger argues, this label appropriates the terms of literature and fine art. The affinity with other more established cultural forms extends into categories and practices of arrangement, borrowing the taxonomy of libraries and archives; software offers the facility to catalogue a collection by title, director or genre. Thus, the practice of film collection is embedded in a matrix of cultural taste that acquires its own forms of legitimacy in reference to established canons of culture and their practices of ordering.

The practices of collection and the cultivation of connoisseurship create a socially meaningful context for digital technology. Preferences not only for film content, but for different forms of technology, generate further symbolic distinctions. In an article entitled 'The Contradictions of Video Collecting' (1997), Charles Tashiro speculates on the fetishization of technological formats as integral to the practice of collecting. Technologies have various status for different users beyond the simple demand of the new. In an autobiographical account of film collecting, Tashiro states a preference for laser discs rather than video tape, a preference which is rooted in a sensual relationship to the object, 'Discs fascinate as objects, their clear, cool surfaces', and a practical appreciation; the laser disc does not degenerate in the way that video tape spoils.[16] The symbolic value of technology shifts in relation to a number of factors such as consumer take-up, reputation for quality and the experiential effect. When technologies are new, their endurance in the marketplace is unknown (beta video provides an example of the random effect of market and monopoly over quality). Conspicuous consumption of the new is also a signifier of poor taste. Technologies that offer forms of social connection, or that enhance experience meaningfully, attain a clearer market value. Yet, the experiential is also a feature of retaining old formats, particularly where the object acquires a biography, to use Appadurai's concept. In music, the preference for vinyl over CDs as a medium that retains the history of its usage (the life of a subject indelibly marked across the object, the object embodying the passage of time), demarcates a particular connoisseur whose cultural capital increases with the rarity of products and scarcity of sales venues. And if laser disc provides a symbol of modern perfection for Tashiro, there is also a reverse pull of nostalgia for film connoisseurs. Celluloid, like vinyl, bears the marks of its history in the form of dropout and glitches, and whilst this is not yet a particularly fetishized experience, with the advent of digital exhibition there is the distinct possibility that it will become so.[17]

'New' technologies, then, acquire value in relation to earlier cultural forms, and the shifting notions of authenticity and perfection. The practice of reformatting 'classic' films with renewed colour and sound provides yet another market for film in eliminating exhibition and production history. In the issue of the reformatted film value shifts again as the new acquires a peculiarly postmodern aura by remixing and versioning the cultural past. In *Modernity at Large* Appadurai writes of the temporal relationship of consumption as the crucial dimension to our understanding of it. He writes 'The pleasure that has been inculcated into the subjects who act as modern consumers is to be found in the tension between nostalgia and fantasy, where the present is represented as if it were already past' (1996: 83). Echoing Jameson's comments on nostalgia and the retro film, Appadurai focuses our attention not on amnesia but on ephemerality: 'This inculcation of the pleasure of *ephemerality* is at the heart of the disciplining of the modern consumer.' If ephemerality, the short-lived, the momentary, the mortal is at the heart of consumer culture, driving us in our pursuit of the moment, the practices of film collection offer a memento of the present, the meaning-ful experience of film within our own lives at particular moments, places and in particular company. Films as material objects represent our own viewing experience like any souvenir. Collections are also an attempt to stave off such thoughts of ephemerality in the material conquest of history displayed, organized and owned (Usai, 2001).[18] Digital film culture of the home provides the post-modern features of accessing any temporal event as a segment, extended storage, data-memory bank, and calms the modernist demand to order time, chronologically placed, controlled, contained.

Digital media offers us different relationships to time; most famously it facilitates a space–time compression, 'speed only made possible because of new communi-cation technologies' (Castells, 1996: 493). Castells also argues that time is manifested differently in different spaces, the timeless time of the exchange of capital across the stock exchange, the extended time of workers in technologically under-developed countries, the promise of eternal time in the compression of data into memory banks. Similar to Appadurai's description of consumption as the oscillation between fantasy and nostalgia, Castells claims '*it is a culture at the same time of the eternal and of the ephemeral*' (1996: 492, italics original). Film has historically held fascination for its representation of a living moment as fleeting, caught in the paradox that time is captured and yet intangible, present and yet absent. Digital film cultures perhaps push this paradox further, into a place where we can live the paradox more easily. Within the home, the cultures of collection provide a control, a containment of time, and in the ancillary products of film we extend the life of the characters and narrative, enter their worlds, make them our own. But once we enter these texts where time is a collage, where we can start again, repeat, move through the layers rather than the narrative of a text, time stretches out into the eternal, 'a flat horizon, with no beginning, no end, no sequence' (Castells: 1996: 493).

The space of the home provides for both narratives of ephemeral fleeting time and of history as object, of postmodernism and modernism. Domestic ritual time is mapped across the space of the home, built into its structure as an arrangement of rooms for different functions and times. It is the place both of face-to-face communication and exchange, and of virtual connection. It connects us to both the nation state through the temporal rhythms of television, and the atemporal flow of a more postmodern existence through digital technologies: 'flows induce timeless time, places are time-bound' writes Castells (1996: 494). Yet the home contains both. They are contradictory logics, pulling us in different directions, into the diverse and confrontational, into the familiar and safe.

projections

If digitalization invokes and invites meditations on the ephemeral and the eternal, flirts coyly with the existential properties of film texts and our experiences of them, it returns us to the nature of film itself: a fleeting, mobile representation of a time that is already past, which can be recalled and replayed but always presents an absence as well as a presence. For some commentators, such as Lev Manovich, digitalization portends a new 'life' to film, undoing the fixity of the single frame and directorial control; the potential for the spectator to reanimate the film text, to mix its parts, to intervene in choice of camera angle and narrative structure, suggests that the edit is no longer the arrest of time, but that film may continue to metamorphosize. This reading suggests a reversal of what Barthes attests to in relation to the photograph as an experience of mortality when confronted with the past as an image, our own death prefigured but never met head on; in place of the gaze, such moments are better thought of as a glance that is always awry.

Such meditations on mortality may be attributed to a millennial discourse with its attendant properties of anxiety, eclipse and apocalypse, a discourse that may have informed Bergson's philosophy a century ago in his ruminations on film, time and memory. Yet, if the project of this book has been in part to read a philosophy and sociology of film together, the material relations that are brought into being and make possible how film is perceived, used and understood necessarily return here. One such attempt to read the effects of digitalization as both a material practice and a philosophically redolent emergence is found in Paolo Cherchi Usai's *The Death of Cinema: History, Cultural Memory and the Digital Dark Age* (2001). As the title suggests, Usai's perception of digitalization is one of loss as the digital threatens the permanent eclipse of celluloid film. Arguing that celluloid remains a distinct cultural form, Usai provides a polemic against the view that the transference of film to a digital format is an act of preservation; in his reading, it is a translation of content into a radically different media with attendant losses and transformations. As a curator, Usai poses some pertinent questions (albeit through a filtre of apocalypse) concerning selection and choice, about which films are preserved, forging a faultline between the abstract possibilities of digitalization and the material uses to which it is put. For Usai, the proliferation of film provided by digitalization, low budget production and dissemination through the Internet further problematizes the already complex issues of which films become history and which are discarded, which films come to represent an age and which film cultures are banished to the waste bin of history. Such choices for Usai are increasingly dictated by economic constraints alone, with the commercial success and further exploitation of film the governing factors.

The argument that Usai makes converges the material and abstract properties of film preservation. For preservation is at once a material matter of political and historical choices, of policy, and also a practice that mitigates against the nature of film as a matter that is in constant dissolution, marked and worn by its history of exhibition: this paradox is neatly summized in the statement 'Preservation of the moving image is a necessary mistake'. According to Usai, digital film as a format is suggestive of an increased production of waste, with the narrowing of audience expectation of what constitutes film cut against the increased production: surplus equals waste. Interestingly, the metaphor to which Usai turns to explicate such a claim is that of the second law of thermodynamics, the same model that Leo Charney invokes in relation to early cinema (see Chapter 1). The second law of thermodynamics posits the rule that the generation of heat involves the encounter of two bodies, producing a third matter different from the original two, and further, that the process of generation necessarily involves an element of irrecoverable waste. Simply put, production necessarily entails loss, excess, negativity.

For Charney, as for Usai, this is a general metaphor for production typifying the eras of modernity and postmodernity respectively. In Charney's account, negative waste is inverted, coming to stand for the disassociated drift, the vacuous, absent decentred self that Charney reclaims as a positive; the model of the decentred subject of early cinema refuses the positivist knowing subject of an imperial past. In Usai's account, waste remains waste, the discarded detritus resulting from new cultural developments, a model that reverses the teleology of technological 'progress'. Yet, in terms of the project of this book, waste can be thought of in another way, as the product of choice, of the exercise of taste. In a culture in which choice speaks the secret of our selves, informs others of who we are and where we come from, the rejection of other tastes, of other film cultures, is a practice of social positioning. What we waste is as important as the matter that we choose, for it is pushed out, refused, constituted as that which is different. And in this sense, the anthropological reading of waste in the work of Lévi-Strauss and Mary Douglas, for example, of expulsion as a ritual act of boundary marking, has a resonance in film culture. For the circulation of film as a familiar, known, identifiable practice and set of norms incurs a refusal of film cultures that are not recognizable; film cultures that are from elsewhere or involve a level of 'alien' culture circulate in increasingly small and select pathways. Furthermore, the taste for other, 'alien' culture, as it resides in the arthouse or gallery, comes to stand for a particular form of class status, a mobility for certain subjects to move across given boundaries, ironically reinstating divisions of class.

Digitalization throws into relief the main dialectic at work in this book: the tension between tradition and revolution, transformation and stasis, modernism and postmodernism. Rather than eclipsing twentieth-century traditions of film making, digitalization is utilized within existing spheres of production; in large budget Hollywood films, digital effects enhance the ability to stage the epic film and historical stories, such as *Gladiator* and *Titanic*, where spectacle and heroism are entwined. In the sphere of alternative and independent production, digitalization facilitates the telling of micro narratives; the economy of digital production, the miniaturization and mobility of new technology allow an exploration of interiority in films such as *The Idiots*, *Julien Donkeyboy* and *The Following*. Technologies provide possibilities for the new, for ways of producing, distributing and viewing film, suggestive of a new form of fluidity. Yet this meets the contours of the existing territory, the ownership of infrastructure, the secured routes of distribution, the prefigured patterns of tastes, the sedimented layers of individual and collective histories. In place of metaphors of productivity versus waste, or heating up versus cooling off, film cultures are produced across and within different, often competing processes.

Notes

1   The lack of agreement about the terminology of the 'new' indicates the level of difficulty in definition of any sort: the different terms in use are new technology, new media, digital culture, electronic media and the, by now rather quaint, 'cyber culture', each representing different preferences and emphases on media forms and their functions for various commentators. And despite the prefix of 'new' in many titles, there is harsh dispute about whether digitalization represents anything new at all; many commentators point to the reproduction of social inequality through differential access, corporate control and the further commodification and privatization of 'life', in short, an extension of the social context in which technologies evolve.

2   See Kember *Virtual Anxieties* (1998) for a further discussion of the neuroses attending digitalization.

3   A discussion document from the 2nd Audiovisual Conference of the Euro-Mediterranean Partnership (September 2000) cites the two risks to the development of European audiovisual markets: the ideology of free market radicalism and the concentration of media industries. The counter-force of such risks are rooted in digital technologies: 'On the other hand, the development of digital techniques and distribution via the Internet is creating decisive new opportunities which must be seized by professionals and institutional decision-makers of the Euro-Mediterranean partnership in order to counter the above-mentioned trends' (8). One of the aims of the three workshops at the conference was 'to explore how new media can assist in bringing together cultures that have become fragmented by inter-country migration in the Euromed area, with a view to encourage better understanding between different cultures' (11). See also the role of new technologies in the report 'Content as a New Growth Industry' (OECD, 1998).

4 Digitalization exists at the intersection of twin axes: a vertical axis of modernism and a horizontal axis of postmodernism. The vertical axis is characterized by hierarchy and structure, giving rise to the identity formations of class, ethnicity and gender. It is an axis that operates through binary structures, of self and other, mind and body; it manifests difference in systems of thought that classify and cast value on subjects and objects. Deriving from a moment in which the status of nation states was at once imperious and in crisis, the vertical axis invokes history as authority, precedence and linearity, and demarcates space in terms of bounded territories. The horizontal axis, by contrast, is characterized by a deterritorialization of space (the nation state, the bounds of the home) and the scrambling of time into repeatable, dislocated segments or loops. The postmodern appears to deconstruct hierarchy through the proliferation of goods and the commodification and aestheticization of life practices, purporting choice over collective judgement. And the horizontal structure reaches out sideways, uncontained by the line of the axis, more like an ebbing fluidity.

The history of the Internet provides another example of the way in which a horizontal, decentralized network developed in conjunction with the fixed and nationally hierarchical agendas of the military; the military development of the Internet developed within specific conditions of national and ideological interest, evolved as a structure uncontained by nation states and open to diverse practices outside and oppositional to the original context of development. Paul Virilio (1989) traces an analogous relation between the development of cinematic technologies and the military.

5 The very public marketing of 'effects' in the film *Star Wars* is read as a particularly significant moment in the development of spectacle and a public engagement with the 'new' possibilities of cinematic experience.

6 'The drive behind much of the technological development in cinema since 1950 has been towards both a greater or heightened sense of "realism" and a bigger, more breathtaking realization of spectacle' (Michael Allen, 1998).

7 Darley also points out that this is not the only way of conceptualizing digital film: 'Unlike Baudrillard, I do not think that these new features now constitute the whole of (visual) culture *per se*, only that they are now so prevalent as to constitute a new and significant dimension of representation within it. Other (and older) orders of representation exist alongside and in contention with this newer one, though they may well be increasingly compromised by its expansion' (2000: 74).

8 Where *Run Lola Run* moves in and out of animation and real time footage, *The Matrix* elides these two forms, mimicking the graphics of cartoon strips. In one scene at the beginning of the film, as the female protagonist is standing with her back to the approaching police agents, the framing of the image replicates the cartoon explicitly. The face of the protagonist is half in frame in extreme close up; her arm above her head, we view the approaching police through the angle of the crook in her arm. The image is shot through a green filter, or coloured green in post-production. The slick lines of the shape of the face and arm reproduce the clean shape-based design of comics. The image also foregrounds the different perspectives

juxtaposing the face of the protagonist (read danger and intent) and the unwitting expression of the police.

9 A narrative of radicalization and digital film making is not confined to academic analyses. The trade press also cites digital film making as 'tantamount to a communist revolution' (Seguin, 'The Politics of Shooting', *Screen International*, 2000).

10 The outcome was perceived to be a triumph for the European contingency, led by Jack Lang (see Chapter 5 for fuller details of the talks). However, the definition of audiovisual services remains problematically indistinct, a situation that will not necessarily work in favour of European states.

11 The complexity of interests at work in the intersection of commercial and public interests, regulation and liberalization, in the development of technological infrastructure is documented in the report conducted by the British government in 1994, 'The British Film Industry'. A memorandum submitted by Polygram, for example, illustrates a perspective at odds with the EU vision, arguing instead for a Hollywood-led infrastructure: 'It is important to capture the Hollywood business not only to attract investment in the British film industry and to create jobs in the industry but because Hollywood is the catalyst for driving new technologies such as video on demand, CD video, CD ROM, etc, which will in turn drive the "high tech" industry. If we do not capture this business we will be severely disadvantaged in the "high tech" race of the future.' Second Report to the National Heritage Committee (1994), Volume 2, HMSO, p. 156.

12 Robert McChesney's discussion is centred on globalization and success and dominance in markets: interestingly he identifies the practice of archiving, along with branding, as a key component of Time–Warner's success.

13 Ethics is increasingly brought into dialogue with new technologies, at times in support of a return to face-to-face interaction as it appears in the work of Levinas (1969), at others, a relocation of ethics to the digital domain. *The Virtual Embodied* (edited John Wood, 1998) provides further discussion, particularly Damien Keown, 'Embodying Virtue', and Lisa M. Blackman, 'Culture, Technology and Subjectivity: an "Ethical" Analysis'.

14 The viewing of film within a national framework had of course already suffered a disruption with the advent of video and the possibilities of timeshift. See Ann Gray (1992), *Video Playtime: The Gendering of a Communications Technology*, and Sean Cubbitt (1991), *Timeshift*.

15 Digital technologies have also reworked the 'ambient' space of the home, which has been consolidated, elaborated and redefined as a viewing space with the technologies of wide screen, surround sound and the precise images of DVD.

16 Manovich points out, however, that the storage and transmission of digital material necessarily involves compression ('lossy compression'), a loss of information to make image files smaller for distribution. Thus, the notion of digital formats exactly replicating analogue forms or being infinitely copied without degradation is,

according to Manovich, a myth. Whilst this may be regarded as a temporary measure in the process of developing storage capacity and faster networks, the widespread industry use of lossy compression suggests that it may emerge as a standard format (Manovich, 2001: 54).

17 The 'value' of existing media in relation to a new form refers us back to Benjamin's reading of film in relation to painting. For Benjamin, film did not remove the aura of the original artwork, but in many ways doubled it. The old form acquires a new authenticity in relation to technology; similarly if Tashiro's reading of nostalgia is right, celluloid may develop such an aura of originality.

References

Abercrombie, N. (1991) 'The privilege of the producer', in R. Keat and N. Abercrombie (eds) *Enterprise Culture*. London: Routledge, pp. 171–86.

Abercrombie, N. (1994) 'Authority and consumer society', in R. Keat, N. Whiteley and N. Abercrombie (eds) *The Authority of the Consumer*. London: Routledge, pp. 45–57.

Adams Sitney, P. (ed.) (1971) *Film Culture: An Anthology*. London: Secker and Warburg.

Aksoy, Asu and Robins, Kevin (1992) 'Hollywood for the 21st century – global competition for critical mass in image markets', *Cambridge Journal of Economics*, 16(1): pp. 1–22.

Alexander, Karen (2000) 'Black British cinema in the 90s: going going gone', in R. Murphy (ed.) *British Cinema of the 90s*. London: BFI, pp. 109–14.

Allen, Michael (1998) 'From *Bwana Devil* to *Batman Forever*: Technology in contemporary Hollywood cinema', in S. Neale and M. Smith (eds) *Contemporary Hollywood Cinema*. London and New York: Routledge, pp. 109–29.

Alloway, Lawrence (1971) *Violent America: The Movies 1946–64*. New York: Museum of Modern Art.

Altman, Rick (1999) *Film Genre*. London: BFI.

Ang, Ien (1992) 'Hegemony-in-trouble: nostalgia and the ideology of the impossible in European cinema', in D. Petrie (ed.) *Screening Europe: Image and Identity in Contemporary European Cinema*. London: BFI, pp. 21–31.

Appadurai, Arjun (1986) 'Introduction: commodities and the politics of value', in A. Appadurai (ed.) *The Social Life of Things: Commodities in Cultural Perspective*. Cambridge: Cambridge University Press, pp. 3–60.

Appadurai, Arjun (1996) *Modernity at Large: Dimensions of Globalization*. Minneapolis and London: University of Minnesota Press.

Appiah, K.A. (1993) *In My Father's House: What Does it Mean to Be an African Today?* London: Methuen.

Armstrong, Isobel (2000) *The Radical Aesthetic*. Oxford: Blackwell.

Auge, Marc (1995) *Non-places: Introduction to an Anthropology of Supermodernity*, trans. J. Howe. London: Verso.

Balio, Tino (1996) 'Adjusting to the new global economy: Hollywood in the 1990s', in A. Moran (ed.) *Film Policy: International, National and Regional Perspectives*. London and New York: Routledge, pp. 23–38.

Balio, Tino (1998) '"A major presence in all the world's markets": the globalization of Hollywood in the 1990s', in S. Neale and M. Smith (eds) *Contemporary Hollywood Cinema*. London and New York: Routledge, pp. 58–73.

Baudrillard, J. (1981) *For a Critique of the Political Economy of the Sign*, trans. C. Levin. St Louis: Telos Press.

Baudrillard, J. (1983) 'The ecstacy of communication', in H. Foster (ed.) *Postmodern Culture*. London and Sydney: Pluto, pp. 126–34.

Baudrillard, J. (1988) *The Ecstacy of Communication*, trans. B. Schutze and C. Schutze. New York: Semiotext(e).

Bauman, Zygmaunt (1989) *Modernity and the Holocaust*. Cambridge: Polity Press.

Bauman, Zygmaunt (2000) *Liquid Modernity*. Oxford: Polity Press.

Beck, Ulrich (1992) *Risk Society: Towards a New Modernity*. London and Newbury Park: Sage.

Beck, Ulrich, Giddens, Anthony and Lash, Scott (1994) *Reflexive Modernization*. Cambridge: Polity Press.

Benjamin, Walter (1936/1999) 'The work of art in the age of mechanical reproduction', in *Illuminations*, trans. Harry Zorn. London: Pimlico, pp. 211–44.

BFI (2000) *Black and Asian Film Research*, conducted by SSMR. London: BFI.

Blackman, Lisa M. (1998) 'Culture, technology and subjectivity: an "ethical" analysis', in J. Wood (ed.) *The Virtual Embodied: Presence, Practice, Technology*. London and New York: Routledge, pp. 132–46.

Bond, R. (1929/1998) 'This montage business', reprinted in J. Donald, A. Friedberg and L. Marcus (eds) *Close Up 1927–1933: Cinema and Modernism*. London: Cassell, pp. 278–80.

Bond, R. (1930/1998) 'Acts under the Acts', in J. Donald, A. Friedberg and L. Marcus (eds) *Close Up: 1927–1933: Cinema and Modernism*. London: Cassell, pp. 301–2.

Bordwell, David and Thompson, Kirstin (1994) *Film History: An Introduction*. New York: McGraw-Hill Inc.

Bordwell, D., Staiger, J. and Thompson, K. (1985) *The Classical Hollywood Cinema: Film Style and Mode of Production to 1960*. New York: Columbia University Press.

Bourdieu, Pierre (1979) *Distinction: A Social Critique of the Judgement of Taste*, trans. Richard Nice. London: Routledge.

Bourdieu, Pierre (1990) *In Other Words: Essays Towards a Reflexive Sociology*, trans. M. Adamson. Cambridge: Polity Press.

Bourdieu, Pierre (1991) *Language and Symbolic Power*, ed. J.B. Thompson, trans. G. Raymond and M. Adamson. Cambridge, MA: Harvard University Press.

Bourdieu, Pierre (1992) *The Rules of Art: Genesis and Structure of the Literary Field*, trans. Susan Emanuel. Cambridge: Polity Press.

Bourdieu, Pierre (1993) *The Field of Cultural Production: Essays on Art and Literature*, edited and introduced by R. Johnson. Cambridge: Polity Press.

Bruno, Giuliana (1987) 'Ramble city: postmodernism and *Blade Runner*', October, 41: pp. 61–74.

Brunsdon, Charlotte (1997) *Screen Tastes: Soap Opera to Satellite Dishes*. London and New York: Routledge.

Buck-Morss, Susan (1989) *The Dialectics of Seeing: Watler Benjamin and the Arcades Project*. Cambridge, MA: MIT Press.

Buck-Morss, Susan (1993) 'Aesthetic anaesthetics: Walter Benjamin's artwork essay reconsidered', in *New Formations*, 20, pp. 123–44.

Bukatman, Scott (1998) 'Zooming out: the end of offscreen space', in J. Lewis (ed.) *The New American Cinema*. Durham, NC and London: Duke University Press.

Burch, Noel (1990) *Life to Those Shadows*. London: BFI.

Burger, Peter (1984) *The Theory of the Avant-Garde*. Manchester: Manchester University Press.

Butler, Judith (1997) *Excitable Speech: A Politics of the Performative*. New York and London: Routledge.

Callinicos, Alex (1990) *Against Postmodernism*. London: Macmillan.

Campbell, Jan (2000) *Arguing with the Phallus: Feminist, Queer and Postcolonial Theory*. London and New York: Zed Books.

Campbell, Jan (forthcoming) *The Embodied Spectator*. Cambridge: Polity Press

Castells, Manuel (1996) *The Rise of the Network Society: Second Edition*. Oxford and Massachusetts: Blackwell.

CAVIAR (1995) *CAVIAR 12: Report of Findings*. London: CAVIAR.

CAVIAR (1997) *CAVIAR 15: Digest of Findings*. London: CAVIAR/BMRB Consortium.

CAVIAR (1998) *CAVIAR 16: Digest of Findings*. London: CAVIAR/BMRB Consortium.

Chambers, Iain (1993) *Migrancy, Identity, Culture*. London and New York: Routledge.

Charney, Leo (1998) *Empty Moments: Cinema, Modernity, and Drift*. Durham, NC and London: Duke University Press.

Chion, Michael (1994) *Audio Vision: Sound on Screen*. Columbia: Columbia University Press.

Christopher, J. (2000) 'Out of the fleapit', *The Times*, 16 February, p. 40.

Christopherson, S. and Storper, M. (1986) 'The city as studio; the world as back lot: the impact of vertical disintegration on the location of the motion picture industry', *Environment and Planning D: Society and Space*, Vol. 4.

Church Gibson, Pamela (2000) 'Fewer weddings and more funerals: changes in the heritage film', in R. Murphy *British Cinema of the 90s*. London: BFI, pp. 115–24.

Clarke, David B. (ed.) (1997) *The Cinematic City*. London and New York: Routledge.

Clifford, James (1988) *The Predicament of Culture*. Cambridge, MA and London: Harvard University Press.

Cohen, Alain. J.-J. (2001) 'Virtual Hollywood and the genealogy of its hyper-spectator', in M. Stokes and R. Maltby (eds) *Hollywood Spectatorship: Changing Perceptions of Cinema Audiences*. London: BFI. pp. 152–63.

Corrigan, Timothy (1991) *A Cinema Without Walls: Movies and Culture After Vietnam*. New York: Routledge.

Cubbitt, Sean (1991) *Timeshift: On Video Culture*. London and New York: Routledge.

Dahlgren, Peter (1995) *Television and the Public Sphere: Citizenship, Democracy and the Media*. London: Sage.

Danan, Martine (2000) 'French cinema in the era of media capitalism', *Media, Culture and Society*. London: Sage, vol. 22, pp. 355–64.

Darley, Andrew (2000) *Visual Digital Culture: Surface Play and Spectacle in New Media Genres*. London and New York: Routledge.

DCMS (1998) 'A bigger picture: The report of the film policy review group', London: DCMS.

de Certeau, Michel (1984) *The Practice of Everyday Life*, trans. Steven Rendall. Berkeley, Los Angeles, London: University of California Press.

Derrida, Jacques (1978a) *The Truth in Painting*, trans. G. Bennington and I. McLeod. Chicago and London: University of Chicago Press.

Derrida, Jacques (1978b) 'Structure, sign and play in the discourse of the human sciences', in *Writing and Difference*, trans. A. Bass. Chicago: University of Chicago Press, pp. 278–94.

Derrida, Jacques (1981) 'Economimesis', *Diacritics* 11: pp. 3–25.

Dittmar, Helga (1992) *The Social Psychology of Material Possessions*. New York: St Martins. Hemel Hempstead: Harvester Wheatsheaf.

Dodona Research (1998) *Cinemagoing Europe*. K.P. Grummitt and K. Couling (ed.). Leicester: Dodona Research.

Dodona Research (2001) *Cinemagoing 9*. K.P. Grummitt and K. Couling (ed.). Leicester: Dodona Research.

Doel, Marcus A. and Clarke, David B. (1997) 'From ramble city to the screening of the Eye: *Blade Runner*, death and symbolic exchange', in D.B. Clarke (ed.) *The Cinematic City*. London and New York: Routledge, pp. 140–67.

Doel, Marcus A. and Clarke, David B. (1999) 'Virtual worlds: simulation, suppletion, s(e)duction and simulacra', in M. Crang, P. Crang and J. May (eds) *Virtual Geographies*. London and New York: Routledge.

Dogme manifesto (1995) www.dogme95.dk

Donald, James, Friedberg, Anne, Marcus, Laura (eds) (1998) *Close Up, 1927–1933: Cinema and Modernism*. London: Cassell.

Donnelly, K.J. (1998) 'The classical film score forever? *Batman, Batman Returns* and post-classical film music', in S. Neale and M. Smith (eds) *Contemporary Hollywood Cinema*. London and New York: Routledge, pp. 142–55.

Dulac, Germaine (1925) 'L'essence de cinema l'idee visuelle', in *Cinema*, Paris, pp. 57–66.

Dyer, Richard (1977) 'Entertainment and Utopia', *Movie*, 24.

Dyer, Richard and Vincendeau, Ginette (eds) (1992) *Popular European Cinema*. London: Routledge.

Eagleton, Terry (1990) *The Ideology of the Aesthetic*. Oxford: Blackwell.

Elsaesser, Thomas (1975) 'The pathos of failure: notes of the unmotivated hero', *Monogram*, 6, pp. 13–19.

Elsaesser, Thomas (ed.) with Barker Adam (1990) *Early Cinema: Space, Frame, Narrative*. London: BFI.

Evans, Graeme and Ford, Jo (1999) 'European funding of culture: promoting common culture or regional growth?', in S. Selwood (ed.) *Cultural Trends*, Issue 36. London: Policy Studies Institute, pp. 55–87.

Featherstone, Mike (1991) *Consumer Culture and Postmodernism*. London: Sage.

Film Council (2000a) *Towards a Sustainable UK Film Industry*. London: London Film Council.

Film Council (2000b) *Film in England: A Development Strategy for Film and the Moving Image in the English Regions*. London: London Film Council.

Finney, Angus (1996) *The State of European Cinema: A New Dose of Reality*. London: Cassell.

168   Foster, Hal (1983) *Postmodern Culture*. London and Sydney: Pluto.

Foucault, Michel (1977) *Discipline and Punish: The Birth of the Prison*, trans. Alan Sheridan. New York: Pantheon.

Foucault, Michel (1980) *Power/Knowledge: Selected Interviews and Other Writings 1972–1977*, ed. Colin Gordon. Brighton: Harvester.

Fowler, Bridget (1997) *Pierre Bourdieu and Cultural Theory: Critical Investigations*. London: Sage.

Friedberg, Anne (1993) *Window Shopping: Cinema and the Postmodern*. Berkeley: University of California Press.

Friedberg, Anne (1998) 'Introduction: Reading *Close Up*, 1927–1933', in J. Donald, A. Friedberg and L. Marcus (eds) *Close Up, 1927–1933: Cinema and Modernism*. London: Cassell, pp. 1–26.

Frow, John (1995) *Cultural Studies and Cultural Value*. Oxford: Clarendon Press.

Fukuyama, F. (1992) *The End of History and the Last Man*. London: Penguin.

Garnham, Nicholas (1983) 'Public service versus the market', *Screen*, 24(1), pp. 6–27.

Garnham, Nicholas (1993) 'Bourdieu, the cultural arbitrary, and television', in C. Calhoun, E. LiPuma and M. Postone (eds) *Bourdieu: Critical Perspectives*. Oxford: Polity Press, pp. 178–92.

Garnham, Nicholas (2000) *Emancipation, the Media and Modernity: Arguments about Media and Social Theory*. Oxford: Oxford University Press.

Geraghty, Christine (2000) 'Re-examining stardom: questions of texts, bodies and performance', in C. Gledhill and L. Williams (eds) *Reinventing Film Studies*. London: Arnold, pp. 183–201.

Giddens, Anthony (1991) *Modernity and Self-Identity*. Cambridge: Polity Press.

Giddens, Anthony (1992) *The Transformation of Intimacy*. Cambridge: Polity Press.

Gilroy, Paul (1993) *The Black Atlantic: Modernity and Double Consciousness*. London and New York: Verso.

Giullory, John (1993) *Cultural Capital: The Problem of Literary Canon Formation*. Chicago and London: University of Chicago Press.

Gledhill, Christine (2000) 'Rethinking genre', in C. Gledhill and L. Williams (eds) *Reinventing Film Studies*. London: Arnold, pp. 221–42.

Gray, Ann (1992) *Video Playtime: The Gendering of a Communications Technology*. London: Comedia/Routledge.

Greenberg, Clement (1940) 'Avant-garde and kitsch', *Parisian Review*, 7 (4) (July–August 1940), pp. 34–49

Grosz, Elizabeth (1995) *Space, Time and Perversion*. New York and London: Routledge.

Gunning, Tom (1990a) 'The cinema of attractions: early film, the spectator and the avant-garde', in T. Elsaesser with Adam Barker (ed.), *Early Cinema: Space, Frame, Narrative*, London: BFI, pp. 56–62.

Gunning, Tom (1990b) 'Non-continuity, continuity, discontinuity: a theory of genres in early film', in T. Elsaesser (ed.) and Adam Barker, *Early Cinema: Space, Frame, Narrative*, London: BFI, pp. 86–94.

Gunning, Tom (1990c) 'Weaving a narrative: style and economic background in Griffith's biograph films', in T. Elsaesser and Adam Barker (eds) *Early Cinema: Space, Frame, Narrative*, London: BFI, pp. 336–47.

Gunning, Tom (1991) *D.W.Griffith and the Origins of American Narrative Film*. Urbana and Chicago: University of Illinois Press.

Habermas, Jurgen (1962) *The Structural Transformation of the Public Sphere – An Inquiry into a Category of Bourgeois Society*. Cambridge: Polity Press.

Habermas, Jurgen (1983) 'Modernity – an incomplete project', in H. Foster (ed.) *Postmodern Culture*. London and Sydney: Pluto, pp. 3–15.

Hainsworth, Paul (1994) 'Politics, culture and cinema in the new Europe', in J. Hill, M. McLoone and P. Hainsworth (eds) *Border Crossing: Film in Ireland, Britain and Europe*. Belfast/London: Institute of Irish Studies/BFI, pp. 8–32.

Hall, Stuart (1996) 'What is this "black" in black popular culture?', in D. Morley and K. Chen (eds) *Stuart Hall: Critical Dialogues in Cultural Studies*. London and New York: Routledge, pp. 465–75.

Hansen, Miriam Bratu (1987) 'Benjamin, cinema and experience: "The Blue Flower in the Land of Technology"', in *New German Critique*, 40: pp. 179–224.

Hansen, Miriam Bratu (1990a) *Babel and Babylon: Spectatorship in American Silent Film*. Cambridge, MA: Harvard University Press.

Hansen, Miriam Bratu (1990b) 'Early cinema – whose public sphere?', in T. Elsaesser (ed.) with Adam Barker, *Early Cinema: Space, Frame, Narrative*. London: BFI, pp. 238–46.

Hansen, Miriam Bratu (1997) 'Introduction to Siegfried Kracauer', *Theory of Film: The Redemption of Physical Reality*. Princeton, NJ: Princeton University Press, pp. vii–xlv.

Hanson, Stuart (2000) 'Spoilt for choice? Multiplexes in the 90s', in R. Murphy (ed.) *British Cinema of the 90s*. London: BFI, pp. 48–59.

Hardy, Forsyth (1992) *Slightly Mad and Full of Dangers: The Story of the Edinburgh Film Festival*. Edinburgh: Ramsay Head.

Harvey, David (1989) *The Condition of Postmodernity*. Oxford: Blackwell.

Harvey, Sylvia (1978) *May '68 and Film Culture*. London: BFI.

Harvey, Sylvia (1996) 'What is cinema? The sensuous, the abstract and the political', in C. Williams (ed.) *Cinema: the Beginnings and the Future: Essays Marking the Centenary of the First Film Show Projected to a Paying Audience*. London: University of Westminster Press, pp. 228–52.

Hay, James (1997) 'Piecing together what remains of the cinematic city', in D. Clarke (ed.) *The Cinematic City*. London and New York: Routledge, pp. 209–29.

Hebdige, Dick (1986) 'A report on the Western front: postmodernism and the "politics" of style', *Block*, 12: pp. 4–26.

Hebdige, Dick (1988) *Hiding in the Light: On Images and Things*. London: Comedia.

Hedetoft, Ulf (2000) 'Contemporary cinema: between cultural globalisation and national interpretation', in Mette Hjort and Scott MacKenzie (eds) *Cinema and Nation*. London and New York: Routledge, pp. 278–97.

Higson, Andrew (1996) 'The heritage film and British cinema', in A. Higson (ed.) *Dissolving Views: Key Writings on British Cinema*. London and New York: Cassell, pp. 232–48.

Hill, John (1992) 'The issue of national cinema and British film production', in D. Petrie (ed.) *New Questions of British Cinema*. London: BFI, pp. 10–20.

Hill, John (1994) 'The future of European cinema: the economics and culture of pan-European strategies', in J. Hill, M. McLoone and P. Hainsworth (eds) *Border Crossing: Film in Ireland, Britain and Europe*. Ulster: Institute of Irish Studies/BFI, pp. 53–80.

Hill, John (1998) 'Film and television', in J. Hill and P. Church-Gibson (eds) *Oxford Guide to Film Studies*. Oxford: Oxford University Press.

Hill, John, McLoone, Martin and Hainsworth, Paul (eds) *Border Crossing: Film in Ireland, Britain and Europe*. Ulster: Institute of Irish Studies/BFI.

Hjort, Mette and MacKenzie, Scott (eds) (2000) *Cinema and Nation*. London and New York: Routledge.

HMSO (1994) Second Report to the National Heritage Committee, Volume 2. London: HMSO.

HMSO (1995) *The British Film Industry: A Policy Document Incorporating the Government's Response to the House of Commons National Heritage Select Committee*. London: HMSO.

HMSO (1998) *A Bigger Picture: The Report of the Film Policy Review Group*. London: HMSO.

Hollows, Joanne and Jancovich, Mark (eds) (1995) *Approaches to Popular Film*. Manchester: Manchester University Press.

Hoskins, Colin, McFadyen, Stuart and Finn, Adam (1997) *Global Television and Film: An Introduction to the Economics of Business*. Oxford: Clarendon Press.

Houston, Penelope (1976) 'Cannes '76', *Sight and Sound*, Summer 45 (3), pp. 148–50.

Huyssen, Andreas (1986) *After the Great Divide: Modernism, Mass Culture, Postmodernism*. London: Macmillan.

Jacobsen, W. (2000) *50 Years Berlinale: Internationale Filmfestspiele Berlin*. Berlin: Film Museum Berlin – Deutsche Kinemathek/Interna.FF.Berlin.

Jameson, Fredric (1985) 'Postmodernism and consumer society', in H. Foster (ed.) *Postmodern Culture*. London and Sydney: Pluto, pp. 111–25.

Jameson, Fredric (1991) *Postmodernism, or, the Cultural Logic of Late Capitalism*. Durham, NC: Duke University Press.

Jenkins, Henry (1992) *Textual Poachers: Television Fans and Participatory Culture*. New York and London: Routledge.

Jenkins, Henry (1995) 'Historical poetics', in M. Jancovich and J. Hollows (eds) *Approaches to Popular Film*. Manchester and New York: Manchester University Press, pp. 100–22.

Jesinghausen, M. (2000) 'The sky over Berlin as transcendental space: Wenders, Doblin and the "Angel of History"', in M. Konstantarakos (ed.) *Spaces in European Cinema*. Exeter and Portland: Intellect Books, pp. 77–92.

Jones, Janna (2001) 'Finding a place at the downtown picture palace: the Tampa Theatre, Florida', in M. Shiel and T. Fitzmaurice (eds) *Cinema and the City: Film and Urban Societies in a Global Context*. Oxford: Blackwell, pp. 122–33.

Kant, Immanual (1790/1952) *The Critique of Judgment*, trans. James Meredith. Oxford: Clarendon Press.

Karsten, Peter and Couling, Katherine (1998) *Cinema Going Europe*. Leicester: Dodona Research.

Karsten, Peter and Couling, Katherine (2000) *Cinema Going Western Europe*. Leicester: Dodona Research.

Karsten, Peter and Couling, Katherine (2001) *Cinema Going 9*. Leicester: Dodona Research.

Kelly, Mary (1981) 'Re-viewing modernist criticism', *Screen*, 22 (3): pp. 41–62.

Kember, Sarah (1998) *Virtual Anxiety: Photography, New Technology and Subjectivity*. Manchester: Manchester University Press.

Keown, Damien (1998) 'Embodying virtue: a Buddhist perspective on virtual reality', in J. Wood (ed.) *The Virtual Embodied: Presence, Practice, Technology*. London and New York: Routledge, pp. 76–87.

King, Barry (1985) 'Articulating stardom', *Screen*, 26 (5): pp. 27–50.

Klinger, Barbara (2001) 'The contemporary cinephile: film collecting in the post-video era', in M. Stokes and R. Maltby (eds) *Hollywood Spectatorship: Changing Perceptions of Cinema Audiences*. London: BFI, pp. 132–51.

Kracauer, Siegfried (1960) *Theory of Film: The Redemption of Physical Reality*. Princeton, NJ: Princeton University Press.

Lee, M. (1993) *Consumer Culture Reborn: The Cultural Politics of Consumption*. London and New York: Routledge.

Lefebvre, Henri (1958) *Critique de la Vie Quotidienne, II: Fondements d'une Sociologie de la Quotidiennete*. Paris: L'Arche.

Levinas, Emmanuel (1961/1987) *Totality and Infinity*, trans. A. Iingis. Pittsburgh: Duquesne University Press.

Light, Jennifer S. (1999) 'From city space to cyber space', in M. Crang, P. Crang and J. May (eds) *Virtual Geographies*. London and New York: Routledge.

Livingstone, Sonia and Lunt, Peter (1992) *Mass Consumption and Personal Identity: Everyday Economic Experience*. Bristol: Oxford University Press.

Lury, Celia (1996) *Consumer Culture*. Cambridge: Polity Press.

Lyotard, Jean-François (1984) *The Postmodern Condition: A Report on the Condition of Knowledge*, trans. G. Bennington and B. Massumi. Minneapolis: University of Minnesota Press.

Malcom, D. (2000) 'Magnolia blossom', *Guardian*, 21 February, p. 9.

Maltby, Richard (1997) ' "Nobody knows everything": Post-classical historiographies and consolidated entertainment', in R. Murphy (ed.) *The British Cinema Book*. London: BFI, pp. 21–43.

Manovich, Lev (2001) *The Language of New Media*. Cambridge, MA: MIT Press.

MacCabe, Colin (1992) 'Subsidies, audiences, producers', in D. Petrie (ed.) *New Questions of British Cinema*. London: BFI, pp. 22–8.

Massey, Doreen (1993) 'Power-geometry and a progressive sense of place', in J. Bird, B. Curtis, T. Putnam, G. Robertson and L. Tickner (eds) *Mapping the Futures: Local Cultures, Global Change*. London and New York: Routledge, pp. 59–69.

McChesney, Robert W. (1998) 'Media convergence and globalisation', in D.K. Thussu (ed.) *Electronic Empires: Global Media and Local Resistance*. London, New York, Sydney, Auckland: Arnold, pp. 27–46.

McGuigan, Jim (1996) *Culture and the Public Sphere*. London and New York: Routledge.

McIntyre, Steve (1996) 'Art and industry: regional film and video policy in the UK', in A. Moran (ed.) *Film Policy: International, National and Regional Perspectives*. London and New York: Routledge, pp. 215–33.

McRobbie, Angela (1994) *Postmodernism and Popular Culture*. London and New York: Routledge.

McRobbie, Angela (1999) *In the Culture Society: Art, Fashion, Popular Music*. London and New York: Routledge.

Miller, Toby (1996) 'The crime of Monsieur Lang: GATT, the screen, and the new international division of cultural labour', in A. Moran (ed.) *Film Policy: International, National and Regional Perspectives*. London and New York: Routledge, pp. 72–85.

Miller, Toby (2000) 'The film industry and the government: "Endless Mr Beans and Mr Bonds?"', in R. Murphy (ed.) *British Cinema of the 90s*. London: BFI, pp. 37–47.

Mingay, David (1996) 'Read Only Memory: the recreation of sensorial experience in 3D and CD ROM', in C. Williams (ed.) *Cinema: the Beginnings and the Future: Essays Marking the Centenary of the First Film Show Projected to a Paying Audience*. London: University of Westminster Press, pp. 207–16.

Monk, Claire (2001) 'The British heritage-film debate revisited', in C. Monk and A. Sargeant (eds) *British Historical Cinema: The History, Heritage and Costume Film*. London and New York: Routledge, pp. 176–98.

Moran, Albert (1996) 'Terms for a reader: film, Hollywood, national cinema, cultural identity and film policy', in A. Moran (ed.) *Film Policy: International, National and Regional Perspectives*. London and New York: Routledge, pp. 1–22.

Morley, David (2000) *Home Territories: Media, Mobility and Identity*. London and New York: Routledge.

Morse, Margaret (1990) 'An ontology of everyday distraction: the Freeway, the Mall and Television', in P. Mellencamp (ed.) *Logics of Television*. Bloomington: Indiana University Press, pp. 193–221.

Mort, Frank (1990) 'What's it worth then?', *Marxism Today*, July.

Mouffe, Chantal (1993) *The Realm of the Political*. London: Verso.

Murphy, Robert (ed.) *The British Cinema Book*. London: BFI.

Musser, Charles (1990) 'The Nickleodeon era begins: establishing the framework for Hollywood's mode of representation', in T. Elsaesser (ed.) with Adam Barker, *Early Cinema: Space, Frame, Narrative*, London: BFI, pp. 256–73.

National Heritage Committee (1998) *A Bigger Picture*. London: HMSO.

Neale, Steve (1981) 'Art cinema as institution', *Screen*, 22(1): pp. 11–40.

Negt, Oscar and Kluge, Alexander (1972/1993) *The Public Sphere and Experience: Toward an Analysis of the Bourgeois and Proletarian Public Sphere*. Minniapolis: University of Minnesota Press.

Nixon, Sean (1997) 'Circulating culture', in P. du Gay (ed.) *The Production of Culture/ Cultures of Production*. London, Thousand Oaks, New Delhi: Sage/Oxford University Press. pp. 177–234.

Nowell-Smith, Geoffrey (2001) 'Cities: real and imagined', in M. Shiel and T. Fitzmaurice (eds) *Cinema and the City: Film and Urban Societies in a Global Context*. Oxford: Blackwell, pp. 99–108.

OECD (1998) *Content as a New Growth Industry*. Paris: OECD.

OECD (2000) *Statement of Prague: Audiovisual Policies and Cultural Diversity in an Enlarged Europe*. Paris: OECD.

Official Journal of the European Communities (2000) 'On the implementation of a programme to encourage the development, distribution and promotion of European audiovisual works', L 336, 30 December.

O'Hagan, A. (2000) 'Berlin Film Festival', *Daily Telegraph*, 18 February, p. 25.

Owens, Craig (1984) 'The allegorical impulse: towards a theory of postmodernism', in B. Wallis (ed.) *Art After Modernism*. New York and Boston: New Museum of Contemporary Art and D. Godine, pp. 203–36.

Parker, Alan (2000) Foreword, in *Towards a Sustainable UK Film Industry*. London: The Film Council.

Petley, Julian (1992) 'Independent distribution in the UK: problems and proposals', in D. Petrie (ed.) *New Questions of British Cinema*. London: BFI, pp. 76–94.

Plant, Sadie (1992) *The Most Radical Gesture: The Situationist International in a Postmodern Age*. London and New York: Routledge.

Pham, Annika and Watson, Neil (1993) *The Film Marketing Handbook: A Practical Guide to Marketing Independent Films*, (ed.) J. Durie. Hampshire: Media Business School.

Pisters, Patricia (2001) 'Glamour and glycerine: surplus and residual of the network society: from *Glamorama* to *Fight Club*', in P. Pisters (ed.) *Micropolitics of Media Culture: Reading the Rhizomes of Deleuze and Guattari*. Amsterdam: Amsterdam University Press, pp. 125–41.

Roberts, James Paul (1992) 'Marketing issues in the film industry today', in D. Petrie (ed.) *New Questions of British Cinema*. London: BFI, pp. 95–111.

Rodowick, D.N. (1988) *The Crisis of Political Modernism: Criticism and Ideology in Contemporary Film Thoery*. Berkeley, Los Angeles, London: University of California Press.

Rose, T. (2000) 'Seriously though, Jovovich is upset', *Evening Standard*, 14 February, p. 9.

Rosenberg, Alfred (1930/1992) 'The myth of the twentieth century', in C. Harrison and P. Wood (eds) *Art in Theory 1900–1990: An Anthology of Changing Ideas*. Oxford and Cambridge, MA: Blackwell, pp. 393–5.

Said, Edward (1992) 'Europe and its others: An Arab perspective', in Kearney (ed.) *Visions of Europe: Conversations on the Legacy and Future of Europe*. Dublin: Wolfhound Press, pp. 107–16.

Sassen, S. (1994) *Cities in a Global Economy*. Thousand Oaks, California Pine: Forge Press.

Schatz, Thomas (1983a) 'The new Hollywood', in J. Collins, H. Radner and A. Preacher (eds) *Film Theory Goes to the Movies*. New York: Routledge, pp. 8–36.

Schatz, Thomas (1983b) *Old Hollywood/New Hollywood: Ritual, Art and Industry*. Ann Arbor/UMI Research Press.

Schlesinger, Philip (1992) 'On national identity (I): Cultural politics and the mediologists', in *Media, State and Nation: Political and Collective Identities*. London: Sage, pp. 140–75.

Schlesinger, Philip (1997) 'From cultural defense to political culture: media, politics and collective identity in the European Union', *Media, Culture and Society*. London, Thousand Oaks, New Delhi: Sage, vol. 19, pp. 369–91.

Schlesinger, Philip (2000) 'The sociological scope of "National Cinema"', in M. Hjort and S. MacKenzie (eds) *Cinema and Nation*. London and New York: Routledge.

Scruton, Roger (1983) *The Aesthetic Understanding: Essays in the Philosophy of Art and Culture*. London and New York: Methuen.

Sedgwick, Eve Kosofsky (1994) 'Epidemics of the will', in *Tendencies*. London: Routledge, pp. 130–41.

Seguin, Denis (2000) 'The politics of shooting', *Screen International*, 18 August, p. 12.

Shields, Rob (1999) *Lefebvre, Love and Struggle: Spatial Dialectics*. London and New York: Routledge.

Shohat, Elaine and Stam, Robert (1996) 'From the Imperial Family to the transnational imaginary: media spectatorship in the age of globalization', in R. Wilson and W. Dissanayake (eds) *Global/Local: Cultural Production and the Transnational Imaginary*. Durham, NC: Duke University Press, pp. 145–70.

Silverstone, Roger (1994) *Television and Everyday Life*. London and New York: Routledge.

Smith, Larry (1999) *Party in a Box: The Story of the Sundance Film Festival*. Salt Lake City: Gibbs Smith.

Smith, Murray (1998) 'Thesis on the philosophy of Hollywood history', in S. Neale and M. Smith (eds) *Contemporary Hollywood Cinema*. London and New York: Routledge, pp. 3–28.

Sobchack, Vivian (1994/2000) 'The scene of the screen: envisioning cinematic and electronic "presence"', in R. Stam and T. Miller (eds) *Film Theory: An Anthology*. Malden, Massachusetts and Oxford: Blackwell, pp. 67–84.

Soja, Edward (1989) *Postmodern Geographies: The Reassertion of Space in Critical Social Theory*. London and New York: Routledge.

Sontag, Susan (1964/1999) 'Notes on "camp"', reprinted in Fabio Cleto (ed.) *Camp: Queer Aesthetics and the Performing Subject: A Reader*. Edinburgh: Edinburgh University Press, pp. 53–65.

Stacey, Jackie (1993) *Star-Gazing*. London: Routledge.

Staiger, Janet (1992) *Interpreting Films: Studies in the Historical Reception of American Cinema*. Princeton, NJ: Princeton University Press.

Stallabrass, Julian (1996) *Gargantua – Manufactured Mass Culture*. London and New York: Verso.

Stallybrass, Peter and White, Allon (1986) *The Politics and Poetics of Transgression*. New York: Cornell University Press.

Stein, Bob (1999) '"We could be better ancestors than this": ethics and first principles for the art of the digital age', in P. Lunenfeld (ed.) *The Digital Dialectic: New Essays on New Media*. Cambridge, MA: MIT Press, pp. 198–213.

Street, Sarah (1997) *British National Cinema*. London and New York: Routledge.

Stringer, Julian (2001) 'Global cities and the international film festival economy', in

M. Shiel and T. Fitzmaurice (eds) *Cinema and the City: Film and Urban Societies in a Global Context*. Oxford: Blackwell, pp 134–44.

Suarez, Juan (1996) *Bike Boys, Drag Queens and Superstars: Avant-Garde, Mass Culture, and Gay Identities in the 1960s Underground Cinema*. Bloomington and Indianapolis: Indiana Univeristy Press.

Swann, Paul (2000) 'The British culture industries and the mythology of the American market: cultural policy and cultural exports in the 1940s and 1990s', *Cinema Journal*, 39(4): pp. 27–42.

Tagg, John (1988) *The Burden of Representation: Essays on Photographies and Histories*. London: Macmillan.

Tashiro, Charles (1997) 'The contradictions of video collecting', *Film Quarterly*, 50(2): pp. 11–18.

Tiratsoo, N. (1999) 'Limits of Americanisation: the United States productivity gospel in Britain', in B. Conekin, F. Mort and C. Waters (eds) *Moments of Modernity: Reconstructing Britain 1945–1964*. London and New York: Rivers Oram Press, pp. 96–113.

Tolson, Andrew (1991) 'Televised chat and the synthetic personality', in P. Scannell (ed.) *Broadcast Talk*. London, Thousand Oaks, New Delhi: Sage, pp. 178–200.

TSO (2001) *Creative Industries Mapping Document*.

Turner, Graeme (1988) *Film as Social Practice*. London: Routledge.

Usai, Paolo Cherchi (2001) *The Death of Cinema: History, Cultural Memory and the Digital Dark Age*. London: BFI.

Virilio, Paul (1989) *War and Cinema*. London: Verso.

Walker, Alexander (2001) 'Ten film turkeys, one juicy plum', *Evening Standard*, 3 January, p. 10.

Wasko, Janet (1994) *Hollywood in the Information Age*. Cambridge: Polity Press.

Wakefield, N. (1990) *Postmodernism: The Twighlight and the Real*. London: Pluto.

Weber, Max (1930) *The Protestant Ethic and the Spirit of Capitalism*, trans. T. Parsons. London: Allen and Unwin.

Welsch, Wolfgang (1997) *Undoing Aesthetics*, trans. A. Inkpin, London, Thousand Oaks, New Delhi: Sage.

Wernick, Andrew (1991) *Promotional Culture: Advertising, Ideology and Symbolic Expression*. London, Thousand Oaks, New Delhi: Sage.

Wheeler, Mark (2000) 'Research note: The "undeclared war" part II', *European Journal of Communication*, 15(2): pp. 253–62.

White, Hayden (1978) *Tropics of Discourse: Essays in Cultural Criticism*. Baltimore, MD: Johns Hopkins University Press.

Willeman, Paul (1994) *Looks and Frictions: Essays in Cultural Studies and Film Theory*. Bloomington and London: Indiana University Press and BFI.

Williams, Raymond (1961) *The Long Revolution*. London: Chatto and Windus.

Wilson, E (1997) 'Looking backward: nostalgia and the city', in S. Westwood and J. Williams (eds) *Imagining Cities: Scripts, Signs, Memory*. London and New York: Routledge, pp. 127–39.

Wood, J. (ed.) (1998) *The Virtual Embodied: Presence, Practice, Technology*. London and New York: Routledge.

Woollen, Peter (1976) 'The two avant-gardes', *Edinburgh Magazine*, 1: pp. 77–84.

Wyatt, Justin (1994) *High Concept: Movies and Marketing in Hollywood*. Austin: University of Texas Press.

Wyatt, Justin (1998) 'The formation of the "major independent": Miramax, New Line and the New Hollywood', in S. Neale and M. Smith (eds) *Contemporary Hollywood Cinema*. London and New York: Routledge, pp. 74–90.

Index

n indicates a note.

access, 27–8
  and connoisseurship, 154–6
active audience, 5
advertising, 84
aesthetics, 5–6, 14
  anti, post or returning, 118–23
  aristocratic (high), 18, 19
  mimesis, replay, reiteration, 123–9
  'popular', 12, 16, 18, 19, 125
  recovering presence, 129–32
  soundtrack, 132–5
  see also art
agency, and structure, 7, 18–19
Aksoy, A. and Robins, K., 99, 103
Altman, R., 79–82, 91*n*
America *see* Hollywood films; United
    States
anti-aesthetic approach, 119–21
Appadurai, A., 69, 154, 156–7
Appiah, K.A., 8, 95
aristocratic (high) aesthetic, 18, 19
Armstrong, I., 19–20, 117, 121, 122–4
art
  and culture, 49–50
  galleries, 42–3, 56
  and life, 19–22, 24, 28, 90–1
    see also Kant, I.
  and technology, 28, 29
  see also aesthetics
arthouse
  vs gallery, 42–3
  vs multiplexes, 39, 40, 52–4
  see also avant-garde; independent films
audience(s)
  active, 5
  disseminated, 81
  identification, 125
  perception, 30–1
  research, 4–5, 83–8

working class, 124–5
aura, 29
  decline of, 30
avant-garde, 23, 25–6, 33–4, 35*n*
  and digitalization, 141–3, 147, 148,
    162*n*
  dual narratives, 42, 50–1
  as independent films, 27–8
  vs mainstream films, 26–8, 40–1, 43–4,
    50, 51, 90
  see also arthouse; independent films

Batman, 133–4
Baudrillard, J., 94, 143
Benjamin, W., 24, 29–32, 33, 34, 129
Berlin Film Festival (IFB), 59, 61–3,
    65–7, 68, 70, 71
BFI *see* British Film Institute
Blade Runner, 1, 93–4, 115*n*
Bordwell, D. et al, 77–8
boundary erosion, 96
Bourdieu, P., 2, 5, 6–7, 14, 15–20, 33,
    49, 56–7
  aesthetics, 121, 124–5, 126, 128
  linguistics, 127
bourgeois conceptions of culture, 33
bourgeois films, 23–4
Britain, 26, 54, 55
  CAVIAR, 51–2, 53–4, 85–6
  Department of Culture, Media and
    Sport, 109
  distribution companies, 99
  London Film Commission, 108
  London Film Society, 63
  National Heritage Committee, 72,
    75*n*, 108
British Film Institute (BFI), 53
British films, 72, 73
  failures, 113–14

funding, 109–13
genres, 114–15
'popular', 109, 112
'Britishness', 109, 110, 114, 115
Brunsdon, C., 152, 153
Buck-Morss, S., 129
Bukatman, S., 101–2
business discourse, 60, 64–5
Butler, J., 126–7, 129, 136n

cable television, 151
camp, 43–4
Cannes film festival, 62, 64–5, 68, 70, 71
Castells, M., 56–7, 105–6, 157
CAVIAR (Cinema and Video Industry
    Research), 51–4, 85–6
censorship, 24
Chambers, I., 55–6
Charney, L., 14–15, 32, 34, 136–7n, 159
Chion, M., 132, 133
Christopher, J., 66, 70
Christopherson, S. and Storper, M.,
    97–8, 99, 100
cinema of attractions, 25–6, 102, 142
Cinemagoing (Dodona Research), 54, 55,
    83
Cinema and Video Industry Research see
    CAVIAR
cities, 54, 56, 61
    global, 65–6
    regeneration, 65, 66–7
class, 17, 27, 36n, 49
    CAVIAR research, 52–4
    relationship to culture, 16–19, 24,
        85–7, 91n, 114
    relationship to space, 56–7
    use of satellite dishes, 152–3
    working class audience, 124–5
Clifford, J., 49–50
climates of change, 32–5
'closeness', 30
Close Up (journal), 26, 27, 28
Cocktail, 81–2
Cohen, A. J.-J., 154
collections, 155–7
commerce see economics; global
    commerce networks; marketing
connoisseurship, 154–6
consumer/commodity culture, 3, 45–8,
    80–1, 88, 156–7
consumer gaze, 46
consumer identification, 84
consumption

as experience, 90
    identity formation and, 94–5
content, 51
    and form split, 19, 142–3
Corrigan, T., 48
Crying Game, The, 100
cultural exchange and translation, 150–1
'cultural industries', 8–9
cultural production, transformations,
    98–9
culture(s)
    art and, 49–50
    bourgeois conceptions of, 33
    and commerce, 69–70, 111–14
    consumer/commodity, 3, 45–8, 80–1,
        88, 156–7
    relationship to class, 16–19, 24, 85–7,
        91n, 114
    taste, 14, 112–13
    technological, 22–3

Darley, A., 138, 140, 142–3, 161n
de Certeau, M., 5, 7, 18, 19
de Hadeln, 65–6, 73
Department of Culture, Media and Sport
    (UK), 109
Derrida, J., 5–6, 121, 125–6, 127
digitalization
    distribution, 107, 148–51
    production, 139–48
    projections, 158–60
    soundtrack, 132–3
disseminated audiences, 81
distinctions thesis see Bourdieu, P.
distracted gaze, 30–1
distribution, 98–100
    digital technology, 107, 148–51
    mainstream/independent, 70–2,
        99–101, 103
Dittmar, H., 89
Dodona Research (Cinemagoing), 54, 55,
    83
Dogme manifesto, 50–1
Donelly, K.J., 133–4
DVD, 154, 155
Dyer, R., 132

Eagleton, T., 19, 20, 121, 135n
early cinema see history
economics
    vs art/culture, 19–22, 69–70, 111–14
    discourse, 60, 64–5
    funding, British film industry, 109–13

GATT talks, 103–4, 105, 106, 149
World Trade Organization (WTO),
     105–6
Edinburgh Film Festival, 63, 68
Edinburgh Film Guild, 63–4
elites, 56–7, 58*n*
ephemerality, 87, 92*n*, 156–7
ethics, and digitalization, 150–1, 162*n*
ethnicity, 53, 57*n*
     see also immigrants
European film festivals, 61–7
European films *vs* Hollywood films, 64,
     70
European identity, 103–7
European modernity, 95
European Union (EU), 106–7, 108,
     149–50, 160*n*, 162*n*
     see also specific countries
exhibition sites, 24, 39, 43, 54–7, 57*n*
     see also multiplexes
experience
     consumption as, 90
     economy, 47–51
expertise, lifeworld and, 95–6

failures, British films, 113–14
Federation Internationale des Associations
     des Producteurs de Film (FIAPF),
     62
Film Council, 110–11, 115
film festivals, 2–3
     discourses, 60, 61
     divisions and enclaves, 67–72
     European, 61–7
     nation states, 72–4
film journals, 26, 27, 28
Film, Le (journal), 26
film societies, 27, 63
film texts *see* text(s)
flânerie, 46
form, 27, 28
     and content split, 19, 142–3
Foster, H., 119–20
Foucault, M., 21, 95
Four Weddings and a Funeral, 110
fragmentation, of production, 96–103
France, 26, 54
     Cannes film festival, 62, 64–5, 68, 70,
          71
     FIAPF, 62
Friedberg, A., 26–7, 32, 34, 40, 45–7
Frow, J., 18–19
Full Monty, The, 110

funding, British film industry, 109–13

galleries, 42–3, 56
Garnham, N., 20, 111
GATT talks, 103–4, 105, 106, 149
gaze
     consumer, 46
     distracted, 30–1
     mobile cultural, 45, 46, 47
     popular, 124–5
genres
     British film, 114–15
     and marketing, 77–83
geographic centralization, 98
Germany, 26, 54
     Berlin Film Festival (IFB), 59, 61–3,
          65–7, 68, 70, 71
Giddens, A., 90, 92*n*
Gilroy, P., 8, 95
Giullory, J., 20–1
global cities, 65–6
global commerce networks, 60–1
global discourses, 103–8
global distributors, 70–2
Greenberg, C., 40–1, 43–4, 57*n*
Griffiths, D.W., 25
Gunning, T., 23–4, 25–6, 32–3, 35*n*, 102

Habermas, J., 81, 87–8, 90, 95
Hansen, M., 29, 31, 37–8*n*
Hardy, F., 63, 64
Harvey, D., 56, 93–4
Harvey, S., 42
Hay, J., 47
high (aristocratic) aesthetic, 18, 19
high concept films, 101–3, 143
Hindi cinema, 53
history
     art and economy split, 19–22
     climates of change, 32–5
     development of industry, 97–8
     excess, 25–8
     film festivals, 63
     narrative in early cinema, 23–6, 35*n*
     'new' technology of film, 22–5, 31
     roots of taste, 15–19
Hollywood films, 27, 44
     vs European films, 64, 70
     fantastic reality, 146
     marketing, 77–8, 79–80
     see also mainstream films
home viewing, 52, 53, 87, 151–9, 162*n*
Huyssen, A., 28, 32–3, 35*n*, 40

idealist–materialist paradox, 89–90
identity
    European, 103–7
    formation, consumption and, 94–5
immigrants, 66, 74–5*n*
    see also ethnicity
independent films, 27–8, 60
    distribution, 70–2, 99–101, 103
    see also arthouse; avant-garde
independent producers, 60, 98
individualism, 88–91
International Film Festival Berlin (IFB)
    see Berlin Film Festival
International League of Independent
    Cinema, 28
Internet, 149, 151, 154–5, 161*n*

Jacobsen, W., 62–3, 65
Jameson, F., 93
journalism discourse, 67–8, 96
Jovovich, M., 59

Kant, I., 22–3, 26, 31, 33, 49, 122, 124,
    125
    critiques/interpretations, 6, 14, 16,
    19–20, 121
Kelly, M., 40–1, 57*n*
kitsch, 40–1, 43–4
Klinger, B., 155
Kracauer, S., 29, 31–2, 34, 36*n*, 37*n*,
    38*n*
Kulturkritik (journal), 26

language, 126–8
laser discs, 155, 156, 162–3*n*
late capitalism, 93, 94
Lefebvre, H., 131–2, 133, 137*n*
Lenauer, J., 27–8
life, art and, 19–23, 24, 28, 90–1
    see also Kant, I.
lifestyle
    choice, 78, 82–3
    marketing, 84–6, 88–91
lifeworld, and expertise, 95–6
London Film Commission, 108
London Film Society, 63
Lumière brothers, 22, 23

MacCabe, C., 19, 107–8
mainstream films
    vs avant-garde, 26–8, 40–1, 43–4, 50,
    51, 90
    digitalization, 147–8

distributors, and independent films,
    70–2, 99–101, 103
    see also Hollywood films
Malcom, D., 70
Maltby, R., 100
Manovich, L., 138, 140–2, 143, 145–6,
    147, 148, 158
marketing
    audience research, 83–8
    genre and, 77–83
    individualism and, 88–91
    lifestyle, 84–6, 88–91
    and production, 81–2, 99–100
mass culture *see* Hollywood films;
    mainstream films
Matrix, The, 143–4, 145, 146, 161–2*n*
Méliès, G., 22, 23, 28, 142
Merleau-Ponty, M., 130, 131
Miller, T., 106
mimesis, 123–9, 136*n*
Miramax, 100–1
mirror metaphor of film, 93–4
mobile cultural gaze, 45, 46, 47
mobility
    social, 48–9
    virtual, 46
    of vision, 32
modernism, 33–4, 95, 96
    division of film cultures, 40–2, 44–5
    political, 120–1, 128–9
    and postmodernism, 1, 7–9, 14–15,
    34–5, 47, 49
    and supermodernity, 146
Morley, D., 151–2
Motion Picture Patents Company
    (MPPC), 24
multifaceted role of film, 8–9
multiple voices, Hollywood studios,
    79–80
multiplexes, 3, 39, 46–8, 49, 54–6
    vs arthouse, 39, 40, 52–4
multivalent text, 81–2
music, 78–9, 101
    see also soundtrack aesthetics
Musser, C., 24–5, 133

narrative(s)
    dual, of avant-garde, 42, 50–1
    early cinema, 23–6, 35*n*
    realism, 145–6
    standardization, 24–5
National Board of Film Censorship
    (US), 24

National Heritage Committee (UK), 72, 75*n*, 108
National Lottery (UK), funding, 112–13
nation states, film festivals, 72–4
nausea, 5–9, 125–6
Neale, S., 43
networks
    of global commerce, 60–1
    spatial, 54–7
    tracing, 3–4, 5
New Line, 100–1
'new' technology, 22–5, 31, 160*n*
    see also digitalization; *specific technologies*
Nightmare on Elm Street, 100
Nixon, S., 84

'objectivity', 17
object–subject division, 121–3, 130–1
O'Hagan, A., 59, 70
oppositional markers, 61
otherness, 6

painting, 141–2
Parker, A., 110, 111
perception, 30–1
'performativity', 126, 128
photography, 123–4, 130, 141–2
political modernism, 120–1, 128–9
politicization of text, 42
POOL collective, 26–7, 36*n*, 64, 74*n*
'popular aesthetic', 12, 16, 18, 19, 125
'popular' cultural engagement, 124–6
'popular' films, British, 109, 112
popular gaze, 124–5
postmodern architecture, 56
postmodernism
    digitalization, 139, 143, 159–60, 161*n*
    fragmentation of production, 96–103
    genres for the nation, 114–15
    global discourses, 103–8
    lifestyle consumption, 88–9
    modernism and, 1, 7–9, 14–15, 34–5, 47, 49
power, 21
presence
    recovering, 129–32
    sound, 133, 134
press screenings, 87
private finance, 109–10
production
    digitalization, 139–48
    fragmentation, 96–103
    and marketing, 81–2, 99–100

production companies (UK), 109–10
product placement, 89, 92*n*
projections, digitalization, 158–60
promotional material, 87
psychoanalytical approaches, 4, 15, 32
psychographic research, 84
public—private funding, 110–11
public—private spheres, 81, 87–8, 91*n*, 154

reinscription, 119–20
reiteration, 127, 129
relational value, 2–3, 49–50
representation, 60, 119
restricted screenings, 87
Rodowick, D.N., 33–4, 120, 128
Rotterdam, 65, 68
Run Lola Run, 143, 144–5, 146, 148, 161*n*

Sassen, S., 66, 74–5*n*
satellite dishes, 152–3
satellite television, 151
Schatz, T., 78
Schlesinger, P., 103–4, 107
Scruton, R., 123–4, 126
Sedgwick, E., 76, 91*n*
self-reflexivity, 90, 92*n*
service industry, 60, 66
sex, lies and videotape, 100
Shields, R., 131
shock, 23–4, 29–33
sites of exhibition *see* exhibition sites; multiplexes
Sobchack, V., 129–30, 132, 134, 136*n*, 148
social class *see* class
social mobility, 48–9
social reproduction, 7, 14, 123
Sontag, S., 43–4
soundtrack aesthetics, 132–5
    see also music
space
    and national identity, 103–4, 107
    relationship to class, 56–7
    see also home
space–time compression, 94, 157
spatial networks, 54–7
spatial–temporal features
    aesthetics, 129–32
    commodity culture, 45–7
special effects, 139–40, 161*n*
sponsorship, 60

181

Stallabrass, J., 138
Stallybrass, P. and White, A., 20, 60
standardization, 24–5, 27, 133
'stars', 70, 97, 101
Star Wars, 101–2, 142
Stringer, J., 72, 73–4
structuralism, 4, 13*n*
structure, agency and, 7, 18–19
stylization, 78–9
Suarez, J., 41
subcultural groups, 88
subjectivity, 32, 47, 48–9
   see also object–subject division
Sundance Festival (US), 71
supermodernity, modernity and, 146
Swann, P., 73

Tashiro, C., 156, 163*n*
taste, 2, 3, 5, 6–7, 9, 14, 125–6
   clusters, 82–3, 84
   cultures, 14, 112–13
   formations, 153
   historical roots, 15–19
   production, 103
technical qualities of film, 51
technology
   and art/culture, 22–3, 28, 29
   'new', 22–5, 31, 160*n*
   see also digitalization; *specific technologies*
television
   cable/satellite, 151
   rights, 100
   terrestrial, 153–4
text(s), 4
   about film, 26
   high concept film, 102
   and marketing, 78, 81–2

   multivalent, 81–2
   politicization of, 42
textual analysis, 4–5, 94
thermodynamics metaphor, 34–5, 159
time *see* emphemerality; space–time
   compression; spatial–temporal
   features
Tiratsoo, N., 62
tourism, film festivals, 60, 62–3, 64–5, 68–9
trade as rights, abstract properties of ownership (TRIPS), 105
tropes, 84, 91*n*

United States, 24, 71, 98
   American *vs* European identity, 103–5
   see also Hollywood films
Usai, P.C., 157, 158–9

value(s), 2–3
   criteria, 69
   discourses, 9
   relational, 2–3, 49–50
Venice Film Biennial, 62, 68, 71
video, 52, 156, 162*n*
virtual mobility, 46
Vow of Chastity manifesto, 50–1

Walker, A., 113–14
Weber, M., 95
Welsch, W., 118–19, 122, 134–5
Wings of Desire, 93–4
Wollen, P., 42
working class audience, 124–5
World Trade Organization (WTO), 105–6
Wyatt, J., 78–9, 82, 100, 101, 143